BRITISH
FOREIGN POLICY
AND THE
COMING OF THE
FRANCO-PRUSSIAN
WAR

Oxford University Press, Amen House, London E.C.4

GLASGOW NEW YORK TORONTO MELBOURNE WELLINGTON
BOMBAY CALCUTTA MADRAS KARACHI LAHORE DACCA
CAPE TOWN SALISBURY NAIROBI IBADAN ACCRA
KUALA LUMPUR HONG KONG

BRITISH
FOREIGN POLICY
AND THE
COMING OF THE
FRANCO-PRUSSIAN
WAR

BY

RICHARD MILLMAN

University of California, Davis

OXFORD

AT THE CLARENDON PRESS

1965

© *Oxford University Press 1965*

PRINTED IN GREAT BRITAIN

TO

LYNN M. CASE

PREFACE

FROM the battle of Sadowa on 3 July 1866 to the end of the Franco-Prussian War the most decisive influence on the future of European international politics was the relationship between two countries, France and Prussia.

This study will analyse British foreign policy during these years against the background of the Franco-Prussian problem. There will be no attempt to consider extra-European aspects of British diplomacy, though some mention will be made of the Eastern question where it seems to affect the main theme.

I first became interested in the present work while writing a seminar paper for Professor L. M. Case of the University of Pennsylvania. His knowledge, guidance, and advice, for which I am in his debt, were essential to this study. The grant of a Penfield Scholarship from the University of Pennsylvania enabled me to go to Europe to continue the necessary research in foreign archives. The staffs of the Haus-Hof-und Staatsarchiv in Vienna and the Public Record Office in London were most helpful, and particularly Mr. Kenneth Timings of the Public Record Office, whose assistance was graciously offered and gratefully accepted. The generous permission of the present Earl of Derby enabled me to see the papers of the fourteenth and fifteenth earls. In this connexion, Mr. Jones of the estate office at Knowsley was extremely helpful. With the kind approval of the Duke of Norfolk and the knowledgeable assistance of Mr. Steer I was able to use a fair amount of the papers of Lord Lyons.

I would like to thank Mr. M. R. D. Foot, Professor Holden Furber, Mr. Kenneth Bourne, and Lord Strang for their kindness at different stages in the preparation of this work, and also Professor Raymond J. Sontag who read the manuscript and made many useful suggestions.

Finally I have to acknowledge the gracious kindness of Her Majesty the Queen for her permission to examine and quote from the Royal Archives at Windsor Castle, where the expert co-operation of Mr. Mackworth-Young and Miss Price-Hill was most valuable.

The new material which I have embodied in this study has, I hope, helped to make a clearer picture of British foreign policy in the years immediately preceding the Franco-Prussian War. The encouragement and intellectual stimulation provided by Mr. Robert Tyler and Mr. Hans Schwarz made the research for this book an extremely pleasant task.

CONTENTS

I

THE FALL FROM THE PINNACLE

BRITISH foreign policy from the latter part of Palmerston's career to the Russo-Turkish war of 1877 has not been thoroughly investigated. There is nothing on this period to compare with the work of Webster and Temperley on Castlereagh, Canning, and the early period of Palmerston. This neglect has been due in part to the lack of great or notable achievements, particularly in the years from 1864 to 1871. Though the outstanding successes of the first part of the century have been much analysed and usually commended, the less striking accomplishments of the 1860's have received less than their due. It is not without significance that the foreign policy of Clarendon, Stanley, and Granville until the Franco-Prussian war was more popular with contemporaries than Castlereagh's, and as popular as Canning's or Palmerston's.

The partial neglect of this period is also a reflection of the assumption that because the foreign policy of England was not dominant in Europe it did not influence events and was therefore unimportant. To say that it did not have the power to control occurrences and therefore greatly to assist or prevent them is but to say the obvious and is itself significant, if only negatively. Even so, in the Luxemburg crisis of 1867 and the Belgian railroads controversy of 1868–9 the voice of England was crucial.

Despite the absence of a general study of the 1860's there has been no lack of smaller essays and monographs on particular episodes and men. Mosse has studied the Austro-Prussian crisis of 1866. Foot has written an article on England and Luxemburg in 1867, and Craig has treated the Belgian railroads affair of 1868–9. There have been several theses of interest from the University of London, such as Anderson's work on Hammond, Bourne's study of Stanley, and Lambert's analysis of parliamentary influence on foreign policy.[1]

[1] Reference to the articles of Mosse, Foot and Craig is contained in the chapters

     B

W. E. Mosse's study of the European powers and the German question appeared in 1958.[1] This is an exceedingly careful work, and no one who is interested in British foreign policy in the nineteenth century should ignore it. Mosse's main concern is with the rise of Germany over a long period, and he relates British diplomacy to this. He is a sound guide, though one may object to some of his conclusions and interpretations.

In analysing British foreign policy in the years before the Franco-Prussian war I have necessarily surveyed some of the same ground, but from a different standpoint. The emphasis of this work is more exclusively on English policy, an emphasis which was impossible for Mosse, concerned as he was with Russian, Austrian, Prussian, and French diplomacy. The foreign office files and the relevant private papers at the Public Record Office were the chief source for my research. The Gladstone papers in the British Museum and the Clarendon letters at Oxford were very helpful, as were portions of Lord Lyons's private papers at Arundel Castle, and the private papers of Derby, Stanley, and Disraeli. I found many useful hints and observations in the British file of the Austrian foreign ministry in Vienna and in the French documents on 'Les origines diplomatiques de la guerre de 1870–71'. For Bismarck's policy I consulted the collected letters in *Die Gesammelten Werke*, as well as the *Auswärtige Politik Preussens*. Though the secondary sources consulted were many, it would be presumptuous to claim that they were complete.

An important problem in this narrative is the position of Belgium and its significance for Britain from 1866 to 1871. Historians have documented British concern for and interest in Belgium and in so doing have assumed without explaining its importance. It is a complicated problem. First, the intensity of English concern for Belgium, though ever present, varied somewhat with different individuals and changing circumstances. Secondly, the justification for this concern is twofold. Was the independence of Belgium really in danger in this period, and if it was, would its loss have adversely affected

---

on Luxemburg and Belgium. The unpublished dissertations of Anderson, Bourne, and Lambert were for the University of London and may be consulted there.

[1] W. E. Mosse, *The European Powers and the German Question 1848–1871* (Cambridge, 1958).

British security or damaged British interests? If so, how, and if not, why the illusions about its importance?

The difficulty of finding an answer to this problem is as evident as the wider implications of it are significant. Because English anxiety for Belgium was so prevalent, the reasons for it are not often defined or documented. This was because the reasons were either illusory or so well understood at the time that they could be assumed. In any case, English concern for Belgium not only dominated British foreign policy from 1866 to 1871 but for the better part of the entire century. This concern is also crucial in explaining British policy toward small or defenceless powers like Portugal and Denmark, which is such an important element in the foreign relations of England in the nineteenth century.

While not pretending to solve the problem completely, I hope to show the connexion between this question and the coming of the Franco-Prussian war.

Great Britain's diplomatic prestige has often been a reflection of her propensity to intervene in Europe and her willingness to associate herself with continental powers.[1] Geography has afforded her the luxury of choice. The necessity to intervene has occurred only when the threat to Europe and its power balance seemed total, or when the independence of the Low Countries was in jeopardy. At these moments when England's commitment to Europe was greatest, her reputation was highest, particularly as victory was the adjunct of effort. 1815 was one of these glorious moments.

After 1815 Castlereagh sought to use British weight and credit for the general security of European peace, and in so doing continued the work of Pitt and set a tradition of close co-operation with European governments. At this splendid Churchillian moment in her history, England had a foreign secretary who interpreted his country's interests in a European sense, and if

---

[1] In 1859 Disraeli wrote to Derby that 'although none know better than the French Government the power and resources of England, it is at this moment the fashion of the Court of France, and the example circulates in all circles, to speak disparagingly of England; that by not taking part in the Italian war, we have sunk into a second-rate Power' (Disraeli to Derby, 27 Oct. 1859, W. F. Monypenny and G. E. Buckle, *Life of Benjamin Disraeli* [London, 1916–25], iv. 265).

he failed to implement this view his failure should be judged by the breadth of the vision which it contained rather than by the lack of success which it occasioned.[1] Within this wider context Castlereagh upheld the specific British concerns for Belgium and the separating of France and Russia with a strong centre between them. Finally, Castlereagh was an interventionist in Europe, if not in the internal affairs of European states. For him intervention was a necessity in order to maintain the balance of power upon which peace depended.

Canning was no less mindful than his predecessor of the importance of the balance of power and the blessings of peace. He was however more conscious of the differences which separated the three conservative powers from England and less willing, being without the overwhelming consideration of an expanding France, to find a common ground for co-operation. In separating his country from the three Eastern powers, Canning was merely maintaining a position towards which events had been forcing Castlereagh at the end of his life. In so doing Canning enunciated another traditional concept of nineteenth-century British diplomacy, isolation from the continent. He did not foreclose on all English interference in Europe, but hoped to limit the occasions for it. In emphasizing the gap separating England from some of her European neighbours, he was consciously separating Britain from her former allies.

Palmerston was a compound of Castlereagh and Canning. He interfered in Europe and co-operated with continental powers more than Canning would have allowed. He did this because, for him as for Castlereagh, the balance of power in Europe was a British goal, especially as it was a guarantee of peace. He wished to be on good terms with France because he felt that alone England could not make her weight felt on the Continent. At the same time Palmerston distrusted France, especially as the threat to Belgian independence was involved. The French annexation of Nice and Savoy in 1860 and the British refusal of Napoleon III's congress proposal in 1863 made Palmerston's wish for a close understanding with France

[1] Hinsley argues that Castlereagh's failure was only temporary and that his conception of Europe triumphed when the Holy Alliance collapsed (F. H. Hinsley, *Power and the Pursuit of Peace* [Cambridge, 1963], pp. 210–12).

almost impossible. This is clearly seen in the Danish dilemma of 1864.

Fear of France, particularly on the part of Palmerston and Russell, frustrated English policy thoughout the Polish affair of 1863 and the Danish crisis of 1864. Mosse points this out in detail and also stresses the change in British opinion, which was now antagonistic to intervention in Europe and the concept of the balance of power.[1] This was reflected by a divided Cabinet and the confused uncertainty of Parliament. The result was an indefinite, wavering policy which brought embarrassment and discredit to the Government. Criticism in parliament was particularly acute, as it seemed that British impotence and her reluctance to fight had been bared for all to see.[2] The glory of 1815 was but a memory, and yet Palmerston obtained a majority of eighteen in the House of Commons, as his past successes in Belgium and at the Straits had not been forgotten.

Mosse interprets 1863 and 1864 as the end of the Anglo-French alliance and of the Palmerstonian era of British foreign policy.[3] Henceforth, he argues, England would withdraw behind the Channel and pursue a course of consistent non-intervention. While this is what Cobden and Bright would have liked, it is not what occurred. The discomfiture and abashment over the Danish business arose because verbal intervention resulted in failure. The relatively small number of convinced isolationists seized the opportunity to discredit intervention and were joined by many who objected to the bitter fruits that interference brought with it. The year 1864 saw no sudden or radical change. If anything, it was the culmination of a long period of British disenchantment with the Continent, which went back at least as far as the end of the Crimean War,[4] an involvement which after

[1] Mosse, pp. 150–2; W. H. Dawson, *Richard Cobden and Foreign Policy* (London, 1926), pp. 93, 97, 102–3; G. M. Trevelyan, *Life of John Bright* (London, 1913), pp. 333–4.

[2] James Joll, *Britain and Europe 1793–1940* (London, 1950), p. 613.

[3] Mosse, pp. 164, 209. See also Mosse, 'Queen Victoria and Her Ministers in the Schleswig-Holstein Crisis, 1863–4', *English Historical Review*, lxxviii (1963), 263–83.

[4] Lord Strang correctly stresses this point in *Britain in World Affairs* (New York, 1961). In 1861 *The Times* commented on the bad after-taste left by the Crimean War: 'Never was so great an effort made for so worthless an object' (B. Kingsley Martin, *The Triumph of Lord Palmerston* [London, 1924], p. 243). On this point see L. M. Penson, 'Obligations by Treaty: Their Place in British Foreign Policy 1898–1914', *Studies in Diplomatic History and Historiography in honour of G. P. Gooch*, ed. by A. O. Sarkissian (London, 1961), pp. 77–78.

the fact also entailed much criticism in England. It would, however, be wrong to disregard the fact that from 1864 to 1871
Britain sought to keep free of new European commitments.
Ironically, she did not succeed, as is seen in the Luxemburg
guarantee of 1867 and the Belgian Treaties of 1870. What she
did was abandon a great deal of the initiative a great power is
entitled and expected to exercise. She went on the defensive.
Therefore it would be a mistake to interpret the changed desire
from more to less involvement as an abrupt transformation in
the nature of British policy. Any change, as that of Canning
when he replaced Castlereagh, was one of degree.

The reluctance to commit herself on the Continent, instead
of preserving British prestige as hoped, actually lowered it in the
eyes of the other European powers, which had grown accustomed
to valuing England to the degree that she made her presence
felt.[1]

There never was a period in wh. England was an object of so much
dislike to all parties in Germany, as at present. Conservatives, Con-
stitutionalists, Ultra Liberals, Unionists, separatists,—all join in one
way only—in repugnance to England, in noting her prosperity, & in
undervaluing her power. . . . France is hated too. But France is
watched with anxiety and respected.[2]

Consequently, the caution and conscious lack of initiative on
the part of the foreign office from 1864 to 1871 seemed like a
recognition on the part of England herself that she was no
longer a great European power. The policy of the Liberal
Government in the Austro-Prussian crisis of 1866 appeared to
confirm the part England would play after Sadowa, when the
relationship between France and Prussia would become
crucial for all the European powers.

The Duchies and Venetia in 1866

With the death of Palmerston in 1865, Russell left the
foreign office to become prime minister and Clarendon suc-

---

[1] Baron Varnbüler, the Württemberg minister, told the British ambassador that
he regretted 'that British policy of late years should have taken the line it has done
of non-intervention' (Gordon to Clarendon, 29 Apr. 1866, Public Record Office
[hereafter cited as PRO], 82/122, no. 49).

[2] Napier to Clarendon, Berlin, 5 Jan. 1866, Royal Archives, Windsor Castle
(hereafter quoted as RA), I 43/1.

ceeded him as foreign secretary.[1] These two men, who would shape British policy during the crisis preceding the Austro-Prussian War, were very unlike.[2] Clarendon was an aristocrat whose familiarity with the Continent made him at least as cosmopolitan as he was patriotic. Russell was known for his willingness to act, a willingness which the mess of 1864 and increasing age had tempered. Clarendon, in 1866, would circumscribe action with enough conditions to make the necessity for it unlikely. Russell went along with Clarendon's cautiousness as reflecting the temper of the cabinet and both political parties. The queen, who in 1863 and 1864 considered the policy of Russell and Palmerston rash and who would from 1866 to 1871 be willing to act more than her ministers would find prudent, was wary of Russell and distrusted Clarendon.[3] Yet all three were agreed, sometimes for different reasons, that the disgrace of 1864, the opprobrium of promising more than was delivered, should not be repeated.[4] In part then, the lack of

[1] Indicative of the British attitude of waiting for crises to occur, Cowley, the English representative at Paris, congratulated Russell on his leaving the foreign office 'without a question of importance to solve' (Cowley to Russell, Paris, 26 Oct. 1865, *The Later Correspondence of Lord John Russell* [hereafter quoted as *Russell*], ed. G. P. Gooch [London, 1925], ii. 339).

[2] 'He [Clarendon] was suave where Lord John was acrimonious, and his suavity was most remarkable in his dispatches—which was just where Lord John's bluntness was most disconcerting' (Martin, p. 110). This writer feels that Professor Temperley's estimate of Clarendon is a just one. 'Clarendon's charm of manner and his high place in society have made some people forget that his views were seldom original, and not seldom diffusely or imprudently expressed' (H. Temperley, 'The Treaty of Paris of 1856 and its execution', *Journal of Modern History*, iv [1932], 399).

[3] Her dislike of Clarendon, which was so pronounced in 1868, was evident in 1865. In a letter to the King of Belgium she wrote that 'I can't say I rejoice to have Clarendon; [as foreign secretary] I don't quite trust him' (Victoria to Leopold, Balmoral, 25 Oct. 1865, *The Letters of Queen Victoria* [hereafter cited as *QVL*], 2nd series, ed. G. E. Buckle [London, 1926], i. 280). There were incidents between Victoria and Clarendon in 1851 and 1863. The queen's German susceptibilities and her fear of having to deal with another Palmerston seemed to have coloured her attitude toward Clarendon (H. Maxwell, *The Life and Letters of Lord Clarendon* [hereafter quoted as Maxwell] [London, 1913], i. 338, 341; ii. 282). A few months before the Austro-Prussian War, Victoria spoke of Clarendon as 'most disagreeable & unmanageable' (Victoria to Crown Princess of Prussia, Windsor, 24 Mar. 1866, RA U/32). On the Austro-Prussian crisis see Mosse's aforementioned article and his 'The Crown and Foreign Policy: Queen Victoria and the Austro-Prussian Conflict, March–May 1866', *The Cambridge Historical Journal*, x (1951), 205–23.

[4] Even so, the queen and Russell were more disposed to action than Clarendon (Russell to Clarendon, 20 Mar. 1866, Maxwell, ii. 311; Victoria to Clarendon, Windsor, 20 Mar. 1866, RA I 43/104).

response by England to the Austro-Prussian crisis of 1866 was due to the fear of commitment. Once Denmark had lost Schleswig-Holstein, its final disposition, even though it involved control by Prussia, was not considered a vital British interest. Intervention was, therefore, out of the question.

At the beginning of March Mensdorff, the Austrian foreign minister, wrote to Apponyi, his ambassador in London, that England's intention of remaining strictly neutral in the quarrel over the Elbe Duchies would in fact favour the aggressor, Prussia. Austria will of course resist Bismarck, the dispatch said, but if she is defeated changes in the balance of power might affect England. 'It will be impossible for the Imperial Govt. to aid the policy of England in the East and assist in the maintenance of the Ottoman Empire'.[1] Clarendon did not rise to the Austrian bait when Apponyi read Mensdorff's letter. He replied that England's advice two years ago was refused, and now, therefore, she could not become concerned over the Duchies and would remain passive over Bismarck's plan to annex them.[2] Privately, however, the foreign secretary was not unhappy that the Austrians were going to stand up to Prussia, and the prospect of doing so successfully was not to him a sad one.[3] England would not therefore intervene officially. The furthest Clarendon seemed willing to go was 'to hold the balance as equally as possible between the belligerents'.[4] Clarendon wrote to Bloomfield in Vienna:

I need not tell you that we shall be neutral & we shall endeavour to prevent our neutrality being in any way injurious to Austria, but it

[1] Mensdorff to Apponyi, 1 Mar. 1866, RA I 43/42, Mosse, p. 223.

[2] Clarendon to Bloomfield, 7 Mar. 1866, confidential, PRO FO 244/208, no. 62. The Prussian minister told Bernstorff, his agent in London, that more intimate relations with the other European powers was in order due to the possibility of a break with Austria (Bismarck to Bernstorff, confidential, Berlin, 3 Mar. 1866, *Die gesammelten Werke* [hereafter cited as *GW*], ed. F. Thimme [Berlin, 1928], v, no. 252).

[3] Clarendon to Bloomfield, 7 Mar. 1866, private, PRO FO 356/33. Clarendon wrote that 'if she [Austria] cd give the Prussians a licking I am sure that Europe wd be glad' (ibid.). Hammond, the under-secretary for foreign affairs, felt the same. He wrote to Bloomfield, 'I confess I should like to see the Prussians well licked' (Hammond to Bloomfield, 20 Mar. 1866, private, PRO FO 356/33).

[4] Clarendon to Bloomfield, 21 Mar. 1866, private, Clarendon Manuscripts (hereafter quoted as Clar. Pap.), C 145. Clarendon wrote to Bloomfield that he was not prepared however to assume that Austria is entirely in the right . . . so if the scales come into my hands I mean to hold them very evenly' (ibid.). This was meant, no doubt, to moderate any Austrian exuberance.

wd be a departure from the rigid rules of neutrality to menace Prussia in the way indicated in Ct. Mensdorff's despatch, & moreover if we took such a course single handed it wd probably do more harm than good. Our experience of 2 years ago has taught us how little the advice and cautions of Engd are regarded in Germany. . . .

I have thought however that there might be a chance of doing some good and not much harm if he [Bismarck] was privately informed of our opinions & I have accordingly written Loftus a letter. . . .[1]

In this private letter to Loftus, the British ambassador in Berlin, Clarendon used strong language which was to be communicated unofficially.

But in the name of all that is rational, decent, humane what can be the justification of war on the part of Prussia. She cannot publicly plead her greed for territorial aggrandizement & she cannot with truth say that the administration of Holstein by the Austrian Authies has been of a kind to constitute a casus belli. . . .[2]

Loftus was told that, while abstaining from making an official communication, he was to suggest to Bismarck that the present difficulty between the two German powers might be referred to a third power as provided for by the Treaty of Paris of 1856.[3] In a friendly and not officious manner, Loftus was to present the following considerations as a deterrent to war.

I am sure [Clarendon wrote] that any grievous injury to her [Austria] such as would destroy the present equilibrium of power would be a misfortune for the rest of Europe and as such would be resented—in fact . . . Prussia will array against her the public opinion of Europe as an aggressive and unreasonable power, and we have no wish for that—setting aside family ties Prussia is the great Protestant power of Europe with which we naturally have kindred feelings, and it would be with deep regret that we should see her regarded as a common enemy, because a wilful disturber of the peace of Europe, and still more in the course of events we found ourselves compelled to take any part against her.[4]

---

[1] Clarendon to Bloomfield, 7 Mar. 1866, private, PRO FO 356/33. Bernstorff reported to Bismarck that Clarendon had told Apponyi that England would remain neutral in an Austro-Prussian war (Bernstorff to Bismarck, London, confidential, 21 Mar. 1866, *Die Auswärtige Politik Preussens, 1858–1871* [10 vols., Oldenburg, 1932 et seq.] [hereafter cited as *APP*], vi. 715–16).

[2] Clarendon to Loftus, ibid.

[3] Granville was to make the same suggestion in July 1870, when it was too late to be effective.

[4] Clarendon to Loftus, 7 Mar. 1866, copy, Clar. Pap. C 145.

Loftus communicated to Bismarck the substance of Clarendon's letter on 11 March. The minister president avoided a direct answer to the mediation proposal but did not hide the fact 'that in his opinion there were no means of deciding the difference with Austria but by the sword, and the present was the most favorable opportunity for Prussia, an opportunity which might not again offer itself for a century'.[1]

A few days later the British ambassador had an opportunity to convey the contents of Clarendon's letter of 7 March to the King of Prussia. Loftus reported that the king was favourably disposed to mediation as an alternative preferable to war.[2] When pressed again, therefore, Bismarck told Loftus that he would instruct Bernstorff, the Prussian minister at London, in the sense of the king's desire.[3] At the same time the crown prince was asked by the king to write to Victoria to ask her to undertake the mediation.[4] The queen communicated the letter to Russell and Clarendon. For a flickering moment it seemed that England's kid glove attempt to avoid war would prove successful. The attempted mediation failed because Bismarck was even more anxious to avoid accepting it than Clarendon was cautious in offering it. The foreign secretary, torn by conflicting desires to avert a war on the one hand and to keep British prestige from further rebuffs on the other, evaded acting decisively to prevent a war which he alternately

---

[1] Loftus to Clarendon, Berlin, 17 Mar. 1866, most confidential, PRO FO 64/591, no. 53. This confirmed what Crowe, who was stationed at Leipzig, had reported to Clarendon. 'At a royal council held in Berlin on the 28th . . . most of the members of the council declared for a breach and a war with Austria' (Crowe to Clarendon, 7 Mar. 1866, PRO FO 68/144, no. 7). Clarendon told Bernstorff that if war occurred the English Government and public opinion would say that Prussia was the aggressor, and there would be no sympathy for Prussia in England (Bernstorff to Bismarck, telegram, 29 Mar. 1866, APP vi. 787).

[2] Ibid.

[3] Loftus to Clarendon, Berlin, 17 Mar. 1866, confidential, ibid., no. 55.

[4] Loftus to Clarendon, Berlin, 17 Mar. 1866, most confidential, ibid., no. 54. Bismarck, angry because the crown prince's letter had been sent without his knowledge, instructed Bernstorff to regard its contents as unofficial (Bismarck to Bernstorff, Berlin, telegram, 20 Mar. 1866, GW v, no. 268). Apparently the King of Prussia was agreed with Bismarck on policy. 'We did not know the King had written to you. He never told us; that he shd lay all the blame on Fritz is very odd; it is really expecting a great deal of Fritz to suppose he is to put disagreeable messages, of wh he entirely disapproves, into acceptable language. That would be Tantamount to furthering the King's Politics, wh Fritz cannot do, as he is completely against them' (Crown Princess of Prussia to Victoria, [?] Mar. 1866, RA I 43/76).

thought would not occur[1] and would be impossible to prevent. On 12 March, Clarendon admitted to Cowley that Prussia appeared to be backing down somewhat, but also that 'it wd have been useless for us to make an official remonstrance agst. Bismarck's peacebreaking proclivities'.[2] On the very next day, in response to Russell's suggestion that the recognition of the duke of Oldenbourg as duke of Schleswig-Holstein might prevent a war from which only France could benefit, Clarendon answered:

> If I thought that war was certain & that any advice of ours wd avert it I shd be prepared to recommend that Oldenbourg or *Couza even* shd reign over the Duchies, but . . . [as] within the last two days the fear of war has rather abated I have come to the conclusion that the practical utility of our recommending Oldenbourg is not so apparent as to counter balance the ill effects it wd have in the Duchies & the certain fix with the Queen who is right I think in saying that we shd advise the states being assembled & the people consulted, if we advise at all.[3]

A few days later Gladstone, the chancellor of the exchequer, made known to Clarendon his opinion that England should not hide from Prussia the impression her iniquitous conduct was creating. The latter responded:

> I was sure that if we had single-handed, made an official representation upon the subject we shd have recd. an insolent answer from Bismarck. . . . The King [of Prussia] is prepared to accept our good offices.
>
> In what sense he expects those good offices to be used remains to be seen, but at all events his request is a present security for the maintenance of peace.[4]

The willingness of the King of Prussia to use English good offices to avert war was less strong than Bismarck's desire not

---

[1] La Tour to Drouyn, 24 Feb. and 4 Apr. 1866, *Les origines diplomatiques de la guerre de 1870–71* (hereafter quoted as *Orig.*), 29 vols. (Paris, 1910 et seq.), vii. 323; viii. 171.

[2] Clarendon to Cowley, 12 Mar. 1866, private, PRO FO 519/180.

[3] Clarendon to Russell, 13 Mar. 1866, PRO FO 30/22, no. 16. Victoria had Grey inform Russell of her opposition to his suggestion (Grey to Russell, 12 Mar. 1866, *Russell*, ii. 344). The queen also informed Clarendon (Grey to Clarendon, 12 Mar. 1866, RA I 43/68).

[4] Clarendon to Gladstone, 18 Mar. 1866, Gladstone Papers (hereafter quoted as Glad. Pap.), pp. 58–59.

to do so, and Clarendon, as he explained to Loftus, was not necessarily putting forth England as the mediator.

I am afraid he [King of Prussia] is under some misapprehension as to our having offered our good offices—such was not . . . [my] intention. I merely wished that the declaration of Paris should be borne in mind by Prussia before she went to war, but by no means that England should have the honour of being the referee. The point is of considerable importance because if our mediation is *offered* we must, if it is accepted, exercise it, whereas if it is *asked for* we are at liberty to say on what terms we will comply with the request. If the pretended casus belli of Prussia is press-grievances and Augustenberg intrigues we might undertake to inquire into such matters . . . but if under the cloak of these foolish complaints it is meant that we should help in annexing the Duchies to Prussia, it is manifest that our honour as well as public opinion here would render the faintest move in that direction impossible. . . . I gave him [Bernstorff] to understand that our good offices had not been offered. . . .

If we act at all in this matter I entirely agree with you that it must be in conjunction with France. . . .[1]

If Clarendon was careful to limit English commitment, he was not ready to close the door completely on English action, particularly since the cabinet on 21 March decided that if asked for 'good offices should be tender'd it [Prussia] . . . and Prussia and Austria should be ask'd what complaints they have to make'.[2] Loftus was no sooner instructed to this effect[3] than Bismarck made it apparent, both through Bernstorff, his minister in London, and Loftus, that any further British effort in this direction would be fruitless. When Clarendon told Bernstorff that England would be willing to inform Vienna of Prussia's complaints, the latter 'answered that they had long ago and in great detail been brought to the knowledge of the Austrian Government, and that no redress had been obtained'.[4] Upon hearing this, Clarendon, who was often more blunt in

---

[1] Clarendon to Loftus, 21 Mar. 1866, private, Clar. Pap. C 145. Eight days before in response to Clarendon's query, Cowley wrote that France saw 'a war between them [Austria and Prussia] . . . as nuts here' (Cowley to Clarendon, 13 Mar. 1866, private, PRO FO 519/232). Clarendon believed this sufficiently to relate it to Bloomfield (Clarendon to Bloomfield, 14 Mar. 1866, private, PRO FO 356/33).

[2] Russell to Victoria, 22 Mar. 1866, RA I 43/110, Mosse, p. 228.

[3] Clarendon to Loftus, 21 Mar. 1866, PRO FO 64/588, no. 26.

[4] Clarendon to Loftus, 22 Mar. 1866, PRO FO 64/588, no. 30; Clarendon to Victoria, 24 Mar. 1866, RA I 43/120.

his conversations with Bernstorff than in his letters to Loftus, said that England would not lift a finger to aid Prussia in annexing the Duchies. When the Prussian ambassador asked why, he was told 'it was a question of principle'.[1] As a parting shot Clarendon asked whether the legislatures of the Duchies might not be allowed to decide their own ruler.[2] The reply was negative since 'they would elect the Duke of Augustenburg'.[3] As a result of this conversation at which Bernstorff read a long letter from Bismarck asserting the Duchies to be 'politically & militarily indispensable to Prussia', Clarendon considered 'all question of good offices . . . at an end'.[4] In Berlin, Bismarck told Loftus that England should attempt to moderate the Austrians as they were 'the party who threatened to be the disturber of the peace'.[5] Bismarck, though not directly negating English mediation, nevertheless made it impossible by refusing to predicate arbitration on any lesser basis than the annexation of Schleswig and Holstein. The intransigence of Bismarck, even to the point of war, was no secret.[6] Russell was sure of it and even hinted to Victoria, hoping she would write to the Queen of Prussia or Fritz or Vicky, that if Bismarck could be cashiered all would be well. How else can this letter to the queen be interpreted:

There is but one remedy—one certain . . . [way] of preserving peace—it is the dismissal of Count Bismarck by the King—

If this can be accomplished by any patriot Prussians who may have access to the King, all may go right—but otherwise—[7]

Perhaps Victoria could, through her family, uncrown the man

[1] Ibid. Bernstorff to Bismark, telegram, 22 Mar. 1866, *APP* vi. 719–20.

[2] Victoria and her private secretary, Grey, had constantly pressed this on Russell and Clarendon. In 1870 Gladstone wished to consult the wishes of the people of Alsace and Lorraine prior to Prussian annexation.

[3] Clarendon to Loftus, 22 Mar. 1866, PRO FO 64/588, no. 30.

[4] Clarendon to Cowley, 22 Mar. 1866, private, PRO FO 519/180. In the letter which Bernstorff read, Bismarck indicated the opposition of both Prussian and German public opinion to the interference of foreign powers in a purely German question involving two German states. The Prussian statesman further alluded to Austrian provocation and suggested England might more justifiably preach moderation at Vienna rather than at Berlin (Bismarck to Bernstorff, very confidential, Berlin, 20 Mar. 1866, *GW* v, no. 269).

[5] Loftus to Clarendon, 24 Mar. 1866, PRO FO 64/592, no. 70; Bismarck to Bernstorff, 20 Mar. 1866, *GW*, ibid.

[6] Crowe to Clarendon, 7 Mar. 1866, PRO FO 68/144, no. 7; Gordon to Clarendon, 3 Apr. 1866, PRO FO 82/122, no. 24.

[7] Russell to Victoria, 27 Mar. 1866, RA I 43, no. 130.

Clarendon referred to as 'the real King of Prussia'.[1] The queen wrote both to the crown prince and princess, but with little effect. She also suggested that France and England together could warn Prussia. The Cabinet, as well as Russell and Clarendon, were cool to this idea.[2] The latter in a long letter to the queen explained that France awaited the impending struggle with bated breath and that, even with France, England could not 'use the language of menace wh. might entail the necessity of action'. Three reasons were given. First, England might have gone to war in 1864 and, having decided not to, it was too late to do so now. Second, the Duchies were a German problem. Third, neither English honour nor interest was involved.[3]

From this it would seem that it is a mistake to argue that without a European ally England could not effectively intervene on the Continent. In Clarendon's words she was not prepared, in the Austro-Prussian crisis, to take action even with France.[4] The foreign secretary still hoped, however, that Prussia might back down. 'There is a chance of Prussia giving way if Germany is stout, and I wrote to the Queen this afternoon that now was the moment for the minor states to exhibit moral courage & to protest agst. the war as groundless & therefore unjustifiable'.[5] Was Clarendon attempting to influence the queen to write to her German relatives and frustrate Bismarck's plans, much as

[1] Clarendon to Bloomfield, 28 Mar. 1866, private, PRO FO 356/33.

[2] Russell to Clarendon, Pembroke Lodge, 30 Mar. 1866, Maxwell, ii. 311. Clarendon's general attitude toward the Austro-Prussian dispute is reflected in his reference to it as a 'banditti quarrel' not worth English blood or money (Clarendon to Russell, 31 Mar. 1866, Russell, ii. 345).

[3] Clarendon to Victoria, 31 Mar. 1866, RA I 43, no. 154; Mosse, p. 230.

[4] In response to the queen's request Clarendon had written to Cowley to sound France on a joint remonstrance to Prussia. Cowley replied that Napoleon felt 'no advantage would result from any advice which France and England might offer' (Clarendon to Cowley, 3 Apr. 1866, PRO FO 519/232).

[5] Clarendon to Russell, 1 Apr. 1866, PRO FO 30/22, no. 16. Clarendon was impressed by the reports from his representatives at the smaller German courts. They were nearly unanimous in reflecting the condemnation of Prussia's policy and particularly Bismarck's desire for war. It was reasonable for the foreign secretary to conclude that the announced intention of Bavaria, Württemberg, Saxony, and Baden to oppose Bismarck if he broke the peace, would prevent him from carrying the King of Prussia to war (Gordon to Clarendon, 14 Mar. 1866, PRO FO 82/122, no. 16; same to same, 19 Mar. 1866, ibid., no. 18; same to same, 26 Mar. 1866, ibid., no. 19; Howard to Clarendon, 10 Apr. 1866, PRO FO 9/173, no. 36; Gordon to Clarendon, 26 May 1866, PRO FO 82/123, no. 73; same to same, 29 Apr. 1866, ibid., no. 49; Howard to Clarendon, 14 May 1866, PRO FO 9/174, no. 78).

Russell had hinted to her? On 3 April he wrote to the queen. 'Ct. Bismarck's case for war is so utterly groundless that Lord C. ventures to think that the king must, before he decides for war, become aware of the truth, notwithstanding all the un-scrupulous contrivances resorted to to conceal it from him'.[1] Three days later Clarendon wrote that he felt 'the best way of opening the King's eyes wd. be a letter to him from the Emperor of Austria . . . stating facts & defying contradictions—the Duke of Coburg might perhaps suggest this course'.[2] And who was better to suggest this to the duke than his sister-in-law, the Queen of England?

At the same time that Clarendon was attempting to use dynastic influence to secure what he was rightly hesitant to attain by more normal diplomatic technique, the prevention of war by the dismissal of Bismarck, he was constantly advising Bloomfield in Vienna that if Austria stood firm but yet allowed Prussia no *'just* cause for complaint' in Holstein, a conflict might be avoided.[3]

In the meantime Victoria, as Mosse points out, without con-sulting the Government,[4] wrote to the King of Prussia. This, however, could hardly have been a surprise to either Russell or Clarendon, as both had intimated to her several times that Bismarck was blinding the king to the reality of the situation and isolating him so that others could not undeceive him. The letter written on 10 April contained a fervent appeal.

Beloved Brother
    At this fearful moment I cannot be silent, without raising my voice earnestly, & in the name of all that is most holy & sacred against the threatening probability of war. . . . You are deceived, you are made to believe that you are to be attacked, & I your . . . Sister hear your honoured name attacked . . . for the faults of one man . . . & if you have any regard for the memory of him who was your friend, (my beloved husband) & for my affection & friendship —pause before you permit so fearful an act as the commencement of

---

[1] Clarendon to Victoria, 3 Apr. 1866, RA I 43, no. 175.
[2] Clarendon to Victoria, 6 Apr. 1866, RA I 43, no. 195.
[3] Clarendon to Bloomfield, 4 Apr. 1866, private, PRO FO 356/33. Clarendon hoped that if war could be put off long enough, Bismarck would be dismissed or a revolution would break out in Prussia. In either case he felt war would be avoided (Crowe to Clarendon, 21 Feb. 1866, PRO FO 68/144, no. 3; Clarendon to Derby, 4 June 1866, Derby Papers [hereafter quoted as Derby Pap.], 105).
[4] Mosse, pp. 230–1.

a war, the responsibility of wh. will rest on *you alone*. . . . I cannot, will not think that I shall have appealed to your heart in vain.[1]

Both Russell and Clarendon were ecstatic over the letter, not the least so in that they had avoided taking the responsibility for its contents and communication.[2] The King of Prussia's reaction to the letter, as reported by Loftus, was that Austria made it difficult to maintain the peace the queen hoped to preserve. In his reply to Victoria he defended Prussia's desire for the Duchies as representing the national will of his people, and both General Grey, the queen's secretary, and Clarendon interpreted his cataloguing of Austrian provocations as the same 'stereotyped accusations . . . wh. Ct. Bismarck has sent forth during the last three months'.[3]

During the month of April another British attempt, unofficial and private, was made to avert war.[4] When it was suggested that Austria might cede Venetia to Italy in return for compensation, Cowley spoke in this sense to Metternich, the Austrian minister in Paris.[5] Two days later the English ambassador was privately instructed by Clarendon to do what he had already undertaken on his own initiative. 'Do press it upon Metternich who from his position at Paris—the supreme umpire's court—may have some influence with his government. . . . I have put the case as strongly as I cd. to Bloomfield'.[6] Russell at the same time was writing privately to Apponyi, the Austrian ambassador in London, explaining the advantages of such a cession.

Avail yourselves of the present moment to make the cession. . . . [This would] have all the grace of a voluntary surrender to national aspirations . . . will satisfy the wishes of England & France . . . may form a lasting friendship with Italy . . . above all Austria may at this

---

[1] Victoria to King of Prussia, 10 Apr. 1866, *QVL* i. 317. The letter was sent to Loftus to be given to the king personally (Clarendon to Loftus, 11 Apr. 1866, private, Clar. Pap. C 145).

[2] Victoria to Russell, Windsor, 10 Apr. 1866, *QVL*, 2nd ser., i. 318; Loftus to Grey, Berlin, private, 14 Apr. 1866, ibid.

[3] Grey to Victoria, 24 Apr. 1866, RA I 44, no. 69; Clarendon to Victoria, 25 Apr. 1866, RA I 44, no. 72. The queen herself was very disappointed with the reply of the King of Prussia.

[4] Chester W. Clark, *Franz Joseph and Bismarck. The Diplomacy of Austria before the War of 1866* (Cambridge, 1934), pp. 408–9.

[5] Cowley to Clarendon, 12 Apr. 1866, most confidential, PRO FO 27/1615, no. 452.

[6] Clarendon to Cowley, 14 Apr. 1866, private, PRO FO 519/180.

moment circumscribe the cession she will make, and establish a frontier which Europe will respect. . . .[1]

Gladstone expressed similar sentiments.[2] Mensdorff was against the suggestion for many reasons, one of which was that after Venetia Italy might claim more.[3]

In the third week of April attempts to suggest suitable compensation for Austria (Silesia, Moldavia and Wallachia, money, &c.) were submerged by reports of the mutual disarming of Austria and Prussia. Bloomfield was instructed:

Her Majesty's Govt. . . . hope that . . . Austria . . . will . . . at once . . . reduce her military force to its original peace establishment, if Prussia will consent to adopt the same course.

H.M.'s Govt. earnestly recommended to the favourable consideration of the Austrian Govt. not to lose the last opportunity that may occur of solving this momentous question in favour of peace.[4]

Hopes for peace died quickly, though hard. Bismarck used Austrian armaments in Venetia as proof of Vienna's insincerity.[5] Clarendon was particularly angry at the spectacle of a peaceful solution being dashed so promptly on the rocks of what he felt to be one man's vanity.[6] To Bernstorff he stated his opinions frankly.

Whether Austria was not entitled, whether she was not compelled, to provide against an attack which appeared so imminent,

[1] Russell to Apponyi, 16 Apr. 1866, PRO FO 356/33; same to same, 16 Apr. 1866, RA I 44/35. The queen was against any official representation on the subject.
[2] Gladstone to Vitzthiam, 18 Apr. 1866, Glad. Pap., vol. ccccli.
[3] Bloomfield to Clarendon, private, Vienna, 26 Apr. 1866, RA I 44/77. In July d'Azeglio asked Stanley his reaction to Italian claims in the Tyrol (Stanley to Cowley, 12 July 1866, PRO FO 146/1257, no. 21).
[4] Clarendon to Bloomfield, 17 Apr. 1866, telegram, PRO FO 146/246, no. 117. Since March Bismarck had been complaining of Austrian armament (Bismarck to Bernstorff, telegram, Berlin, 27 Mar. 1866, GW v, no. 281).
[5] Bismarck to German missions in London, St. Petersburg, and Paris, telegram, Berlin, 11 Apr. 1866, GW v, no. 301; ibid., 19 Apr. 1866, GW v, no. 306; ibid., 30 Apr. 1866, GW v, no. 317; ibid., 4 May 1866, GW v, no. 323.
[6] On 26 April Loftus had written that Bismarck had told him that 'my illness & possible death may prevent war—nothing else will—' (Clarendon to Cowley, 27 Apr. 1866, private, PRO FO 519/180). Bismarck surely said this for effect, knowing it would be reported to London. He hoped perhaps that Clarendon would press Vienna to give in on the Duchies since Prussia meant to go to war, or else have England so convinced that Prussia wanted war, that she would make no more attempts to prevent it because of the futility of so doing.

knowing, as she must know, the understanding for offence as well as defense which existed between Prussia and Italy.

Speaking for my own inmost conviction, I said that if civil war should break out in Germany, if Europe should take part in such a war, if revolution should ensue . . . the person who would be responsible in the estimation of mankind for the evils . . . would be Count Bismarck.[1]

At the end of April, Napleon III put out feelers for a congress. Informed of this by Cowley, Clarendon's reaction was favourable yet wary.[2] He himself prepared a draft in which England would make an appeal to Prussia and Austria, but the Cabinet had vetoed this as being too clear a manifestation 'that France was not agreed'.[3] With this in mind, and failing to see how a conference could solve the problems of Venetia and the Duchies, the foreign secretary made another suggestion.

England & France . . . [should invoke] the declaration of Paris . . . [and] appeal to the honour, the Christian feelings & the true interests of the three powers, should call upon them to resume the status quo & declare that the power which persisted without sufficient cause in provoking an unjustifiable war must in the eyes . . . of the whole civilized world, be held responsible for all the calamities which it would cause. Her Majesty's Government would further suggest that Russia . . . should be invited to join in this appeal.[4]

Both Napoleon and his foreign minister, Drouyn de Lhuys, vetoed this proposal.[5] Drouyn told Cowley that France could not sustain a rebuff from Germany which such a step might entail.[6] The reason for France's refusal to co-operate was, however, Venetia. If it is true, as Mosse maintains, that Napoleon's Rhine dreams prevented Anglo-French co-operation in 1863 and 1864,[7] such was not the main stumbling-block in 1866.

---

[1] Clarendon to Loftus, 29 Apr. 1866, PRO FO 64/588, no. 81; same to same, 29 Apr. 1866, RA I 44/93.

[2] Clarendon to Cowley, 30 Apr. 1866, private, PRO FO 64/588, no. 81.

[3] Victoria memorandum, 6 May 1866, QVL, 2nd ser., i. 325–6; ibid., RA I 44/144.

[4] Clarendon to Cowley, 2 May 1866, secret and confidential, PRO FO 27/1604, no. 600. This suggestion of a joint appeal was approved by the Cabinet.

[5] Cowley to Clarendon, 4 May 1866, private, PRO FO 519/232; same to same, 4 May 1866, telegram, PRO FO 27/1616, no. 381; same to same, Paris, secret and confidential, 5 May 1866, RA J 81/110.

[6] Cowley to Clarendon, 4 May 1866, secret and confidential, PRO FO 27/1616, no. 587.

[7] Mosse, p. 128.

Napoleon wanted Italy to have Venetia at any price,[1] and Britain's appeal to the status quo did not take this into account. England could not and would not be so generous, particularly since Venetia was guaranteed to Austria by treaty.[2] Napoleon told Cowley:

> The annexation of Venetia to Italy must form the first item of any arrangement to which he could consent either in a congress, or in a more limited understanding[3] with one or two powers. To effect this His Majesty would willingly join Her Majesty's Government and that of Russia. This question once settled . . . Germany might be left to solve her own difficulties.[4]

Napoleon's price for co-operation was clear. Cowley realized this when he informed Clarendon that the 'foundation of any understanding with His Majesty must be the transfer of Venetia from Austria to Italy'.[5] England could not sanction formally what Russell, Gladstone, and Clarendon had attempted to do unofficially when they had tried to persuade Austria to cede Venetia. Any remaining hope of an understanding with France was shattered by the explosion of the emperor's speech at Auxerre.[6] Clarendon referred to it 'as the worst & most ominous thing he has done since his accession.'[7]

Having failed either to dissuade Prussia or to achieve co-operation with France, Clarendon advised Italy to remain neutral[8] and the German states to remain firm.[9] The Italian

---

[1] La Tour to Drouyn, 8 June 1866, *Orig.*, vol. ix.

[2] Clarendon privately informed Cowley that 'we cannot join in an attempt to coerce any power to give up territory that it is entitled to hold' (Clarendon to Cowley, 10 May 1866, private, PRO FO 519/180).

[3] This was in reference to Clarendon's suggestion of a joint appeal by England, France, and Russia.

[4] Cowley to Clarendon, 5 May 1866, secret and confidential, PRO FO 27/1616, no. 591.

[5] Ibid.; Cowley to Clarendon, 7 May 1866, private, PRO FO 519/232.

[6] Napoleon in this speech castigated the Vienna Treaties. Victoria, however, offered to write to Napoleon in order to persuade him to prevent war. Russell and Clarendon were cool to this (Clarendon to Victoria, 7 May 1866, RA J 81/113).

[7] Clarendon to Bloomfield, 9 May 1866, private, PRO FO 356/33.

[8] Clarendon to Cowley, 6 May 1866, telegram, PRO FO 146/1249, no. 623. Before making this proposal, Napoleon had ascertained confidentially that Britain was not opposed to a congress (Clarendon to Victoria, 2 May 1866, RA J 81/102).

[9] Clarendon to Cowley, 9 May 1866, confidential, PRO FO 146/1249. Clarendon also had the queen write a letter to 'Fritz'. This action had no apparent effect.

reply was that this was impossible and Italy must await the circumstances of fortune.[1]

Napoleon now proposed a preliminary conference of the three powers to frame proposals to be set before a more general congress to which Prussia, Austria, and Italy would be invited. Venetia would of course be on the agenda.[2] Clarendon reacted favourably to this overture, but did not conceal his anxiety about the motives of the emperor or the limits beyond which English commitment could not go.[3] He wrote privately to Cowley that 'we cannot join in an attempt to coerce any power to give up territory that it is entitled to hold or [sic] can we be parties to forcing the Duchies to accept the yoke of Prussia'.[4] The Cabinet, the prime minister, the foreign secretary, and Cowley feared that the proposed congress might be a trap to commit England to the cession of Venetia to Italy.[5] Drouyn de Lhuys removed the main English objection to a congress when he informed Clarendon that he understood Britain's reluctance to bind herself beforehand, and this would not be necessary since 'each power would . . . retain full liberty of action' in the event of differences of opinion at the conclusion of the congress.[6] Though the French foreign minister silenced any official English objections, Cowley was still attempting to ascertain the 'real motives of France calling a congress'.[7] If the English Government showed more suspicion of France when she was trying to co-operate with her than when the two were isolated, it stemmed from the fact that Clarendon did not wish to be pulled into any Continental imbroglio he could not justify in Parliament or before public opinion,[8] nor did he feel confidence

---

[1] Clarendon to Cowley, 8 May 1866, telegram, PRO FO 146/1249.

[2] Clarendon to Cowley, 10 May 1866, PRO FO 27/1605, no. 650; Drouyn to La Tour, 8 May 1866, confidential, *Orig.* ix. 534.

[3] Clarendon to Cowley, 10 May 1866, PRO FO 27/1605, no. 657. Clarendon emphasized that England would not support the use of force (and so of course nothing would be done) to impose any resolutions decided upon (La Tour to Drouyn, 12 May 1866, *Orig.* ix. 114–16).

[4] Clarendon to Cowley, 10 May 1866, private, PRO FO 519/180.

[5] Ibid.; Clarendon to Cowley, 10 May 1866, PRO FO 27/1605, no. 67; Cowley to Clarendon, 11 May 1866, private, PRO FO 519/232; Russell to Clarendon, 6 May 1866, RA J 38/151.

[6] Clarendon to Cowley, 11 May 1866, PRO FO 27/1605, no. 660; Clarendon to Cowley, 12 May 1866, private, PRO FO 519/180.

[7] Cowley to Clarendon, 15 May 1866, PRO FO 27/1617, no. 645.

[8] Clarendon to Cowley, 12 May 1866, private, PRO FO 519/180. Clarendon

in a government which refused one idea for peace (Clarendon's plan of a joint appeal by England, France, and Russia) while at almost the same time suggesting a step similar to it, a preliminary congress of the same three powers.[1]

In the end Clarendon agreed to a congress which he thought would do no good[2] because the responsibility for a refusal appeared to outweigh the possible commitments involved in acceptance.[3] When it was learned that Austria attached conditions to her acceptance of the congress, conditions which the French Government felt rendered the meeting useless, London was not unduly saddened. Hammond, the under secretary,[4] Grey, the queen's private secretary, and Clarendon[5] himself sympathized with Austria's decision, the foreign secretary being particularly relieved that the failure of the congress to meet could not be laid at England's door.[6] Even the Prince of Wales and the English press were on Austria's side.[7]

The difficulty in co-operating with France led Clarendon once more to make use of the queen, a step which had the particular merit in the foreign secretary's eyes of being unofficial and therefore not committing the British Government. He made the following suggestion to the queen:

wrote privately to Cowley that 'we are willing to do anything for the maintenance of peace except committing ourselves to a policy of action that we cd. not justify & wh. wd. not be sanctioned by public opinion at home' (ibid.). Cowley feared for Clarendon's position in parliament if a congress failed.

[1] Clarendon to Cowley, 15 May 1866, PRO FO 146/1250, no. 678. Both Cowley and Clarendon disliked Drouyn and thought he was a liar, a fact which did nothing to foster Anglo-French harmony (Clarendon to Bloomfield, 16 May 1866, private, PRO FO 356/33). They also thought that Drouyn hoped to use the congress to hasten war (Clarendon to Cowley, 18 May 1866, private, PRO FO 519/180; Cowley to Clarendon, private, Paris, 8 May 1866, RA J 81/122; same to same, private, Paris, 15 May 1866, ibid., no. 151; same to same, private, Paris, 17 May 1866, ibid., no. 158).

[2] Ibid.

[3] Clarendon to Cowley, 26 May 1866, private, PRO FO 519/180. Bismarck's acceptance of a congress was probably due to the futility of holding it (Bismarck to missions in London, Paris, and St. Petersburg, Berlin, 29 May 1866, *GW* v, no. 360).

[4] Hammond to Cowley, 2 June 1866, private, PRO FO 519/192.

[5] Clarendon to Cowley, 14 June 1866, private, PRO FO 519/180.

[6] Ibid.

[7] Apponyi to Mensdorff, 7 Apr. 1866, Haus-Hof und Staatsarchiv, Wien (hereafter quoted as HHSA), England, no. 31. La Tour to Drouyn, 8 June 1866, confidential, *Orig.* ix. 80–81; Sir Sydney Lee, *King Edward VII. A Biography* (New York, 1925), i. 258–9. Cowley, Bloomfield, and Loftus were also pro-Austrian (Bloomfield to Cowley, 11 June 1866, private, PRO FO 519/201).

To write to the Crown Prince [of Prussia that] it has occurred to Your Majesty that a reference of the question of the Duchies to the Diet might solve all the difficulties. . . . If the King [of Prussia] shd . . . consider Himself . . . not to allow the intervention of the Diet in the question of the Duchies H[is] M[ajesty] might be [persuaded] . . . to do so by a Congress . . . at the request of the Great Powers.

Your Majesty wd. probably request the Crown Prince to lay the letter before the King.

The crown prince delivered the queen's letter to the King of Prussia but it did not have the effect hoped for by the queen and her foreign secretary.[1]

At the beginning of June it was obvious that war was imminent. On 8 June Goltz, the Prussian minister in Paris, told Fane that Prussia had resolved on an immediate war.[2] There was no eleventh hour attempt on England's part to avert a conflict. Why? The queen's offer to write again to the King of Prussia as well as her suggestion of an English appeal to Prussia, Austria, and Italy were vetoed.[3] Undoubtedly Clarendon felt the futility of England's doing anything at the beginning of June to be overwhelming, and the prospect of an Austrian victory, which most thought likely, was enough to sweeten the bitterness of the frustration of previous efforts to prevent war.[4] He did not hide his feelings from Napoleon III. 'Her Majesty's Government had arrived at no fixed opinion which would have admitted of their at once assenting to the proposi-

---

[1] Clarendon to Victoria, 15 May 1866, RA I 44/178; Victoria to Crown Princess of Prussia, Windsor, 16 May 1866, ibid., U/32; Crown Princess of Prussia to Victoria, Neue Palais, 19 May 1866, ibid., I 44/189.

[2] Fane to Clarendon, 8 June 1866, secret and confidential, PRO FO 27/1618, no. 20.

[3] The queen's frustration was expressed in a letter to her daughter, the Crown Princess of Prussia. 'I & the Govt. (& Ld. Clarendon behaves extremely well) have done all we can but the Empr. N[apoleon] will do nothing—& he cd! . . . This state of suspense is fearful—& I wish Fritz wd. be firm & say he refuses to take part in such an iniquitous war!' (Victoria to Crown Princess of Prussia, Osborne, 9 May 1866, RA U/32). Victoria was not in doubt as to the parties wanting war. This can be seen from her comments on Clarendon's draft circular to all the German courts. 'She [the Queen] thinks that in stating the suspicions attaching to the three Powrs who threaten the peace of Europe, Austria ought not to be classed exactly with Prussia & Italy. . . . Prussia & Italy have not concealed their determination—the one to annex the Duchies—the other to lose no opportunity of obtaining Venetia' (Grey to Clarendon, Windsor, 9 May 1866, RA I 44/158).

[4] He told Cowley 'that what wd. please everybody in Europe wd. be that Italy got Venetia, Austria, Silesia & Prussia a licking' (Clarendon to Cowley, 12 May 1866, private, PRO FO 519/180).

tion . . . that it was desirable to secure for that power [Prussia] greater strength in the north of Europe'.[1] It was consistent with this attitude that on 21 June, after war had begun and Prussia had announced that the Germanic Confederation was no more, Clarendon wrote to Cowley that the British Government felt that no single state should dissolve an institution which owed its existence 'to the general assent of all the Powers of Europe'. Cowley was to ascertain the views of the French Government on this question.[2] While Napoleon was not receptive to this point of view,[3] the Russian Government was. Prussia's victories in the field, however, soon made the existence of the Confederation an academic question.

During the crisis which led to war there was little discussion of European affairs in a parliament preoccupied with reform. In the House of Lords, Clarendon justified the Government's position by stating that 'we have stood alone, and alone we could do nothing against the determination that war was the most effective means . . . of giving effect to an ambitious policy'.[4] Earl Grey, almost a lone voice from the Palmerstonian past, spoke in reply:

It was at that time 1864 ostentatiously laid down as the political rules of conduct of this country that we were never to interfere with foreign states except when our interests were directly and immediately threatened. The rule or principle of non-intervention . . . was abused to this extent. . . .

My Lords, I say this is a new doctrine . . . for the first time acted upon in a manner which has left a stain on the fair name of this country some two years ago. . . .[5]

Russell, in an uncharacteristic refrain, argued that 'if you enter a war merely for the sake of preserving the general balance of power in Europe, without your interests or honour being involved, you ought to see whether you are not likely to

[1] Clarendon to Cowley, 16 June 1866, PRO FO 27/1606, no. 846. Palmerston had been willing, at least in private, to admit this (Palmerston to Russell, 13 Sept. 1865, Mosse, p. 222). Russell was not greatly opposed to this prospect either (Clarendon to Cowley, 11 April 1866, private, PRO FO 519/180).
[2] Clarendon to Cowley, 21 June 1866, PRO FO 146/1255, no. 869; ibid., PRO FO 27/606, no. 869.
[3] Cowley to Clarendon, 21 June 1866, most confidential, PRO FO 27/1619, no. 824; Drouyn to Benedetti, 2 July 1866, *Orig.* x. 303–4.
[4] Hansard, *Parliamentary Debates* (3rd series), clxxxiii. 573.
[5] Ibid., pp. 514–75.

produce much more evil than you are likely to remedy'.[1] This statement was more in the tradition of Canning[2] than of Castlereagh[3] or Palmerston,[4] who assumed that the European balance of power was identical with British interest. Clarendon of course never considered going into a war the extent of which he hoped to limit,[5] and he undoubtedly wished to avoid any discussion of foreign affairs in Parliament that might embarrass his Government in the midst of pushing through a reform bill.[6] He could not afford the kind of explosive condemnation his party had received in 1864, particularly since the popularity and prestige of Palmerston were no longer available to see them through. Consequently Clarendon moved cautiously and in so doing kept in step with the majority in the Cabinet and Parliament. He acted this way not merely because it was politically expedient at home, but because like almost everyone else he underestimated Prussia and Bismarck. He saw the danger to Britain's position from out of the past, and thus allowed Napoleon III, and to a lesser extent Alexander II, to obscure the future. He argued that he could not effectively prevent the war because no real British interests were involved in it, and in consequence intervention and appeals on the ground of morality or humanity[7] had no chance of success. His failure, however, was hardly complete, because his willingness to co-operate with France and Russia, though motivated as much by a suspicion of their designs as by a community of interests, resulted in a conflict in which Paris and St. Petersburg were not involved. It is true, of course, that Clarendon could not have prevented Napoleon III from entering the war, and it is clear that he greatly feared the consequences of such a development.

The effectiveness of any English mediation, even unofficial

[1] Ibid., p. 576.

[2] Harold W. V. Temperley, *The Foreign Policy of Canning 1822–27* (London, 1925), p. 459.

[3] Charles K. Webster, *The Foreign Policy of Castlereagh 1815–22* (London, 1925), i. 199, 208, 493.

[4] Charles K. Webster, *The Foreign Policy of Palmerston 1830–41* (London, 1951), ii. 792.

[5] Clarendon to England's representatives in Germany, 9 April 1866, most confidential, PRO FO 146/1245. Apponyi interpreted British passivity partly as a reflection of English concern over Ireland and the state of the navy (Apponyi to Mensdorff, 8 Apr. 1866, HHSA, England, no. 53).

[6] Apponyi to Mensdorff, 20 Mar. 1866, HHSA, England, no. 20 E.

[7] La Tour to Drouyn, 25 Mar. 1866, *Orig.* viii. 64.

mediation, was destroyed when the Venetian question became entangled in the German issue. The moral disinterestedness of John Bull needed to be backed up by the threat of French bayonets, a threat which ironically Clarendon feared almost as much as Bismarck. When, however, the Italian cause was tied to the Prussian, France's value as an ally for peace was negated because of Venetia. The English Government found itself in a position where it could not publicly advocate the sacrifice of Venetia, which was guaranteed to Austria by treaty, in order to gain French support to prevent war. Not having stopped the original spoliation in 1864, why frustrate a war between the two German powers over the division of the spoils? As far back as 9 April, Clarendon had instructed the English representatives at all the German courts that 'however much this country may regret to see Germany a prey to civil war, yet so long as the war is confined to Germany there is not British interest of sufficient magnitude to render imperative the tender of British good offices, though . . . they would, if invited . . . [aid] in conjunction with those . . . other powers, in the cause of peace'.[1] Had it been uttered in 1815 even the Cabinet might have found this response wanting. It would seem that the fall from the pinnacle was a self-acknowledged one.

Clarendon, though possessed of diplomatic experience, lacked the political vision and personal generosity of Palmerston. Bismarck's attempt to trap his support for the Prussian annexation of the Duchies was frustrated, as was Napoleon III's endeavour to obtain British backing for the joining of Venetia to Italy. The foreign secretary was cautious enough to keep England free of commitment. He was far less successful, however, in using his mediatorial position effectively. His imagination was handicapped by the memory of 'drifting' into the Crimean War.[2] Consequently, his advice to Austria and the other German states was to remain firm and so avert being pushed into hostilities. With Prussia, Clarendon's moral appeals were irrelevant, and the gamble on Bismarck's dismissal failed.[3]

[1] Clarendon to England's representatives in Germany, 9 Apr. 1866, most confidential, PRO FO 146/1245.

[2] During the Polish crisis of 1863 Disraeli wrote that the British 'ambassador at St. Petersburg says we are again "drifting into war" ' (Disraeli to Mrs. Brydges Williams, confidential, 21 July 1863, Monypenny and Buckle, iv. 339).

[3] Gordon reported from Stuttgart that 'the feeling against Count Bismarck here

His acceptance of Britain's inability to prevent war was both a realistic estimate of her military unpreparedness and a niggardly evaluation of her European interests. One is left with the impression that the difficulty in preventing war was subordinate in Clarendon's mind to the anxiety he felt at committing his country even for the preservation of peace.[1]

is becoming if possible more bitter than before and I have heard that 100 florins were lately publicly offered in a club here towards a subscription for procuring the assassination of the Prussian minister' (Gordon to Clarendon, 29 Apr. 1866, PRO FO 82/122, no. 49). 'I think the King [of Prussia] might be induced to part with B[ismarck] for he is now aware of his dangerous policy' (Loftus to Clarendon, Berlin, 21 Apr. 1866, RA I 44/55).

[1] America was certainly on his mind. 'Lord Clarendon, when I spoke to him, seemed more alarmed about the Fenian business, and its influence on American diplomacy than about any of these European complications' (Stanley to Carnarvon, private, 7 July 1866, *Stanley Papers*, Cabinet).

II

THE AFTERMATH OF WAR AND COMPENSATION

The Principalities

THE insignificant role played by England in connexion with the French demands for compensation after the Austro-Prussian War was one manifestation of the deterioration of Britain's relations with both Prussia and France. The inability to combine with France, to prevent the iniquitous conduct of Prussia[1] from leading to war, provoked Clarendon to comment on 'the sort of chestnuts that he [Napoleon III] means to get out of the great European conflagration that he might have prevented & for wh. his responsibility is only second to that of Bismarck'.[2] The coolness produced by the Austro-Prussian crisis was compounded by contemporaneous events in the Principalities,[3] and caused further friction in Anglo-French and Anglo-Prussian friendship.

Clarendon felt the selection of a foreign prince would endanger the peace of Europe, and 'Her Majesty's Government would not therefore be inclined to entertaining any proposal

[1] Morier called her 'a rampant & profligate Govt. bent on territorial aggrandisement with the primary object of crushing liberty at home, & debauching public opinion by the prestige of military success' (Morier to Grant-Duff, Vienna, 9 June 1866, Mrs. Rosslyn Wemyss, *The Memoirs and Letters of Sir Robert Morier 1826–1876* [London, 1911], ii. 65).

[2] Clarendon to Cowley, 7 May 1866, private, PRO FO 519/180. When he thought that Prussia had suffered a military reverse, Clarendon wrote Cowley 'the Prussians seem to have got a licking and the joy thereat in London knows no bounds—I believe that the Queen will be as well pleased as Her subjects provided of course that the Crown Prince comes to no harm' (Clarendon to Cowley, 28 June 1866, private, Clar. Pap. C 144).

[3] In February of 1866, Couza, the ruler of the two provinces of Moldavia and Wallachia, was overthrown and a provisional government began to search for a suitable candidate to replace him. In this crisis Clarendon sought close co-operation with France in case Russia decided upon intervention (La Tour to Drouyn, 26 Feb. and 18 Mar. 1866. *Orig.* vii. 335; viii. 18; Clarendon to Buchanan, 26 Feb. 1866, private, Clar. Pap. C 143). As well, France wished to march in step with England (La Tour to Drouyn, 18 Mar. 1866, *Orig.* viii. 24). For a recent study of the crisis see W. E. Mosse, *The Rise and Fall of the Crimean System 1855–71* (Macmillan, 1963).

for placing a member of any reigning family in Europe at the head of the United Principalities'.[1] The foreign secretary was even more strongly opposed to the cession of the Principalities to Austria (as an exchange for giving up Venetia), arguing that Russia, Austria, and Turkey were against it.[2] His concern for national self-determination was more acute in the Principalities, where it was consistent with his desire to maintain intact the Ottoman Empire, than it was in the Duchies, the disposal of which less directly affected English interest. And of course there was no Prussian objection to consulting the wishes of the people in the East as there was in the case of Schleswig-Holstein.

At the end of March, while the powers were arguing pro and con at Paris over a foreign prince,[3] the provisional government at Bucharest offered the vacant position to Charles, the son of Prince Anton of Hohenzollern-Sigmaringen and in April held a plebiscite which confirmed the offer. Having tried to work closely with France, Clarendon was thoroughly disenchanted with the conduct of Napoleon III who he felt had intrigued behind his back to select a Hohenzollern.[4] Further he felt it was 'a very stupid choice . . . for besides being excluded, according to usage, by his connexion with one of the royal houses represented at the conference, how cd. Drouyn suppose that at this particular moment a Prussian Lieut. wd. be allowed to place himself on the Austrian frontier & to make use of 4 millions of savages on her flank in the event of her going to war with Prussia'.[5] To Loftus he wrote that Charles 'is connected moreover with the Royal Family and that alone, if there was no other reason, would suffice for his exclusion'.[6]

The attitude of the Prussian Government to the offer was similar to the one they were to adopt in July of 1870—insincere indifference and feigned ignorance.[7] Clarendon expressed his displeasure with Prussia to Bernstorff. 'The King of Prussia had

---

[1] Clarendon to Cowley, 8 Mar. 1866, PRO FO 146/1239, no. 275.
[2] Clarendon to Cowley, 12 Mar. 1866, PRO FO 27/1602, no. 292; La Tour to Drouyn, 27 Feb. and 9 Mar. 1866, *Orig.* vii. 343, vii. 395–6; Apponyi to Mensdorff, 20 Mar. and 27 Mar. 1866, HHSA, England, no. 20 c, no. 24 AB.
[3] Russia and Turkey against, France and Italy in favour.
[4] Apponyi to Mensdorff, 25 Apr. 1866, HHSA, England, no. 29 A–C.
[5] Clarendon to Cowley, 18 Apr. 1866, private, PRO FO 519/180.
[6] Clarendon to Loftus, 18 Apr. 1866, private, Clar. Pap. C 145.
[7] Loftus to Clarendon, 21 Apr. 1866, PRO FO 64/593, no. 138.

declared . . . that he would not allow him [Charles] to accept the offer unless it was desired by the conference.'[1] Since the conference of the powers at Paris did not so desire,[2] Clarendon told the Prussian ambassador that his 'King had not adhered to his declaration . . . in order that the Principalities might be Prussianized, and become a thorn in the flank of Austria'.[1]

Throughout the crisis in the Principalities British policy was subordinated to the technique or means by which it would be carried out. Clarendon's flexibility concerning the union or separation of the two provinces, and whether they would have a native or foreign ruler, was not extended to the manner in which a decision might be reached. From the beginning he was firm on two points: first, that the powers should act collectively and impose a European solution, and secondly that England should co-operate as closely as possible with France. He reasoned that complications were less likely to occur while the powers were discussing the issues in conference at Paris, and English intervention in the crisis could be justified at home because it could be said that the Government was merely acting with the other powers which were co-guarantors of Turkey.[3] Clarendon was concerned more in preventing a war over the Eastern question, particularly when it seemed that one was already likely between Prussia and Austria, than in any particular solution short of hostilities. Hence his readiness to accept a 'patch up'.[4]

Accord with France was essential as an insurance against Russian designs, as well as being necessary in order to implement effectively British policy. In 1853 'the real grounds of England's going to war with Russia was the pressure of British public opinion, which ultimately regarded Turkey as a lamb and Nicholas as a brutal and ravening wolf'.[5] In 1866 there was not 'much feeling in her [Turkey's] favour in England'.[6] The lack of pro-Turkish feeling was accompanied by a decline

---

[1] Clarendon to Bloomfield, 22 May 1866, PRO FO 146/1252, no. 114.

[2] The vote was four to three against.

[3] Gladstone to Clarendon, 5 Mar. 1866, Glad. Pap., p. 57.

[4] Clarendon to Cowley, 19 May 1866, PRO FO 519/180.

[5] H. Temperley and L. M. Penson, *Foundations of British Foreign Policy 1792–1902* (Cambridge, 1938), p. 138.

[6] Lyons to Cowley, Constantinople, 6 June 1866, Lyons Papers, Arundel Castle (hereafter quoted as Lyons Pap.), RD I.

of British prestige at Constantinople. The best of England's foreign representatives, Lord Lyons, observed that the Turks 'think we are too friendly for them to have anything from us & not friendly or resolute enough to protect her effectually from France or Russia. . . . We have here, as elsewhere, a great deal to do to recover the loss of reputation entailed by the Danish business'.[1] It seemed that co-operation with France was as necessary in 1866 as in 1853 when Clarendon ordered the fleet to Constantinople.

If Clarendon's failure in the Austro-Prussian crisis was incomplete, his success in the Principalities was partial. War was avoided but the prestige and integrity of the Ottoman Empire were weakened with the election of Charles. This was the price paid for the lack of Anglo-French harmony. In fact, for the moment, it appeared that France had replaced Russia as Britain's bogy-man in the East. Clarendon did not doubt that Drouyn was attempting 'to carry out the French policy of the dismemberment of Turkey'.[2] The tragic position of British foreign policy in this period was that intervention on the Continent, when England chose not to abstain, could be effective only with the concurrence of France, the power she feared more than any other.

Stanley

After the defeat of the Liberals on the Reform Bill, a Conservative Government took office with Lord Derby as prime minister and his son Stanley as foreign secretary. Clarendon thought him able[3] but was concerned over his 'strange theories about our being only a manufacturing nation and that we have no business to meddle with Foreign Affairs'.[4] 'He says himself

[1] Lyons to Erskine, Constantinople, 4 July 1866, Lyons Pap. RD I.

[2] Clarendon to Russell, 24 May 1866, PRO FO 30/22, no. 16.

[3] Apponyi felt he was talented but little communicative and not a good leader (Apponyi to Mensdorff, 27 Mar. 1866, HHSA, England, no. 24 A–B).

[4] Clarendon to Loftus, 20 June 1866, private, Clar. Pap. C 145. Though stating that Stanley was honest and talented, Apponyi concurred with Clarendon's view of the new foreign secretary (Apponyi to Mensdorff, 8 Apr. 1866, HHSA, England, no. 53). Russell was almost violent. 'I own I should dread Stanley at the Foreign Office if Derby were not over him to keep up the traditional policy of England. I should dread Stanley as Prime Minister as a fore-runner of the downfall of this country' (Maxwell, ii. 321).

that he knows and cares nothing about Foreign Affairs[1] but he is clever, industrious, and just so I hope he will do well, but at any rate he must do better than the aspirant to this office, Disraeli.'[2] Bloomfield, at Vienna, felt he was 'inexperienced in diplomatic affairs & habits' and hoped his father, Lord Derby, would guide him.[3] The queen had instructed Derby to offer the post of foreign secretary to Clarendon in the hope he would remain in office:[4]

> She owns she is greatly alarmed at Lord Stanley's inability for that office!
> She would wish in perfect frankness to ask Lord Derby whether he thinks the For. Office just the one best suited to him? . . . May he not be inclined to go too far in the line of noninterference, which might become serious, when matters take a form which would require us in the interests of humanity & Europe in general, to take a prominent part in conjunction with Fr., to put a stop to further bloodshed?[5]

As Clarendon refused Derby's offer on party grounds,[6] the Earl responded with Stanley.

> He [Derby] does not think that the Foreign Office is the one best suited to Lord Stanley; but on the other hand he is satisfied that Lord Stanley is better suited to the Foreign Office than any other person whose services he can command.

---

[1] To his father Stanley said 'I am in your hands, but the place in question [foreign secretaryship] is that of all others for which I judge myself least fit. Nor do I think, if it can be avoided with honour, that you ought to hold office without a majority' (Stanley to Derby, private, 27 Apr. 1866, Derby Pap. 105).

[2] Clarendon to Lyons, 28 June 1866, private, Clar. Pap. C 143. Nevertheless, Clarendon hoped that the more experienced Malmesbury would become foreign secretary (Clarendon to Admiral Harris, 3 July 1866, private, Clar. Pap. C 143). Derby had sounded Malmesbury who begged off because of health (Malmesbury to Derby, 20 Apr. 1866, Derby Pap. 105).

[3] Baroness Georgianna Bloomfield, *Reminiscences of Court and Diplomatic Life* (2 vols., 2nd ed., New York, 1883), ii. 223.

[4] Clarendon to Cowley, 30 June 1866, PRO FO 519/180. Whatever her personal feelings for Clarendon, the queen recognized his diplomatic experience and the esteem in which he was held by European sovereigns and statesmen (Algernon Cecil, *British Foreign Secretaries 1807–1916* [London, 1927], p. 232; Lord Edmund Fitzmaurice, *Life of the Second Earl of Granville* [2 vols., London, 1905], ii. 26; John Morley, *Life of William Ewart Gladstone* [4 vols., New York, 1903], i. 254–5; Apponyi to Mensdorff, 8 Apr. 1866, HHSA, England, no. 53).

[5] Victoria to Grey, 30 June 1866, *QVL* i. 352–3.

[6] Clarendon's dislike of Derby and hatred of Disraeli were well known.

It is unfortunate that so few of our public men give much of their attention to foreign affairs.[1]

Just before he surrendered the seals of office, Clarendon had a long talk with Stanley and advised him on policy,[2] so that Derby was able to tell the French ambassador that the foreign policy of the new Government would not differ from that of the old.[3]

It would be unkind to say that Stanley succeeded to a greater extent than some of his contemporaries expected.[4] His hatred of war was only exceeded by his fear of it, and this coupled with a natural reserve made him appear more cautious than he sometimes intended—though it is true that he often paraded his cautiousness to foreign ambassadors in the hope that they would not expect more than he was willing to give.[5] Stanley's effacement had the same purpose as Clarendon's caution, the avoidance of commitment, so that the change in British policy when the former replaced the latter was one of degree only. Because in Mosse's words he made a 'virtue of necessity',[6] foreign diplomats were made much more conscious of English abstinence. Clarendon pointed this out to Stanley: 'I begged him however not to proclaim our determined inaction on every opportunity that arises—the policy of not meddling is of course the right one but it is not necessary that all mankind shd. be let into the secret twice a day'.[7] He feared that the result would be that 'Engd. will become more & more isolated . . . [and] will cool & render indifferent such friends as we may still have'.[8] Victoria was also concerned about the reserve of her foreign secretary. 'It is quite right that we shd. avoid, as much as possible, being

---

[1] Derby to Victoria, 1 July 1866, *QVL*, 2nd ser., i. 353–4.

[2] Clarendon to Cowley, 4 July 1866, private, PRO FO 519/180.

[3] La Tour to Drouyn, 1 July 1866, *Orig.* x. 299.

[4] A contemporary author observed 'how admirably he [Stanley] had conducted the foreign affairs of this country' (T. H. Higginson, *English Statesmen* [New York, 1876], p. 224). The official biographers of Disraeli commented: 'For Stanley was pre-eminently a statesman who trusted, and was trusted by, the middle classes. His plain common-sense and love of peace appealed to them almost as much as did Palmerston's good-humour and bounce, and on Palmerston's death he largely succeeded to his place in their favour' (Monypenny and Buckle, iv. 186).

[5] Stanley to Cowley, 7 July 1866, PRO FO 27/1607; Temperley and Penson, pp. 306–7. The diplomatic corps in London did not particularly like Stanley (Bernstorff to Bismarck, 12 Dec. 1866, *APP* viii. 209).   [6] Mosse, p. 164.

[7] Clarendon to Cowley, 14 July 1866, private, PRO FO 519/180.

[8] Clarendon to Cowley, 21 Aug. 1866, private, PRO FO 519/180.

mixed up in these continental troubles—but it will hardly do, H.M. thinks, for England to stand so completely aloof, as to be totally disregarded abroad, & to abdicate her position as one of the great European powers'.[1]

Stanley seemed more consciously aware of the balance of power than Clarendon, but in trying to act consistently and logically on the basis of non-intervention he created a circumspection which seemed like indifference, and this prevented his acting effectively within the framework of that balance of power to which he gave lip service.[2]

On 6 July, Drouyn asked England to support the French plan for an armistice at Berlin and Florence.[3] Stanley quickly acceded[4] for the sake of peace, though he was unwilling to become entangled further if Prussia objected to the interference.[5] When, however, the Austrians asked him 'to take any step . . . which might tend to bring about an immediate armistice', Stanley refused mediation as its success seemed questionable.[6] His reaction was no more favourable nine days later when Apponyi read a dispatch from Mensdorff asking for 'the good offices of H.M. Govt.' and hoped 'that England & Russia . . . should exercise their right of interfering, in order to check the excessive pretensions of Prussia'.[7] On the evening before, in the House of Commons, Stanley expressed his belief that 'a strong and compact power in the north of Germany . . . [was] neither injurious nor inconvenient to England'.[8] He told Apponyi 'that the danger of disturbance to the peace of Europe lay in the weakness rather than in the strength of Germany'.[9] La Tour had no doubt but that English opinion supported the views of the foreign secretary.[10]

[1] Grey to Derby, 2 Aug. 1866, RA A 77, no. 8.

[2] K. Bourne, 'The Foreign Secretaryship of Lord Stanley, July 1866–December 1868' (University of London Thesis, 1955), pp. 35, 197.

[3] Drouyn to La Tour, 6 July 1866, telegram, *Orig.* x. 328.

[4] Stanley to Cowley, 6 July 1866, PRO FO 27/1607.

[5] Stanley to Cowley, 7 July 1866, private, PRO FO 519/182.

[6] Stanley to Cowley, 12 July 1866, PRO FO 27/1607. He wrote Bloomfield that 'the Emp. of the French by his precipitate offer of a mediation which has been rejected almost with contempt by the victors . . . has placed himself in a disagreeable position' (Stanley to Bloomfield, 14 July 1866, PRO FO 356/33).

[7] Stanley to Bloomfield, 21 July 1866, PRO FO 146/1256, no. 12.

[8] Ibid.; La Tour to Drouyn, 21 July 1866, *Orig.* xi. 147–8. Clarendon was not as definite about this as Stanley.   [9] Stanley to Bloomfield, loc. cit.

[10] La Tour to Drouyn, 26 July 1866, *Orig.* xi. 233–4.

In the meantime the Russian Government had broached the idea of a congress to sanction those changes in the Europe which all the powers had helped create in 1815. Why should such important European issues 'be decided' under the mediation of one power? The Russian ambassador, Brunnow, had spoken to Stanley in this sense on 23 July and again on 28 July,[1] without receiving a definite answer from the British minister who, however, showed little enthusiasm for a congress.[2] Cowley expressed the English attitude when he wrote, 'Yet what can be done but ratify the behests of Prussia'.[3] As Russia had also approached France concerning a congress, La Tour asked Stanley his reaction to the proposal. The foreign secretary said that he doubted whether Prussia would be willing to discuss the gains acquired by war, nor would it enhance the dignity of the powers merely 'to ratify accomplished facts', but he would have to consult his colleagues before he could give a formal answer.[4] Brunnow called again on 31 July to ask Stanley for 'the views of H.M.'s govt. as to the expediency of holding a congress', and was told that the British government 'would probably not refuse to go into a congress'.[5] It was clear that Stanley felt the uselessness of a congress only a little less than the responsibility of refusing one. He told Cowley that he suspected Russian motives[6] and informed La Tour of his answer to Brunnow after having consulted Derby and Disraeli.[7] Even when it was learned that Napoleon III was lukewarm and Bismarck refused a congress,[8] the persistence of Russia continued. France

[1] Stanley to Buchanan, 23 July 1866, PRO FO 181/444, no. 11, Mosse, p. 243; Stanley to Buchanan, 28 July 1866, ibid., no. 21; same to same, 28 July 1866, RA I 46/111.   [2] La Tour to Drouyn, 29 July 1866, *Orig.* xi. 284.

[3] Cowley to Bloomfield, 30 July 1866, PRO FO 519/233.

[4] La Tour to Drouyn, 30 July 1866, *Orig.* xi. 303; Stanley to Cowley, 30 July 1866, PRO FO 27/1607, no. 84. Cowley advised Stanley on this point (Stanley memorandum, 13 July 1866, Stanley Papers (hereafter quoted as Stan. Pap.).

[5] Stanley to Buchanan, 31 July 1866, PRO FO 146/1259, no. 22.

[6] Stanley to Cowley, 31 July 1866, private, PRO FO 519/182. Loftus, a few days earlier, indicated to Stanley that a congress 'might . . . compromise our position' (Loftus to Stanley, private, Berlin, 28 July 1866, RA I 46/115).

[7] La Tour to Drouyn, 31 July 1866, *Orig.* xi. 321; Stanley to Cowley, 31 July 1866, PRO FO 27/1607, no. 92. Disraeli was almost as vocal as Gladstone on government economy but unlike Stanley was prepared to admit 'that there may . . . be occasions in which it may be the duty of E. to interfere in European wars' (Buckle, iv. 467).

[8] Stanley to Cowley, 1 Aug. 1866, telegram, PRO FO 27/1608, no. 94; Stanley to Loftus, 2 Aug. 1866, confidential, PRO FO 64/889, no. 41.

was asked to join Russia and England 'in a declaration to be made to the Belligerent Powers, that no changes affecting the treaties to which the three powers are parties, can be made without their sanction and participation'.[1] Drouyn refused in as much as Napoleon III as mediator had already agreed to 'certain changes'.[2] Stanley informed Bloomfield that 'we shall decline to join in any declaration, protest, or whatever it may be called, that has for its object a demonstration of hostility or jealousy towards Prussia on the score of her recent increase of power'.[3]

On 6 August the French Government asked Stanley's opinion concerning the latest Russian proposal. After consulting with his colleagues, Stanley replied:

That, with regard to the Treaties of Vienna, the present is not the first instance in which they have been violated, without any protest being made on the part of the powers by whom they were signed.

That if the only object of the Russian proposition was, to reserve freedom of action for the neutral powers, that end could be obtained simply by abstaining from an active cohesion to the new arrangements, and no declaration on the subject was required.

That Her Majesty's Government will not join in any such declaration as may have the appearance of a protest against what is passing in Germany.

And that . . . [England has] no cause to object to such increase of power on her [Prussia's] part.[4]

Stanley further pointed out to the French minister 'the extreme favour with which English public opinion sees the aggrandizement of Prussia'.[5]

[1] Cowley to Stanley, 7 Aug. 1866, PRO FO 27/1621, no. 136.

[2] Ibid.

[3] Stanley to Bloomfield, 7 Aug. 1866, PRO FO 356/33. Derby felt that Stanley was 'over-cautious as to the expression of any opinion on the state of Germany; & especially undisposed to run the risk of receiving a snub from Prussia' (Derby to Grey, 5 Aug. 1866, Derby Pap. B 190/2). The queen was concerned lest 'England [should] . . . stand so completely aloof, as to be totally disregarded abroad' (Grey to Derby, 2 Aug. 1866, RA A 77/8).

[4] Stanley to Cowley, 8 Aug. 1866, PRO FO 27/1608, no. 118; Baude to Drouyn, 8 Aug. 1866, telegram, Orig. xii. 33. Stanley admitted privately to Malmesbury that 'I have imposed conditions which made its [a congress] being assented to by Prussia impossible. . . . Before I wrote the despatch I had ascertained that the Prussians would refuse' (Stanley to Malmesbury, 2 Aug. 1866, Stan. Pap., Cabinet).

[5] Baude to Drouyn, 8 Aug. 1866, Orig. xii. 34. The foreign secretary was no more willing to intervene against Italy, when it seemed that Austro-Italian negotiations for an armistice would fail due to Italy's demand for the Tyrol. Stanley refused

Renouvin has claimed that the British Government before Sadowa hoped for a localized conflict in which there would be no French or Russian intervention.[1] A short engagement quickly resolved was the ideal. When Sadowa provided this, London was content to see the rise of a new force offset the power of France and Russia. In Stanley's words, 'we must make up our minds to consider Prussia as a leading—perhaps the leading military power of Europe'.[2] Such an estimate caused him no anxiety.

The growing jealousy of Russia, and I suspect France also, against Prussia is natural. We should feel the same in their position. But to us there is no loss,[3] rather a gain, in the interposition of a solid barrier between the two great aggressive powers of the continent.[4]

To Bloomfield, Stanley affirmed that 'if anything wanted to convince me of what is our interest in this matter, I should find it in the evident jealousy of the two great nations, between which Prussia is interposed as a barrier'.[5]

Parliamentary feeling supported the views of the foreign secretary.[6] Gladstone argued:

The influence of England is best maintained by refraining from

Austria's appeal to use English influence at Florence and Berlin (Stanley to Cowley, 8 and 9 Aug. 1866, PRO FO 27/1608, no. 117, no. 123).

[1] Pierre Renouvin, *Histoire des relations internationales: Le XIX siècle de 1815 à 1871* (Paris, 1954), p. 368.

[2] Stanley to Cowley, 14 July 1866, PRO FO 519/182.

[3] Cowley was almost alone in seeing the growth of Prussia as a possible future danger to Britain. 'I have no faith in the friendship of Prussia and if ever she becomes a naval power she will give us trouble' (Cowley to Bloomfield, 30 July 1866, PRO FO 519/233). Howard at Munich was also apprehensive. 'Can we see it [the aggrandizement of Prussia] with unmixed satisfaction when it is coupled with . . . the disruption of Germany, and when we reflect, from the past conduct of Prussia, that we have no security against her not allying herself with Russia, and with France even, or at all events conniving in a policy in the East detrimental to our interests? Who knows whether at this present moment Russia has not been induced to remain a passive spectator of the subversion in the West . . . by the prospect held out to her of having full liberty of action left to her in the East, when the time . . . arises' (Howard to Stanley, 21 Aug. 1866, PRO FO 9/176, no. 69).

[4] Stanley to Cowley, 7 Aug. 1866, PRO FO 519/182. At the outbreak of the Austro-Prussian war, the following article appeared in *The Times*. 'Whether under Prussian or Austrian hegemony, the country must emerge more consolidated than at present, more capable of preserving peace within its limits and repelling aggression from abroad. If, then, events shall prove that the Confederation is now a thing of the past, there may be no reason to regret the change' (*The Times*, 15 June 1866).

[5] Stanley to Bloomfield, 7 Aug. 1866, private, PRO FO 356/33.

[6] Hansard, *Parliamentary Debates* (3rd series), clxxxiv. 1221–57.

continued interference. The influence of England does not depend on elaborate schemes for magnifying our old reputation & our old performances. It does depend, first, on the strength of the country, and secondly, upon the credit that may be given to the country for the honesty of its purpose, & for the disinterestedness that is so favoured by our insular position.[1]

In announcing and defending the Government's policy Stanley declared:

Ours will be a pacific policy, a policy of observation rather than action.

I think there never was a great European war in which the direct national interests of England were less concerned . . . if North Germany is to become a single great power, I do not see that any English interest is in the least degree affected.[2]

In the debate no 'voice was raised in favour of Austria, except that of Sir G. Bowyer, who speaks in the ultra-Catholic sense'.[3] In the midst of the great continental changes the passiveness of the British Government reflected public opinion,[4] and England's foreign policy seemed to grow more and more indifferent toward continental questions.[5] This lassitude was shaken when it was learned that France was seeking compensation to balance the enlarged Prussia. What interrupted the governmental languor was concern for Belgium.

Compensation

As early as 16 June, Napoleon III made it clear (to England if not Prussia) that Prussian control of northern Germany would necessitate French compensation.[6] When Bismarck learned through Benedetti, the French ambassador at Berlin,

---

[1] Ibid., p. 1245.

[2] Ibid., pp. 1253–6. Stanley seemed to reflect perfectly the feeling in the House of Commons 'to keep out of the quarrel as completely as possible' (Stanley to Cowley, private, 17 July 1866, Stan. Pap., France). 'The feeling for nonintervention is, I think, stronger in the House of Commons and among the public than I ever saw it before' (Stanley to Loftus, private, 18 July 1866, ibid., Prussia).

[3] Stanley to Cowley, 21 July 1866, PRO FO 519/182.

[4] Baude to Drouyn, 24 Aug. 1866, *Orig.* xii. 181–2.

[5] La Tour to Drouyn, 29 July 1866, *Orig.* xi. 293–4.

[6] Cowley to Clarendon, Paris, 16 June 1866, private, PRO FO 519/232; same to same, 18 June 1866, most confidential, PRO FO 27/1619, no. 799. One Briton anyway, Morier, agreed with this view (Morier to his father, 20 June 1866, Morier, ii. 67).

of Napoleon's desire to mediate and end the war, he sent Reuss to Paris to ascertain the demands of the emperor. He also wired Goltz, his representative at Paris, to learn 'what non-German compensations France would be led to demand . . . by our fully annexing Saxony, Hanover, Hesse-Cassel, Upper Hesse, and Nassau'.[1] Reuss was received in Paris by both Napoleon and Eugenie and listened, no doubt to his dismay, to the suggestion of a Rhenish buffer state. The proposal was made also to Goltz, who remained firm both on this and on the emperor's next suggestion of a return to boundaries of 1814.[2] Three days later the emperor made another attempt to secure Goltz's acquiescence to a Rhenish buffer state and again he was turned down. On 15 July, Benedetti sent word to Drouyn, the French foreign minister, that Bismarck felt France and Prussia could 'modify their territorial state' if they were bound by engagements.[3]

While these negotiations were in progress, Britain became anxious for Belgium.[4] Clarendon, just before he left office, wrote to Cowley about Leopold's wanting 'to put Antwerp in a complete state of defence'.[5] Cowley replied:

I do not think that at the present it would be wise or prudent to say anything about Belgium [to the French] unless a conversation shd. naturally lead to the subject.

I should not like to trust Drouyn on so delicate a subject.

What makes the K. of the Belgians suppose that he is likely to be attacked by the Prussians? . . . I suppose . . . that it is against the latter [the French] that the King really desires to be prepared. I quite share your opinion that H.M. had better not move. . . . Should the present state of affairs lead to any armaments on the part of France . . . we should perhaps do right to ask for explanations, but at

---

[1] Avet to La Mamora, Pardulutz, 7 July 1866, *Ancora un po piu di luce*, p. 394 (Paul Bernstein, 'The Rhine Problem during the Second Empire' [Univ. of Penn. dissertation, 1955] [hereafter cited as Bernstein], pp. 233–4).

[2] Reuss to King of Prussia, Paris, 10 July 1866, Hermann Oncken, *Die Rheinpolitik Kaiser Napoleons III von 1863 bis 1870 und der Ursprung as Rheinpolitik* [hereafter cited as *Rheinpolitik*] (3 vols., Berlin, 1926), i. 330–1.

[3] Benedetti to Drouyn, Brunn, 15 July 1866, *Orig.* xi. 53–54. On 5 July Hammond wrote Cowley that 'the urgent point now is to ascertain what bargain, if any, has been made between France and Prussia' (Hammond to Cowley, 5 July 1866, private, PRO FO 519/192).

[4] The King of Belgium and his Government continually reminded the court and the English Government of threats, real and supposed, on Belgian independence.

[5] Clarendon to Cowley, 5 July 1866, private, PRO FO 519/180.

present, unless we are prepared to go further, we had better ask no questions.[1]

Again on 20 July, Van de Weyer, the Belgian minister in London, in a conversation with Stanley expressed the hope that France might be told that 'an attack on Belgium' would bring about a break with England. Stanley replied that the emperor knew the English position on Belgium.[2]

On 23 July, Drouyn again pressed the question of compensation for France. Benedetti was told to request the boundaries of 1814 and Luxemburg.[3] The French ambassador saw Bismarck three days later at Nikolsburg and relayed Drouyn's instruction. After examining a map before him, Bismarck replied that as far as he was concerned there would be no difficulty in re-establishing the frontier of 1814, but how was the King of Holland to be indemnified for the loss of Luxemburg? Bismarck's parting comment was to mention Belgium.[4] Two days later Benedetti was told to ask for the boundary of 1814 plus that part of Hesse and Bavaria on the left bank of the Rhine.[5] On 5 August, Benedetti gave Bismarck a draft of a French demand for the entire left bank of the Rhine as far south as Mainz and withdrawal of the Prussian garrison from Luxemburg. Goltz was ordered to reply in the negative at Paris, and in Berlin Benedetti was told that Prussia would not accede to these requests.[6]

Stanley, while reluctantly admitting the justice of French claims for compensation, told La Tour that England would not oppose such claims as long as Egypt, Constantinople, and Belgium were not affected.[7] It was not until 7 August, however, when Cowley telegraphed that 'France has demanded of

---

[1] Cowley to Clarendon, Paris, 6 July 1866, private, PRO FO 519/233. Cowley did believe that Prussia offered Belgium and the Palatinate to France (Cowley to Stanley, Paris, 13 July 1866, PRO FO 27/1620, no. 19).

[2] Stanley to Cowley, 20 July 1866, PRO FO 27/1607, no. 51. Hammond wrote to Bloomfield that 'if Belgium is let alone, I conceive no possible circumstances occurring on the Continent which could induce us to take a prominent part' (Hammond to Bloomfield, 21 July 1866, private, PRO FO 356/33).

[3] Drouyn to Benedetti, 23 July 1866, confidential, *Orig.* xi. 164.

[4] Benedetti to Drouyn, Nikolsburg, 26 July 1866, ibid., pp. 219–25.

[5] Drouyn to Benedetti, Vichy, telegram, 29 July 1866, ibid., pp. 281–2.

[6] Ibid., pp. 241–2; Bismarck to Goltz, Berlin, 5 Aug. 1866, *Rheinpolitik*, ii. 22; Benedetti to Drouyn, Berlin, 8 Aug. 1866, *Orig.* xii. 22–23.

[7] La Tour to Drouyn, London, 29 July 1866, *Orig.* xi. 293–4.

Prussia the frontiers of 1814',[1] that Stanley learned of specific indemnifications. Victoria was greatly disturbed.

> The Queen has been much alarmed by the telegram from Lord Cowley, which she received this morning, in which he says that 'Fr. has asked Pr. for the frontier of 1814, & even more'.
>
> E. cannot remain a passive spectator of such proceedings, & the Queen relies on Lord Derby & his cabinet giving this his immediate & serious consideration.[2]

A Cabinet was held and Cowley was instructed to obtain assurances concerning Belgium.[3] The English minister wired back that Belgium was safe.[4]

It was now thoroughly evident to Stanley that the stability of Napoleon's dynasty depended on the prestige which compensation would bring to France.[5] It was with this in mind that Drouyn dispatched a Danish journalist, Jules Hansen, to Berlin with the proposal for a Rhenish buffer state. On 16 August, unable to see Bismarck, Hansen spoke to the counsellor of the legation, Keudell, who replied that Prussia had not asked France to mediate and therefore owed her nothing for it. Prussia would rather go to war than give France territory or buffer states.[6] Drouyn was now relieved as foreign minister.[7] Before his successor took office, Rouher, the French statesman, after much discussion with Napoleon III, instructed Benedetti on 16 August to hold out for Landau, Saarlouis, Saarbrücken, and Luxemburg by 'public treaty'. He was also to ask for Belgium as well as an offensive and defensive alliance with

[1] Cowley to Stanley, Paris, telegram, 7 Aug. 1866, PRO FO 27/1621, no. 134. This was confirmed by Loftus (Loftus to Stanley, Berlin, telegram, 8 Aug. 1866, PRO FO 64/599, no. 125).

[2] Victoria to Derby, Osborne, 8 Aug. 1866, QVL, 2nd ser., i. 364–5.

[3] Derby to Victoria, 10 Aug. 1866, ibid.; Stanley to Cowley, telegram, 10 Aug. 1866, PRO FO 27/1608, no. 129. Drouyn reassured Cowley on Belgium even before the British ambassador was directly instructed to this effect (Cowley to Stanley, Paris, 10 Aug. 1866, confidential, PRO FO 27/1621, no. 154).

[4] Cowley to Stanley, Paris, telegram, 14 Aug. 1866, PRO FO 27/1621, no. 161; ibid., no. 166. Cowley had asked for an audience with the emperor, but he was assured by Drouyn that concern was unnecessary as there were no French designs on Belgium (ibid., Baron Napoleon Beyens, *Histoire du Second Empire vu par un diplomate belge* [2 vols., Paris, 1924–6], ii. 194).

[5] Rouher to Conti, Crécy, 6 Aug. 1866, *Orig.* xi. 393; Stanley to Cowley, 15 Aug. 1866, private, PRO FO 519/182.

[6] Bernstein, pp. 245–6. Loftus informed Stanley of Hansen's mission (Loftus to Stanley, private, 26 Aug. 1866, Stan. Pap., Prussia).

[7] Goltz thought this 'the adoption of a definitely friendly policy toward Prussia' (Goltz to Bismarck, 30 Aug. 1866, *APP* viii. 53).

Prussia. If the above was not well received, Benedetti was to insist only on Luxemburg and Belgium, and if this brought objections, he was to suggest making Antwerp into a free city in order to pacify England.[1] Bismarck told Benedetti that the cession of Landau, Saarlouis, and Saarbrücken was impossible since German territory was involved. As for Belgium and Luxemburg, Bismarck felt William would object, especially as the king did not wish to alienate England. Bismarck was not adamant, however, and Benedetti wrote out a draft with Bismarck dictating portions of it.[2] Negotiations were never officially broken off, but Bismarck now had the famous draft treaty which he later used to insure England's neutrality during the Franco-Prussian war.

The British Government knew that something was up through Crowe, one of its ministers, who had obtained a copy of the letter Napoleon III had written to La Valette.[3] On 10 September, Leopold II asked Victoria to say something at Berlin as Bismarck 'positively offers us continually to France'.[4] A few days later the British minister at Brussels, de Walden, wrote that 'it has long been a matter of notoriety in Belgium that Count Bismarck has more than once proposed to the Emperor Louis Napoleon to take possession of Belgium as a compensation or set off against the aggrandizement of Prussia'.[5]

---

[1] Rouher to Benedetti, 16 Aug. 1866, *Orig.* xii. 116–17. At practically this very moment Napoleon reassured Cowley that France was not seeking Belgium (Cowley to Stanley, 17 Aug. 1866, H. R. C. W. Cowley, *Secrets of the Second Empire*, ed. by F. A. Wellesley [New York, 1929], p. 306).

[2] Bismarck to Goltz, Berlin, 20 Aug. 1866, *Rheinpolitik*, ii. 87–88. This draft treaty had five articles: 1. Napoleon recognized Prussian annexations in northern Germany. 2. Prussia would help France get Luxemburg from Holland. 3. France agreed not to oppose a union of the south German states and the North German Confederation. 4. Should France wish to annex Belgium, Prussia would assist her. 5. An alliance would be concluded between France and Prussia. Loftus's suspicions at the time were not far wrong. 'Benedetti who is returned [to Berlin] brings words of conciliation & peace. We must look out that France and Prussia do not come to an understanding at the expense of Belgium' (Loftus to Stanley, private, Berlin, 18 Aug. 1866, RA I 47/14).

[3] Crowe to Stanley, 25 Aug. 1866, RA J 92/74. 'I should like to know how M. Crowe got hold of the Emperor's letter to La Valette. I have no doubt that it is genuine and it confirms what Goltz told me that a convention had been sent in draft to Benedetti to be proposed to the Prussian govt. Drouyn . . . today said that the whole question of a cession of territory etait tombee dans l'eau' (Cowley to Stanley, Paris, 28 Aug. 1866, private, PRO FO 519/233).

[4] King of Belgium to Victoria, Ostend, 10 Sept. 1866, 2nd ser., *QVL* i. 367–8.

[5] De Walden to Stanley, Brussels, 16 Sept. 1866, PRO FO 10/271, no. 25.

Thoughts of Belgium were soon submerged by the publication of the La Valette circular. This document was interpreted as an official repudiation of the policy of compensation as well as an attempt to hide the fact that that policy had failed. The success of Prussia was recognized as an accomplished fact. The circular was paraded on the front page of the *Moniteur* in order to placate French public opinion which was still vigorously demanding compensation.[1]

The British reaction was favourable if not ecstatic. Cowley thought it would 'do good', and Clarendon felt it was 'very clever'. Generally the Government saw it as a sign of peace 'which is the main and nearly unique object of English politics'.[2] Berlin was pleased but quiet about the circular. There, too, it had 'a tranquilizing effect . . . on the public mind'.[3] A temporary lull now ensued before the Luxemburg affair would produce another Franco-Prussian crisis.

Once Bismarck had succeeded in unifying northern Germany the means he had used to do so were forgotten in the flush of glorious success. Whereas his conduct had been labelled unscrupulous and without principle, its results were now praised. The expansion of Prussia, instead of alienating England, drew her sympathy.

At this time [August] I [Loftus] wrote to Lord Stanley that I could not view with any dissatisfaction or fear of danger to E. an increase of power to Prussia. She was the great Protestant State of Continental Europe. . . . She will become a Power of great importance in maintaining the peace of Central Europe. . . . We have much in common with her—our race, our religion, our mutual interests are all interwoven with Pr., & our political interests should be identical. . . . A strong Germany will always look to E. for moral support, & will naturally seek the alliance of a great maritime power.[4]

---

[1] L. M. Case, *French Opinion on War and Diplomacy during the Second Empire* (Philadelphia, 1954), pp. 221–5.

[2] Cowley to Stanley, Paris, 18 Sept. 1866, private, PRO FO 519/233; ibid., most confidential, PRO FO 27/1622, no. 260. Clarendon to Hammond, the Grove, 19 Sept. 1866, private, PRO FO 391/4; Baude to La Valette, London, 19 Sept. 1866, *Orig.* xii. 315. Disraeli was not particularly impressed. 'I thought the French circular a tissue of maladroit & contradictory humbug' (Disraeli to Derby, Hughenden Manor, 30 Sept. 1866, Derby Pap. 146/2).

[3] Loftus to Stanley, Berlin, 29 Sept. 1866, confidential, PRO FO 64/601, A, no. 241.

[4] Lord Augustus Loftus, *The Diplomatic Reminiscences of Lord Augustus Loftus: 1862–1879*, 4 vols. (London, 1892–4), i. 99–100. 'It is not our business to become

The queen was of the same mind.

The queen thinks it is highly important that E. should not appear utterly indifferent to what passes in Ger., a country allied in so many ways to her, else the effect would be very injurious to the position & influence of E.

Germany's wish is to be united under the supremacy of Pr., & not divided into N. & S., the result of which would be to throw the latter into the arms of Fr.—than which nothing could be worse.

A strong, united, liberal Ger. would be a most useful ally to E.[1]

In a letter to Cyrus Field, Gladstone wrote that 'we live in times of great events'. 'Europe has not often seen greater than those of the present year, wh. apparently go far to complete the glorious work of the reconstruction of Italy, & wh. seem in substance both to begin & complete another hardly less needed work in the reconstruction of Germany'.[2] Baude, the acting French minister in London, noted the 'marked satisfaction' in England over the larger, more powerful Prussia. 'The entirely passive attitude of the English government, in the midst of European complications, certainly conforms to the true state of opinion in England'.[3]

Stanley also approved the aim, if not the method, of Prussian policy. He saw with satisfaction the rise of a strong counterweight to France and Russia,[4] but at the same time evinced some apprehension:

If the Emperor gives way [on compensation], this new defeat, following the Mexican failure, and shortly to be followed by a surrender of Rome, which I assume to be inevitable, will be the most serious shock his dynasty has yet undergone.

partisans of either side, but the advantage to England of a strong Prussia is so obvious, that in my judgement it may fairly be set against the disapproval which we should otherwise feel of acts which however useful in their ultimate result, have undoubtedly been violent and arbitrary' (Stanley to Loftus, confidential, 8 Aug. 1866, Stan. Pap., Prussia). Among most of the German states hatred for Prussia turned to adulation (Gordon to Stanley, 24 July 1866, PRO FO 82/123, no. 19; same to same, 13 Aug. 1866, ibid., 82/124, no. 34).

[1] Victoria to Stanley, Osborne, 7 Aug. 1866, *QVL*, 2nd ser., i. 364. The queen herself was doubtful however that a liberal Germany was what had resulted. 'But oh! if only Papa's gt. maxim of Germany & Prussia becoming a gt. German Empire cd. be realized—& not merely a large Prussia with annexations to the exclusion of South Germany! Oh! if Fritz & the liberals wd. only insist on this' (Victoria to Crown Princess of Prussia, 11 Aug. 1866, RA U/32).

[2] Gladstone to Cyrus Field, 28 Aug. 1866, Glad. Pap., vol. ccccli.

[3] Baude to Drouyn, London, 24 Aug. 1866, *Orig.* xii. 181–2.

[4] Stanley to Loftus, private, 26 Dec. 1866, Stan. Pap., Prussia.

If he does not give way, it is war.
We do not want Napoleon upset, nor do we want a new war.[1]

It was war and the ensuing complications which he feared. 'We have only as yet seen the first act of the great drama. The more complete union of Germany will probably be next— and then a war with France'.[2] His desire to forestall armed conflict did not include the support of French claims for compensation which would greatly obviate the need for war as a concomitant of German unification. Instead of trying to influence events towards a desired end, he eschewed action[3] and hoped that his fears would prove illusory. When questioned in Parliament about a French demand upon Prussia for territorial compensation, Stanley was evasive and replied that he was not certain of the communications on this question between France and Prussia.[4]

Though his party had a minority in the House of Commons, Stanley's reticence and lack of initiative were not due primarily to this fact.[5] Clarendon had been more aware of the connexion between foreign policy and a parliamentary majority than his successor.[6] Abstention under Stanley, however, was the more marked because it stemmed from conviction and was not handled with Clarendon's diplomatic finesse. This abnegation was supported by British opinion as a natural reaction from the unpleasantness which verbal exclamations had caused in 1864. For the sake of English prestige, therefore, Stanley inter-

---

[1] Stanley to Cowley, 15 Aug. 1866, private, PRO FO 519/182.
[2] Stanley to Bloomfield, 28 Aug. 1866, private, PRO FO 356/33; ibid., 21 Aug. 1866, private, PRO FO 356/33.
[3] Bourne has pointed out that 'Stanley's policy was based on the avoidance of action—no doubt his personal interpretation of nonintervention' (Bourne, pp. 448-9).
[4] Hansard, *Parliamentary Debates* (3rd series), clxxxiv. 2163.
[5] Stanley was concerned about the Alabama claims and Fenians in Canada. 'I see with surprise and not without anxiety the development of the war-spirit in that country' [United States] (Stanley to Mr. Smith, private, 18 Aug. 1866, Stan. Pap., Miscellaneous). 'The only question as to which I feel nervous is the American' (Stanley to Disraeli, private, 22 Aug. 1866, Stan. Pap., Disraeli). Additional troops were sent to Canada due to Fenian difficulties (Stanley to Cowley, private, 30 Aug. 1866, Stan. Pap., France).
[6] Clarendon's desire for office far exceeded Stanley's and he blamed the fall of the Liberal Government in 1866 on Gladstone. 'Gladstone's obstinacy has been the cause [of the Government's resigning] and it is clear to me that his temper unfits him for supreme command' (Clarendon to Cowley, private, 26 June 1866, Clar. Pap., C 144).

vened only where such intervention could be confidently implemented by force. He 'intervened forcibly only where right and ability were well-matched'[1]—in Abyssinia and Spain. The lack of a sure continental ally made his European policy one of utmost circumspection, a circumspection which probably caused as much harm to Britain's reputation as Russell's former enthusiasm.

The general opinion seems to be that he is doing well but I think that under his regime Engd. will become more & more isolated—he will not, like the Earl [Russell] create a host of enemies but he will cool and render indifferent such friends as we may still have. It is perhaps best, tho not glorious, that we shd. try to efface ourselves for we are in a horribly defenseless position.[2]

To have officially endorsed French claims for territory, the equity of which he did not deny, might have involved England in a Franco-Prussian quarrel. As he already felt a war between those two powers to be ineluctable, the main thing was to keep Britain free and clear of commitment.

Bismarck's success in 1866, instead of bringing France and England closer together, had the opposite effect of separating them still further, as Belgium was the natural compensation for France to balance Prussia's gains. Napoleon III, not wishing to excite Britain, attempted to obtain German territory, and Bismarck refused on grounds of national sentiment and his king's objections. The Prussian minister then dropped hints about Belgium and Luxemburg, realizing that this might embroil France with England and perhaps drive a real wedge between the two. Napoleon, hesitant to move towards Belgium without a definite understanding with Prussia, decided to acquire Luxemburg.

---

[1] Bourne, abstract.
[2] Clarendon to Cowley, the Grove, 21 Aug. 1866, private, PRO FO 519/180. The 'horribly defenseless position' was due to military as well as diplomatic circumstances. 'Any proposal for an augmentation of the army would be most unpopular, and I am sure we could not carry it in the House of Commons unless there is a prospect of war, which God forbid' (General Peel to Derby, 11 July 1866, Derby Pap. 161/11). Disraeli pointed out 'the obstinacy with wh. the Adm[iralty] has declined building iron ships' (Disraeli to Derby, confidential, 29 Aug. 1866, Derby Pap. 146/2). Malmesbury had 'been for a long time anxious about the state of our *navy* wh. from unavoidable circumstances does not bear nearly the same relative position as regards other navies wh. it formerly did' (Malmesbury to Derby, 13 Sept. 1866, Derby Pap. 105).

III

LUXEMBURG: PRIVATE
NEGOTIATIONS

WITH the dissolution of the German confederation, of which
Luxemburg was a member, the status of the grand duchy
became uncertain.[1] It had figured prominently, along
with the Palatinate and the Rhineland, in French suggestions
for compensation in July and August of 1866.[2] Furthermore, as
Bismarck told Loftus, Prussia was not affected by its disposition.

> Prussia had no personal interest or wish with respect to Luxem-
> burg; . . . Prussia was quite ready . . . to withdraw her garrison . . .
> it is a question which does not materially or politically affect
> Prussia, and we are prepared for any arrangement which may be
> agreeable to the King Grand Duke.[3]

The British ambassador was satisfied with the veracity of this
reply, the more so as it was later confirmed that the Prussian
military believed that the fortress no longer had much importance.[4]

It is not surprising, therefore, that Napoleon, still determined
on acquiring territory, concentrated on Luxemburg. In the
middle of October he requested Prussian support in order to
obtain the grand duchy.[5] The absence of Bismarck from Berlin

---

[1] By a treaty made with the Netherlands in 1816, Prussia contributed the major
part of the garrison for the fortress of Luxemburg, which was one of a number of
strongholds on the eastern frontier of France intended to prevent any future
French expansion. The grand duchy in which the fortress lay was the personal
property of William III, King of the Netherlands, and had belonged both to the
German Confederation and the Zollverein. Though the treaty of Prague dissolved
the former, the Prussian garrison remained in the fortress (M. R. D. Foot, 'Great
Britain and Luxemburg 1867', *English Historical Review*, lxvii [1952], 352).

[2] Luxemburg had been mentioned specifically on 23 and 29 July and 16 August
(Drouyn to Benedetti, 23 July 1866, confidential, *Orig.* xi. 164; Bismarck to Goltz,
29 July 1866, *Rheinpolitik*, ii. 12, no. 141; Rouher to Benedetti, 16 Aug. 1866, *Orig.*
xii. 116–17).

[3] Loftus to Stanley, Berlin, 1 Sept. 1866, PRO FO 64/600, no. 195; ibid., *APP*
viii. 55.

[4] Loftus to Stanley, Berlin, 29 Sept. 1866, PRO FO 64/601 A, no. 243.

[5] Goltz to Thile, Paris, 14 Oct. 1866, *APP* viii. 110.

enabled Goltz to justify Prussian evasiveness. No arrangement
was possible while his chief was away.[1] The minister president's
return did not, however, greatly change the situation, as Goltz
was told that Prussia could not publicly show fear of France by
offering to yield Luxemburg or give up the right to garrison the
fortress.[2] An alliance was out of the question.[3] Benedetti's
attempts to question Bismarck on Luxemburg and to conclude
the draft treaty came to nothing; the Prussian leader avoided
seeing the French ambassador.[4] Moustier, the new French foreign
minister, tried to achieve by threat what he failed to gain by
negotiation. He told Goltz that if Prussia would not sign the
draft treaty France would be forced to seek an alliance with
Austria or south Germany.[5] When Bismarck finally saw Benedetti,
he told him that the French Government should arrange demonstrations in Luxemburg and then present Europe with an accomplished fact. A Franco-Prussian alliance would have to wait,
according to Bismarck, until the Prussian garrison had been
withdrawn from the fortress.[6]

Sensing Bismarck's insincerity, the French Government
decided to withhold further requests, and permit Prussia to
demonstrate her friendliness by taking the initiative concerning
Luxemburg and the draft treaty.[7] Moustier told Goltz that
France would provoke no anti-Prussian demonstrations in
Luxemburg and make no demand for compensation.[8]

French expectancy was of short duration. The need for a
glittering stroke to soothe public opinion and quiet Thiers had
become obsessive. Napoleon, of course, felt this more than
Moustier. Consequently, Rouher, on 3 January 1867, told

---

[1] Goltz to Thile, Paris, 27 Oct. 1866, *APP* viii. 121. Loftus confirmed this
(Loftus to Stanley, Berlin, 8 Dec. 1866, confidential, PRO FO 64/603, no. 369).

[2] Bismarck to Goltz, Berlin, telegram, 19 Dec. 1866, *Rheinpolitik*, ii. 143–4.

[3] Ibid. ii. 148.

[4] Benedetti to Moustier, private, Berlin, 8 Dec. 1866, *Orig.* xiii. 226–7; same to
same, confidential, Berlin, 14 Dec. 1866, ibid., p. 273.

[5] Goltz to Bismarck, telegram, Paris, 17 Dec. 1866, *Rheinpolitik*, ii. 136–7; same
to same, Paris, 18 Dec. 1866, *APP* viii. 217–22.

[6] Bismarck to Goltz, telegram, Berlin, 19 Dec. 1866, *Rheinpolitik*, ii. 151; Benedetti to Moustier, telegram, Berlin, 19 Dec. 1866, *Orig.* xiii. 305; same to same,
private, Berlin, 20 Dec. 1866, ibid., pp. 322–4.

[7] Benedetti to Moustier, private, Berlin, 24 Dec. 1866, *Orig.* xiii. 366–71; same
to same, private, Berlin, 26 Dec. 1866, ibid., p. 375; Goltz to Bismarck, Paris,
28 Dec. 1866, *APP* viii. 246–7.

[8] Ibid.

Goltz that France must have Luxemburg, the acquisition of which would lead to the signing of the alliance treaty.[1] France could not gain Luxemburg until Prussia withdrew her garrison from the fortress and Bismarck informed Benedetti that his king was still opposed to this. He then repeated his advice of December, that France should arrange popular demonstrations in the duchy for the removal of the garrison.[2] Moustier now tried to bring matters to a head by preparing a draft treaty of cession.[3] This was premature and the optimism was unjustified. Benedetti was getting nowhere with Bismarck,[4] and the end of January and beginning of February saw France no nearer to acquiring Luxemburg than before.

Moustier was now apparently convinced that Bismarck only meant to frustrate the cession of Luxemburg to France. He therefore decided to open negotiations directly with the Netherlands and present the *fait accompli* to Berlin that Bismarck had advised him to present to Europe.[5] This procedure was not necessary, however, as the Prussian Government sanctioned direct negotiations with the King of Holland.[6] The overtures which France had already made at the Hague now seemed to have full Prussian approval.

The British Government was ill-informed concerning these negotiations and apparently misinterpreted what information it did receive. While Loftus put little trust in Bismarck, he was pro-German in sentiment.[7] Cowley was old and getting very deaf; he wished to retire and only Stanley's appeal kept him at his post. He disliked Drouyn and Moustier and was very suspicious of Napoleon III.[8] The sympathy which Loftus felt

---

[1] Goltz to Bismarck, Paris, 3 Jan. 1867, *APP* viii. 157–62.

[2] Benedetti to Moustier, private, Berlin, 11 Jan. 1867, *Orig.* xiv. 77–80.

[3] Baudin to Moustier, private, Paris, 13 Jan. 1867, *Orig.* xiv. 98–99.

[4] Benedetti to Moustier, private, Berlin, 4 Feb. 1867, *Orig.* xiv. 231.

[5] Moustier to Benedetti, private and confidential, Paris, 18 Feb. 1867, *Orig.* xiv. 319–20.

[6] Benedetti to Moustier, private, Berlin, 8 Mar. 1867, ibid. xv. 38–41; Moustier to Benedetti, Paris, 4 Mar. 1867, *Rheinpolitik*, ii. 229.

[7] Granville thought that Loftus was 'wanting in tact, and a great bore, although he has some merits' (Granville to Victoria, 14 Nov. 1870, RA I 67/30). Young thought Loftus was 'a stupid man' (*Young*, pp. 103–4).

[8] Moustier 'hates business, it seems, and prefers the society of ballet dancers to all others. Nobody has understood the infatuation of the E[mperor] for him. . . . "Birds of a feather" I suppose' (Cowley to Stanley, private, Paris, 2 Sept. 1866, RA J 82/84).

for a united Germany was not counterbalanced in Paris where Cowley distrusted French motives, showing only occasional feeling for the emperor's position after Sadowa. The two 'B's', Bloomfield at Vienna and Buchanan at St. Petersburg, merely transmitted what they were told. Britain's best ambassador, Lyons, was at Constantinople, though he would shortly replace Cowley at Paris.

British withdrawal and the very nature of the Franco-Prussian talks further kept the English Government in the dark. There were always rumours about Belgium being in danger, a Franco-Prussian alliance, and the like, but little sure information. One of the reasons why Stanley and Victoria were not more excited when Crowe got hold of a copy of Napoleon's letter to La Valette mentioning a proposed convention with Prussia was that such reports were in almost constant circulation.[1] But at least Stanley knew of the proposed alliance that was to cause such a sensation when Bismarck disclosed it in 1870. If it excited any attention when it first reached his eyes it was soon forgotten in the glare of the La Valette circular.

Governmental opinion in England floated upon wave after wave of unverified news only to break upon the rock of concern for Belgium. At the end of December Disraeli wrote to Stanley:

I have just heard from a first rate quarter, that at the last Cabinet Council at the Tuileries, a proposition from Bismarck, suggesting an arrangement by which the Southern States of Ger. should blend with Pr., and that Fr. should take possession of Belgium, was absolutely brought forward & favoured by several of the Ministers, principally by La Valette. It was opposed by the Minister of Foreign Affairs.

Can this be true? And if so . . . what are Bismarck's relations with us? Have you heard anything from our Goosey Gander at Berlin, a pretty instrument to cope with the Prussian Minister!

The Emperor is like a gambler who has lost half his fortune & restless to recover; likely to make a coup, which may be fatally final for himself.

I doubt whether this country would see any further glaring case

---

[1] Stanley did ask Loftus what he made of the emperor's letter. The reply of the British ambassador did not allude to a possible Franco-Prussian convention (Loftus to Stanley, 1 Sept. 1870, *APP* viii. 77, Note).

of public violence & treachery with composure. Reaction is the law of all human affairs; & the reaction from non-intervention must sooner or later set in. I would rather, however, try to prevent mischief—i.e., as long as we can.[1]

When Stanley questioned Bernstorff as to the existence of a Franco-Prussian deal involving Belgium and south Germany, the Prussian ambassador maintained that no such arrangement existed.[2] Victoria had Grey write to Stanley in the same vein:

In the present state of feeling in Fr. where everything seems to show how much the Emperor has lost in public estimation, one cannot shut one's eyes to the possibility (not to say probability) of his attempting, by some such means as the annexation of Belgium, to recover his lost prestige.

But Her Majesty trusts that her ministers both at Paris & Berlin are instructed to keep an anxious watch over the course of events, & to neglect no opportunity in conversation, where the subject might happen to be broached, of letting it be understood, beyond the possibility of mistake, that E. will never stand quietly by, or remain a passive spectator of any attempt against the integrity or independence of Belgium.[3]

---

[1] Disraeli to Stanley, Grosvenor Gate, 30 Dec. 1866, Buckle, iv. 469. At the end of December, Gordon at Munich reported 'a rumour' that Prussia and the south German states had signed secret defensive alliances. Loftus did not believe in the 'rumour' but qualified his disbelief. 'Altho no formal instrument . . . was concluded, a written engagement has been entered into by which Bavaria (and I believe the other two governments) is bound in the event of an aggressive attack on Prussia by France to place her military forces at the disposal of the King of Prussia' (Stanley to Loftus, 2 Jan. 1867, PRO FO 64/615, PRO FO 64/617, no. 29; same to same, confidential, Berlin, 19 Jan. 1867, ibid., no. 36). Howard at Munich confirmed Loftus's report (Howard to Stanley, most confidential, 31 Dec. 1866, PRO FO 9/177, no. 164).

[2] Bismarck to Bernstorff, secret, Berlin, 14 Jan. 1867, GW vi, no. 652. Bismarck informed Bernstorff that for Prussia Belgium was a pawn to be used to obtain either Parisian acquiescence to German consolidation or active British support on the Continent. Bismarck did not fear a land war with France but did express concern about the damage a French fleet might impose, and it was this danger that England could obviate. But as England was abstaining from the Continent, Prussia might, if necessary, use Belgium to buy off France unless, of course, London would be willing to pay for Prussian support for Belgium by an active and friendly policy on the Continent (ibid.). In his reply to Bismarck, Bernstorff questioned the wisdom of Prussia's conniving in a French annexation of Belgium because this would damage Anglo-Prussian friendship. It would, he felt, also hurt Prussia in Germany because British interest in the rise of Prussia was a reflection of the prospect of an enlarged Prussia as a counterpoise to France and Prussia (Bernstorff to Bismark, secret, 18 Feb. 1867, APP viii. 403–7; ibid., 3 Apr. 1867, APP viii. 575–6).

[3] Grey to Stanley, Osborne, 9 Jan. 1867, QVL, 2nd ser., i. 386–7. 'Nothing that is known here encourages the supposition that there is any understanding between

The foreign secretary replied almost immediately that he had no news of a French move on Belgium, but he was not reassuring about its continued independence.

I have no doubt that B. (& probably the K. of Pr.) would be glad to see Belgium sacrificed, if that act would avert the jealousy so generally felt in Fr. of the increase in Ger. power: & thus save Germany from being involved in war, which, as matters stand, seems a very possible event.

I speak of a Franco-German war as a 'very possible event', but I do not mean that it seems to be probable. I should say the chances were considerably against it: The Fr. are growing every yr. a more peace-loving & commercial people. . . . Still it is on the cards: & I do not believe that a French invasion of Belgium is, except under circumstances very different from the present.[1]

The British Government would have been even more concerned had it been aware of Bismarck's letter to Bernstorff, his minister in London, about Belgium. The ambassador was told that Prussia did not attach great weight to the existence of Belgium, especially as undesirable political and ecclesiastical influences had spread from there into the Rhine provinces. Its importance for Germany lay in the good relations with France its cession could achieve.[2]

In February British concern for Belgium was temporarily interrupted by a representation from The Hague. The Dutch Government was worried about Prussian designs,[3] and Stanley was so informed by Bentinck.

They are anxious to ascertain confidentially what course England would pursue in the event of an unprovoked attack being made on the Netherlands. They deprecate however any enquiry being made as to the intentions of Prussia; and looking at the result which attended the intervention of foreign Powers in the affairs of Denmark,

him [Napoleon III] and Bismarck' (Stanley to Disraeli, 31 Dec. 1866, Stan. Pap., Disraeli).

[1] Stanley to Grey, 10 Jan. 1867, *QVL*, 2nd ser., i. 387. 'France and Germany may fight out their quarrel with little harm to us' (Stanley to Cowley, 27 Nov. 1866, Stan. Pap., France).

[2] Bismarck to Bernstorff, 14 Jan. 1867, *Rheinpolitik*, ii. 185; Bismarck to Bernstorff, secret, Berlin, 14 Jan. 1867, *GW* vi., no. 652.

[3] Holland feared that the new North German Confederation would demand the province of Limburg which had been a member of the old Germanic Confederation.

they have no wish to invite any such intervention in those of the Netherlands.[1]

The foreign secretary avoided commitment with an honest reply:

[It] would be premature to express an opinion as to the designs imputed to Prussia. There could be no doubt that an unprovoked attack by Prussia on the Netherlands would be regarded with extreme dissatisfaction in England; and that all moral support would be given to prevent or resist any such attack. More I could not at present promise.[2]

At approximately the same time Baron Zuylen, the Dutch foreign minister, applied for French support against possible Prussian expansion.[3] Moustier used this as an opening to obtain Luxemburg through direct negotiations with the Dutch. Baudin, the French ambassador at The Hague, was directed to propose a defensive alliance against Prussian attack. If this were acceptable, he was then to suggest the cession of Luxemburg. The consent of the people of the duchy as well as Prussian approbation were stipulated as preconditions.[4]

The reaction at The Hague to the French proposal of an alliance was favourable, but cession of Luxemburg elicited a lukewarm response.[5] Zuylen wished the prior approval of Prussia, as he felt the cession of the duchy to France might provoke a German demand for Limburg.[6] Moustier disregarded this and made the cession of Luxemburg the first condition of a Franco-Dutch alliance, maintaining that once the transfer of the duchy was completed Prussia would automatically withdraw her troops from the fortress.[7] On 16 March the foreign minister's frustration was manifested in a telegram to Baudin. The minister was to explain to the King of Holland that France

[1] Stanley to Loftus, confidential, 25 Feb. 1867, PRO FO 64/615, no. 50, Foot, p. 356.
[2] Ibid. At the beginning of March Stanley was not unduly concerned about the Netherlands nor by any news he had on Luxemburg, since he wrote to Bloomfield that 'There is happily not much in the foreign line that is urgent' (Stanley to Bloomfield, private, 5 Mar. 1867, PRO FO 356/33).
[3] Zuylen to Lightenvelt, The Hague, 20 Feb. 1867, *Orig.* xiv. 336-9.
[4] Moustier to Baudin, Paris, 28 Feb. 1867, ibid., pp. 380-3.
[5] Baudin to Moustier, private, The Hague, 4 Mar. 1867, ibid. xv. 13-17.
[6] Same to same, telegram, The Hague, 14 Mar. 1867, ibid., pp. 66-67.
[7] Moustier to Baudin, telegram, Paris, 9 and 12 Mar. 1867, ibid., p. 45, p. 56.

must have Luxemburg, after which his remaining territory, including Limburg, would be guaranteed him by Paris. If the king refused this request he was to be told that the result would be French enmity towards the Netherlands, and the assent to any ambitions concerning Holland which Belgium might contemplate.[1]

French pressure coincided with Dutch acquiescence. On 19 March, William III agreed to sell Luxemburg to France, a transaction which would be accompanied by a treaty guaranteeing the integrity of the Kingdom of the Netherlands. What seemingly had been won by waiting soon proved to be a completely hollow victory for Moustier and Napoleon III. The ensuing failure to gain Luxemburg was particularly frustrating when its acquisition had been so nearly arranged.

Criticism of the emperor's Germany policy, led by Thiers, increased when on 19 March Bismarck publicly announced the existence of offensive and defensive treaties with the south German states which had been signed in August 1866. This declaration caused the Dutch Government second thoughts about selling the duchy.[2] Matters were made more difficult as reports and rumours of the impending cession became frequent.

On 26 March, William III decided to ask the King of Prussia for his consent to the sale of the duchy.[3] As no Prussian veto was placed on the transaction, both Moustier and Baudin assumed the cession to be practically completed. The error of this assumption was quickly exposed by a harsh confrontation with reality. On the last day of March Goltz requested the French Government to drop the negotiations with The Hague because German opinion was opposed to the cession of Luxemburg to France. Moustier was furious and told the Prussian ambassador that his request was impossible. Not even the possibility of war would make his government withdraw.[4] The new Prussian position was confirmed by Benedetti at Berlin. The French ambassador had been told by Bismarck that he was to be questioned the next day in the Reichstag and he wished

---

[1] Same to same, telegram, Paris, 16 Mar. 1867, ibid., p. 80.

[2] Baudin to Moustier, telegram, The Hague, 21 Mar. 1867, ibid.

[3] William III to Napoleon III, The Hague, 26 Mar. 1867, ibid., p. 166; Baudin to Moustier, telegram, The Hague, 26 Mar. 1867, ibid., p. 165; Perponcher to William I, The Hague, 26 Mar. 1867, *APP* viii. 512–13.

[4] Moustier to Benedetti, telegram, Paris, 31 Mar. 1867, *Orig.* xv. 211.

to be able to say that he was not aware that the sale of Luxemburg had been concluded.[1]

The French foreign minister refused to back down. He wired Benedetti that Bismarck could tell the Reichstag that the cession was already completed and the Prussian Government had been notified too late to object. France would not retreat, and if Prussia prevented the sale war might result.[2]

Until the end of March the British Government knew little of what was happening over Luxemburg. The foreign office seemed more preoccupied with rumours that Bismarck had made some sort of engagement with the south German states. Cowley, however, had heard something. On 12 March he wrote to Stanley 'that he was "almost sure that there is something in the wind" about Luxemburg'.[3] The foreign secretary's reply revealed his indifference.

La Tour had seen the Luxemburg story in the papers, but knew nothing of its truth or falsehood. I suppose you will telegraph if it is confirmed. Prussia will be furious. I do not see, as at present advised, that England has any reason to object. This explains why the Dutch government was so much alarmed at the possibility of Prussian aggression.[4]

Cowley's attempt to elicit information from Napoleon failed. 'I tried in vain to get a rise out of H.M. as to Luxemburg. . . . I saw in a moment that the subject was a disagreeable one'.[5] From the Berlin embassy came more definite news. 'The simultaneous arrival at Paris of Monsieur Benedetti and of Monsieur Baudin, the French minister at The Hague, has given rise to the report that a sale of the Duchy of Luxemburg by Holland to the French government is about to be negotiated.'[6]

A few days before official publication of the Prussian alliance treaties with south Germany, Bernstorff communicated their existence privately to Stanley. The foreign secretary told the

[1] Benedetti to Moustier, telegram, Berlin, 31 Mar. 1867, Orig. xv, pp. 209–10.
[2] Moustier to Benedetti, telegram, Paris, 31 Mar. and 1 Apr. 1867, ibid., pp. 215–16, 222.
[3] Cowley to Stanley, private, Paris, 12 Mar. 1867, Foot, p. 358. Fane sent him a similar report (Fane to Stanley, private, 12 Mar. 1867, Stan. Pap. X 6).
[4] Stanley to Cowley, private, 13 Mar. 1867, PRO FO 519/182. Stanley probably felt that Prussia was as unaware of the contemplated sale of Luxemburg as England had been.
[5] Cowley to Stanley, private, Paris, 14 Mar. 1867, PRO FO 519/233.
[6] Lowther to Stanley, Berlin, 16 Mar. 1867, PRO FO 64/619, no. 6.

ambassador that he 'was glad in the interest of European peace, to hear of the union of Germany for defensive purposes being effected'.[1] Stanley's approbation was overshadowed by 'a great explosion of irritation' at Paris when the treaties were made public.[2] French efforts to obtain Luxemburg continued with renewed intensity.

As complications arose, Stanley became alive to the negotiations for the cession. He wrote to Cowley giving him his impressions. 'What Prussia will say remains to be seen. On the French side it will no doubt be accepted as a tolerably adequate set off to the Prussian gains of last summer.'[3] Cowley, more acutely aware of the emperor's position, replied that 'if the peace of Europe is to be maintained, Prussia must be prepared to make some sacrifice'.[4] Whilst recognizing the emperor's need for Luxemburg as a factor in preserving the European balance of power, Stanley refused to lend any support to his move to gain the duchy. He told Apponyi, the Austrian ambassador, that the question 'does not affect the interests of England'.[5] His hesitancy in exercising any initiative was partly due to his ignorance of the details of the Luxemburg negotiations,[6] and his reluctance to becoming blindly involved persisted even though he admitted war might result.[7] The possibility of armed

[1] Stanley to Loftus, confidential, 16 Mar. 1867, PRO FO 64/615, no. 71; Stanley to Cowley, ibid., 27/1652, no. 22. Loftus reported these sentiments to the King of Prussia. William 'heartily concurred in these opinions, observing that Germany would not take the offensive but that she would always be prepared to defend herself' (Loftus to Stanley, most confidential, Berlin, 23 Mar. 1867, *APP* viii. 504–5; same to same, ibid., PRO FO 64/619, no. 152). 'The defensive alliance between North and South Germany is thoroughly satisfactory' (Stanley to Lyons, private, 19 Mar. 1867, Stan. Pap., Prussia).
[2] Cowley to Stanley, Paris, 21 Mar. 1867, PRO FO 27/1659, no. 57.
[3] Stanley to Cowley, private, 21 Mar. 1867, Foot, p. 358.
[4] Cowley to Stanley, Paris, 22 Mar. 1867, ibid. Clarendon was of the same opinion as he wrote the following to Cowley: 'I mean therefore to tell the Queen [of Holland] that in my opinion a disposition shd be shewn to treat with France, but that instead of an ex post facto guarantee Holland wd require the Empr to obtain the full consent of Prussia before any arrangement is come to' (Clarendon to Cowley, private, 23 Mar. 1867, PRO FO 519/181).
[5] La Tour to Moustier, confidential, London, 24 Mar. 1867, *Orig.* xv. 156–7.
[6] Ibid.; Stanley to Cowley, 25 Mar. 1867, PRO FO 27/1652, no. 50. 'Luxemburg is farther advanced than we thought. An intercepted telegram states that the demand for it is about to be made' (Stanley to Disraeli, secret, 27 Mar. 1867, Disraeli Papers, 111).
[7] Stanley to Cowley, 25 Mar. 1867, Foot, p. 359; same to same, confidential, 26 Mar. 1867, PRO FO 27/1652, no. 56.

conflict did not move Stanley to take steps to prevent it; it caused him to abjure all interest in order to avoid becoming involved. His psychological incapacity for action was most pronounced when events became grave. On the other hand he had such a strong feeling about the implications of commitment that he was not likely to lure with false hopes or complicate crises by an unnecessary intrusion.

As Stanley's knowledge of the dispute increased, so also did his sympathy for France:

It is idle for Prussia to complain of breach of treaties.[1] When her own proceedings have been founded on the ignoring of such obligations when they stand in the way of her designs. And it is even more unreasonable for her to complain of a slight increase of territory on the part of France, after having swallowed up half a dozen small states in the last year.[2]

On 28 March he told La Tour that such compensation to France was only fair.[3] Moustier, who at this moment was pressing Holland to cede the duchy, telegraphed to Baudin that Cowley had told him confidentially that the English Government was even willing 'to support our negotiations'.[4] It is difficult to know whether Cowley actually said this, or whether in the heat of the situation Moustier convinced himself that sympathy meant support. As Baudin was demanding Luxemburg at The Hague, the knowledge of British approval might tip the scale and seal the bargain.

By the end of March Stanley's apprehension had diminished. Under the impression that Bismarck was a consenting party, he looked upon the cession as settled.[5] His contentment was not disturbed by any anxiety for Belgium, which he considered unaffected by the sale of Luxemburg.

I see the Belgians are preparing for an outcry, but not much will come of that, and certainly I shall not encourage it. I do not know

---

[1] Stanley is referring to Prussia's treaty with Holland which concedes her right to garrison the fortress.

[2] Stanley to Cowley, private, 27 Mar. 1867, PRO FO 519/182.

[3] La Tour to Moustier, confidential, London, 28 Mar. 1867, *Orig.* xv. 193. Stanley informed both the Prussian and Russian ambassadors of his personal opinion (ibid.).

[4] Moustier to Baudin, telegram, Paris, 28 Mar. 1867, *Orig.* xv. 183.

[5] 'The Luxemburg affair is a mystery—The belief here is that the sale—if not effected—will be effected' (Loftus to Stanley, private, 30 Mar. 1867, Stan. Pap., Prussia).

whether it will be expedient to place our views on record in a despatch: perhaps not, at least for the present; I am sure to be questioned in the H. of C. and can say with more effect there whatever has to be said.[1]

When questioned in the House of Commons on 1 April, however, the foreign secretary said only that the transaction had not taken place and more he did not know.[2] On the same day that Stanley was questioned in Parliament, Bismarck was faced with an interpellation of his own devising in the Reichstag.[3]

Crete

In the winter and spring of 1866–7 Luxemburg was the least of British worries. The Irish question and the Fenian movement were constant preoccupations of the Government.[4] There was also concern with the Alabama claims and the introduction of a new reform bill,[5] and, of course, Belgium.[6] Stanley's biggest foreign problem, however, was the revival of the Eastern question.

In the preceding summer a revolt had erupted in Crete, and Greece was aiding the insurrection against Ottoman rule. There were some who felt that this, coupled with the election of Charles in Roumania, would be enough to kill the 'sick man'. Stanley's anxiety manifested itself in a letter to Lyons:

I have to instruct you to inform H.H. [Aali Pasha] that H.M.'s

---

[1] Stanley to Cowley, 30 Mar. 1867, Foot, p. 360.

[2] Hansard, *Parliamentary Debates* (3rd series), clxxxvi. 909.

[3] Erich Eyck, *Bismarck and the German Empire* (London, 1950), p. 155.

[4] Kalnoky to Beust, London, 5 Dec. 1866, HHSA, England, no. 73c; Derby to Stanley, 10 Nov. 1866, Stan. Pap., Derby.

[5] Apponyi to Beust, London, 6 Feb. 1867, ibid., no. 11; Stanley to Derby, 10 Nov. 1866, Stan. Pap., Derby. On the introduction of a reform measure, Stanley told Apponyi that the ministry had a minority in commons, and that all depended on the attitude of the moderate whigs who do not follow Bright (same to same, London, 30 Jan. 1867, HHSA, no. 8c). 'If we wish to commit political suicide, it is not difficult to do so. . . . I accepted office very unwillingly, but having accepted it, I mean to keep it as long as I can . . . but, in our position, to propose it [a reform bill] wd. be to court immediate defeat. . . . Our object must be to affirm principles, & Postpone details as far as possible' (Derby to Pakington, confidential, 4 Dec. 1866, Derby Pap. 193/1).

[6] 'I do not believe any French ruler can take Belgium by sheer force—such a proceeding would shock even the not very acute sense of France. . . . Whether we should fight in that quarrel I don't know: but I am sure no other power would' (Stanley to Fane, private, 6 Feb. 1867, Stan. Pap., France).

Govt strongly advise the Porte to deal with the Cretans with the utmost forebearance and in a conciliatory spirit to redress any grievances of which they may have cause to complain.

In the present state of the Continent it would be a great misfortune to Turkey if any question were to arise which should excite the sympathies of Europe in favour of the Christian subjects of the Porte.[1]

The British ambassador thought the situation was serious,[2] sentiments which the foreign secretary echoed:

I am afraid the Cretan affair is likely to become serious. The grievances put forward by the islanders are not very clearly stated. . . . My impression is that the movement is directed rather against Turkish rule in general than against any particular act committed, or system adopted, by the Porte. . . . Agents from Greece with the support of the Greek government have . . . been active. . . . The population of Crete itself I take to be much divided.[3]

At the end of August the Turkish Government sent a special commissioner to the island. At the same time the Russian Government suggested to both Paris and London that the three powers should urge the Porte to satisfy the rebels.[4] Advice to the Porte would be most effective if, as Gorchakov suggested, it was joined by the despatch of warships to Crete.[5] Stanley, upon receipt of the Russian proposal, asked for time to consider it and instructed Lyons to 'urge the Porte of the absolute necessity if his [the Sultan's] authority is to be maintained of measures being taken for the removal of such grievances as exist in Crete'.[6] Wishing to act with Paris, Stanley ascertained the French reaction to Gorchakov's proposition before giving his reply to Brunnow. As the French Government felt that intervention was not yet necessary, the foreign secretary told the Russian ambassador that his chief's proposal was premature.[7]

[1] Stanley to Lyons, copy, 13 Aug. 1866, PRO FO 146/1260, no. 37.
[2] Lyons to Stanley, private, Constaninople, 29 Aug. 1866, Lyons Pap. RD I.
[3] Stanley to Gladstone, private, London, 3 Sept. 1866, Glad. Pap., pp. 21–22.
[4] Stanley to Fane, 6 Sept. 1866, PRO FO 27/1608, no. 9; Stanley to Lyons, 6 Sept. 1866, PRO FO 78/1905, no. 52.
[5] Gorchakov to Budberg, 20 Aug./1 Sept. 1866, Orig. xii. 249, Mosse, p. 254. Stanley told Brunnow, the Russian ambassador, that a British 'warship already had been sent to Crete but only to protect British subjects' (Stanley to Cowley, copy, 6 Sept. 1866, PRO FO 146/2161, no. 52).
[6] Stanley to Lyons, 6 Sept. 1866, PRO FO 78/1905, no. 52.
[7] Stanley to Fane, 8 Sept. 1866, PRO FO 27/1608, no. 12; Stanley to Lyons, 8 Sept. 1866, PRO FO 78/1905, no. 55.

For the moment . . . I see nothing to do. Civil war has begun: and it is idle to advise conciliation when an armed insurrection has to be dealt with. . . . When we act, we must act altogether. . . . It seems to me quite in the cards that the final collapse may be at hand.[1]

Stanley's feeling that the Turk was nearly dead was not borne out by Lyons, who reported the rebel cause as hopeless,[2] but the foreign secretary's preference for the collective action of the powers was no doubt due to the possibility of Turkish collapse:

I do not believe in the Turkish Empire: it seems to be worn out and unable to maintain itself: and if Greece were like Piedmont or Prussia, a well governed and civilized state, the solution of the problem would be simple. But Greece is the very reverse of this: bankrupt, anarchical, without an honest politician or a class which can be trusted with power. I see no natural heir to the sick man.[3]

In October Brunnow asked England to join France and Russia in defending the Cretans from Turkish retaliation. Stanley refused, as he felt any step in this direction would be interpreted as 'sympathy for the cause of the insurgents'.[4] At this point the British Government hoped that Crete would remain in Turkish hands, since the latter was a friendly power. In a foreign office memorandum prepared in September, the strategic importance of the island to England was underlined.

The deep interest felt by England in the island of Candia may be traced to its important position with regard to the maintenance of the Egyptian route to India. From its situation it may be considered as one of the chain of sentries which, in connection with Gibraltar, Malta, and Cyprus, serve in friendly hands to keep open this important connection with our Eastern Empire. Candia and Cyprus have more than once been described as the keys of Egypt,

---

[1] Stanley to Cowley, private, 15 Sept. 1866, PRO FO 519/182. Four days later, however, Stanley was talking of a 'Turkish victory in Crete' (Stanley to Derby, private, 19 Sept. 1866, Derby Pap. 161/2).

[2] Lyons to Stanley, private, Therapia, 19 Sept. 1866, Lyons Pap. RD I. On 24 Sept. the foreign secretary was sure 'that the Turks have been beaten' (Stanley to Derby, private, 24 Sept. 1866, Derby Pap. 161/2).

[3] Stanley to Cowley, private, 25 Sept. 1866, PRO FO 519/182. Stanley's view of Turkish collapse was shared and wished for by the Russian Government (Gould to Stanley, confidential, St. Petersburg, 26 Sept. 1866, PRO FO 146/1261). Derby had no sympathy with the 'Eastern Christians' and hoped for a speedy end to the insurrection (Derby to Stanley, private, 23 Sept. 1866, Stan. Pap., Derby).

[4] Stanley to Lyons, 12 Oct. 1866, PRO FO 146/1262, no. 81.

and there is no doubt that in the possession of a maritime power hostile to England, they might be a great menace for our route across the Isthmus.[1]

The situation became more serious when the Cretan rebellion was complicated by a Serbian demand that the Turks should evacuate the fortress in Belgrade.[2] France seemed well disposed to act with England, particularly as Stanley was more willing to grant concessions to the Serbs than he was to the Cretans.[3] Stanley instructed Lyons to suggest to Turkey that she act spontaneously in evacuating the fortress and by so doing keep the Serbs from the clutches of Russian support. 'She [Russia] naturally seeks in the advocacy of Christian interests in Turkey, the means at least of bringing herself into notice, if not of retrieving in some form or other the disastrous effects of the Crimean War.'[4] The foreign secretary's suggested compromise was that the sultan would give up garrisoning the fortress but retain full sovereignty over it.[5]

In the meantime the insurrection in Crete lingered on, and the Russian Government attempted to turn it to her advantage by means of an agreement with France.[6] Budberg proposed to Moustier that Crete should be granted autonomy,[7] and the French minister, while negotiating with Russia, hinted to Fane that Crete might be made a 'Princedom'.[8] The failure of France

---

[1] Stanley to Lyons, 12 Oct. 1866, PRO FO 195/183, no. 27, Bourne, p. 236.

[2] Lyons to Stanley, private, Constantinople, 21 Nov. 1866, Lyons Pap. RD I; Moustier to La Tour, Paris, 21 Nov. 1866, *Orig.* xiii. 140–1.

[3] Stanley to Cowley, 23 Nov. 1866, PRO FO 27/1608, no. 325; La Tour to Moustier, London, 24 Nov. 1866, *Orig.* xiii. 148. Other than the fact that it was more important for England to keep Turkey in Crete than in a fortress on the Danube, Stanley's hesitancy to press Cretan grievances on the Porte was due to his ignorance of them (Lyons to Stanley, private, Therapia, 24 Oct. 1866, Lyons Pap. RD I). Lyons had to tell the British consul in Crete to furnish more information on events occurring there and not merely repeat Turkish reports originating in Constantinople (Lyons to Cowley, private, Constantinople, 21 Nov. 1866, ibid.).

[4] Stanley to Lyons, confidential, 11 Dec. 1866, PRO FO 146/1265, no. 140; same to same, ibid., 146/1290, no. 10. Lyons thought that both Russia and Greece were working for the disintegration of the Ottoman Empire (Lyons to Stanley, private, Constantinople, 19 Dec. 1866, Lyons Pap. RD I).

[5] Stanley to Lyons, 12 Dec. 1866, PRO FO 146/1290, no. 11.

[6] 'It is very obvious that there has been a little coquetting between France and Russia on the Eastern question' (Fane to Stanley, private, 1 Jan. 1867, Stan. Pap., x 6).

[7] Moustier to Talleyrand, 24 Dec. 1866, Mosse, p. 259.

[8] Fane to Stanley, Paris, 27 Dec. 1866, PRO FO 27/1625, no. 61.

and Russia to get together[1] coincided with a French proposal
to Britain 'that the Porte should be advised by the Powers
collectively to abandon the Servian Fortresses and to give the
inhabitants of Crete local autonomy'.[2] Stanley, whose purpose
it was to keep his country free and uncommitted, pointed out
that he had already advised the Porte to evacuate the fortress.
As to Crete, the foreign secretary told La Tour that separation
of the island from Turkey was out of the question, although at
the same time he appeared to admit the possibility of some
kind of autonomy.[3] On 19 January he wrote to Lyons:

> We are willing to support the proposition of France and Russia
> for giving local autonomy to Crete. . . . We disclaim all idea of put-
> ting any pressure on the Porte. . . . We do not understand by the
> word local autonomy anything in the nature of a separation of
> Crete from the rest of the Empire.[4]

No sooner had Stanley stated the British position than the
French Government, solicitous of Russian support in the West,
proposed to St. Petersburg and London the complete separation
of Crete from Turkey.[5] It seemed that there was a European
conspiracy against Britain's position in the East, for hard upon
this news Austria suggested to England and France the abroga-
tion of the demilitarization of the Black Sea and a conference
of the powers on the Eastern question. Stanley replied that
'England and France would never consent to abandon the
principle of the neutralization of the Black Sea'.[6]

Moustier again brought up the cession of Crete to Greece.[7]
Stanley replied to La Tour that he needed time for his Government's answer, but that personally he did not favour so drastic

---

[1] Mosse, pp. 259–62; A. J. P. Taylor, *The Struggle for Mastery in Europe* (Oxford,
1954), pp. 179–80.

[2] Stanley to Fane, 8 Jan. 1867, PRO FO 27/1651, no. 17.

[3] Stanley to Fane, 9 Jan. 1867, PRO FO 27/1651, no. 27; La Tour to Moustier,
London, 9 Jan. 1867, *Orig.* xiv. 63–65. Stanley told La Tour that British opinion
and parliament had changed since 1856, and war for England in the east was
impossible (ibid.; Stanley to Buchanan, private, 8 Jan. 1867, Stan. Pap., Russia).

[4] Stanley to Fane, 19 Jan. 1867, PRO FO 27/1651, no. 52.

[5] Moustier to Talleyrand, 23 Jan. 1867, Mosse, p. 261; Fane to Stanley, confidential, Paris, 24 Jan. 1867, PRO FO 27/1656, no. 98.

[6] Stanley to Fane, 30 Jan. 1867, PRO FO 146/1288, no. 90. The foreign secretary writing to Fane on 30 Jan. was not sure whether the Austrian proposal was
made to him 'two or three days ago' (ibid.).

[7] Moustier to La Tour, Paris, 30 Jan. 1867, *Orig.* xiv. 193–6.

a solution.[1] The Government's difficulty in working with Paris
was summed up by Lyons: 'If France makes such sudden and
violent changes [from autonomy to complete separation] as
this last proposal about Crete, it must be impossible to act
with her and we can do little more than let things take their
course and keep free from entanglements'.[2] Turkey's evacuation
of the fortress in Belgrade and her apparent success in quelling
the Cretan uprising confirmed Stanley in his opposition to
cession.[3] Consquently when Moustier again pressed London to
support the separation of Crete from Turkey Stanley refused,
adding 'that if the Porte were willing to agree to the cession
[the foreign secretary was sure that it would not] Her Majesty's
Government would not oppose it'.[4]

The failure of Paris and St. Petersburg to conclude an agreement on the cession of Crete, of which negotiations the British were unaware,[5] resulted in English apprehension about
the unpredictability of French policy.[6] But the need to work
with France in the East was recognized, as 'our object must
be to prevent isolated action, or what would be worse the
joint action of France and Russia'.[7] Stanley admitted this,[8] but
also knew that 'France and Russia can do almost anything they
please with the Porte, unless we interfere to prevent it, wh. I
suppose we shall certainly not do'.[9] Stanley's position was not
an easy one. Admitting British interest in Constantinople and
Egypt and recognizing Crete as a link with those two places,
the foreign secretary dismissed from his mind, particularly as
opinion was against involvement, the possibility of an English
war in the East. Yet with whom was he to co-operate to prevent

---

[1] Stanley to Fane, 1 Feb. 1867, PRO FO 146/1288, no. 93; La Tour to Moustier,
London, 2 Feb. 1867, *Orig.* xiv. 227–9.

[2] Lyons to Stanley, private, Constantinople, 13 Feb. 1867, Lyons Pap. RD I.

[3] La Tour to Moustier, London, 1 Mar. 1867, *Orig.* xiv. 399.

[4] Stanley to Cowley, 13 Mar. 1867, PRO FO 27/1652, no. 15; same to same,
13 Mar. 1867, Derby Pap. 54/3, no. 15.

[5] Cowley to Stanley, private, Paris, 14 Mar. 1867, PRO FO 519/233; Clarendon
to Cowley, private, Egerton Crescent, 16 Mar. 1867, PRO FO 519/181.

[6] It seemed that France had temporarily given up obtaining any close understanding with Russia. Moustier 'has no intention at present of setting the East in
a flame. . . . [The emperor] has ordered Moustier to hold his hand' (Cowley to
Stanley, private, 21 Mar. 1867, Stan. Pap. X 6).

[7] Cowley to Stanley, Paris, 25 Mar. 1867, PRO FO 27/1659, no. 59.

[8] Stanley to Cowley, private, 27 Mar. 1867, PRO FO 519/182.

[9] Lyons to Cowley, private, Constantinople, 27 Mar. 1867, Lyons Pap. RD I.

an explosion in the Ottoman Empire from resulting in strife? Gorchakov was working to destroy the Turks whom Stanley was trying to maintain, and France seemed as disposed to act with Russia for support in the West as with her old Crimean war ally.[1]

The isolation of England in the East, a condition apprehended and feared by Victoria, Clarendon, Cowley, and Lyons, was not due to Stanley's policy in the Levant so much as to his attitude and position in the West. His acquiescence in and approval of Prussian aggrandizement[2] was not balanced by any corresponding desire to support France's quest for compensation. Napoleon attempted to play Russia's game at Constantinople in return for the active support over Luxemburg and Belgium that Britain would not give.

At the beginning of April London's isolation in the East was forgotten when the secret Luxemburg negotiations erupted into a public dispute. Though Stanley tried very hard to avoid involvement he was unsuccessful. In the ensuing crisis his sympathy for France was manifest, but his circumspection neutralized his feelings and prevented any significant contribution to the stabilization of the balance of power upset by Bismarck. Peace was preserved temporarily but a Franco-Prussian war became more than ever probable.

[1] Stanley was only too conscious of Britain's position (Stanley to Grey, 30 Mar. 1867, RA B 23/37.

[2] 'Bismarck's retirement would now be a misfortune, whatever might have been the case two or three years ago' (Stanley to Loftus, private, 10 Oct. 1866, Stan. Pap., Prussia).

IV

LUXEMBURG: PUBLIC DISPUTE

ON 1 April 1867, Benningsen, one of the leaders of the National Liberal party, made a speech in the form of a question in the Reichstag:

We should have no doubt in Germany or abroad as to our intention of defending this portion of Germany [Luxemburg]. . . . Let us show that we do not fear war. . . . We do not seek a war . . . if it breaks out the responsibility will rest with France.

Is the Prussian Government in a position to inform the Reichstag —all parties of which will unite their utmost endeavours to repel any attempt at separating an old German country from the united Fatherland—that they in common with their confederates are determined to secure the connection of the Grand Duchy of Luxemburg with the rest of Germany, and especially the right of Prussia of garrisoning the fortress of Luxemburg, permanently from all danger.[1]

Bismarck's reply to the interpellation, which it seems he had previously arranged with Benningsen, was a moderate one in that no veto was placed on the cession of the duchy to France.

A few days ago the King of Holland personally requested our minister at The Hague to express an opinion as to what the Prussian Govt. would think if the King of the Netherlands were to dispossess himself of . . . Luxemburg. Count Perponcher was instructed to answer that for the moment there was no reason why the Prussian government and her confederate allies should express any opinion on the subject: that we must leave to H.M. alone the responsibility of his own negotiations, and that this govt. before it expressed any opinion whatever upon the question—in the event of its being obliged to do so—would inform itself beforehand as to how the question was viewed by Her German confederates, by the signatories of the treaties of 1839, and by public opinion in Germany.[2]

Moustier instructed Baudin to conclude the cession immediately.[3] On the same day Bismarck gave his private interpretation

---

[1] Loftus to Stanley, Berlin, 1 Apr. 1867, PRO FO 64/619, no. 177, no. 178.
[2] Ibid.
[3] Moustier to Baudin, telegram, Paris, 2 Apr. 1867, *Orig.* xv. 250–1.

of his public reply to the Reichstag interpellation by again pressing the French Government to cancel negotiations with Holland.[1] At an interview with Napoleon III, Goltz cautioned him that the German people would not shrink from war as an alternative preferable to the cession of Luxemburg to France.[2] On 3 April the Dutch requested that negotiations should be suspended as the Prussian minister at The Hague warned that war might otherwise result.[3]

As Paris also contemplated armed conflict, Bismarck had approached the British Government on the last day of March. Bernstorff read Stanley two telegrams. The first requested England for the sake of peace to influence the Dutch Government against the sale. The second, containing a hint at the geographical proximity of the duchy to Belgium, expressed the fact that Prussia considered Luxemburg as well as Belgium to be under the guarantee of 1839. Was this also the view of the British Government? Stanley refused to bite, and told Bernstorff that he needed time to consider the proposals.[4] The next day he replied:

The guarantee . . . was meant for the protection of the King of Holland, but if the King were an assenting party to the transfer, the question of protecting his interests would not arise. The Prussian government appeared to regard it as a question affecting the integrity of the German territory, which for them was a natural point of view, but it had certainly never been contemplated by England to guarantee the integrity of Germany.

It did not seem therefore that the possession of Luxemburg would materially affect the future of Belgium.

It would not be the duty of Her Majesty's Government to

---

[1] Benedetti to Moustier, telegram, Berlin, 2 Apr. 1867, ibid., p. 251.

[2] Goltz to Bismarck, Paris, 2 Apr. 1867, *APP* viii. 569.

[3] Baudin to Moustier, telegram, The Hague, 3 Apr. 1867, *Orig.* xv. 366.

[4] Stanley to Cowley, 1 Apr. 1867, PRO FO 27/1652, no. 68; Stanley to Loftus, 1 Apr. 1867, PRO FO 64/615, no. 88; Bismarck to Bernstorff, Berlin, telegram, 30 Mar. 1867, *GW* vi, no. 724; ibid., no. 728. In recounting the interview to Cowley, Stanley wrote that he told Bernstorff that 'if by so small a re-arrangement of territory the irritation now undoubtedly existing in Europe could be allayed, and the peace of Europe thereby secured, I should have thought so great an advantage cheaply purchased' (Stanley to Cowley, ibid.). But in his report to Loftus, the foreign secretary omitted the above opinion and wrote that he had told the Prussian minister that 'he did not consider that the arrangement, whatever might be its precise character, was one of a nature to call for the intervention of England' (Stanley to Loftus, ibid.).

interfere in the matter which seemed to be one entirely between France and Germany.[1]

On 3 April Bernstorff came again with a dispatch from Bismarck.

He [Bismarck] did not see how war could be avoided, and in the event of its taking place, and of France obtaining any success, the position of Belgium would become exceedingly precarious. He was anxious therefore to know whether in the event of a war being forced on Prussia by France, Her Majesty's government would take part in it, and to what extent they would give their cooperation to Prussia?

Stanley said England was not involved in the quarrel and any armed interference on either side was out of the question.

As to Belgium that was a different question. England was pledged in the strongest manner to assist in maintaining the independence of that country. . . . But there was a wide distinction between taking up arms in case of necessity for the protection of Belgium, in fulfilment of promises solemnly and repeatedly given, and joining in a war between France and Germany, in which no English interest was involved.[2]

Needless to say Bismarck was thoroughly disenchanted with Stanley's answer.[3] Though the foreign secretary did not admit any danger to Belgium, the queen did, and at her behest he wrote to Cowley 'to encourage any disposition which may be shown . . . to renounce any views of aggrandizement at the expense of Belgium'.

It would be a great satisfaction to Her Majesty's government to receive in some formal and authentic shape an assurance that whatever may be the issue of a war between France and Prussia on account of Luxemburg, if war should unfortunately break out, the

---

[1] Stanley to Cowley, 2 Apr. 1867, PRO FO 27/1652, no. 77; Bernstorff to Bismarck, telegram, London, 2 Apr. 1867, *APP* viii. 599.

[2] Stanley to Cowley, 3 Apr. 1867, PRO FO 27/1652, no. 83; Bismarck to Bernstorff, Berlin, telegram, 2 Apr. 1867, *GW* vi, no. 735. Stanley told Bernstorff that no British Minister could justify to Parliament England's joining a Franco-Prussian war over Luxemburg (Bernstorff to Bismarck, confidential, 3 Apr. 1867, *APP* viii. 575–6).

[3] Bismarck to Bernstorff, Berlin, telegram, 3 Apr. 1867, *GW* vi, no. 73. Convinced that he could not count on the British fleet, Bismarck was ready to consider the sacrifice of Belgium to France as a distinct possibility if an accommodation with France was desirable (ibid.).

independence and territorial integrity of Belgium as now constituted will be respected by France.[1]

Victoria approved Stanley's position and felt war was probable,[2] as the foreign secretary thought also after receiving Cowley's telegram concerning Napoleon III.[3] On the next day Cowley confirmed his telegram of 3 April, though personally he felt that France was not yet ready for hostilities. 'Goltz . . . added that the Emperor . . . had given him to understand that there was no option for him between the possession of Luxemburg and war'.[4] The French Government was seriously considering war as preferable to humiliation. Moustier's frustration was embittered by what he considered the unscrupulousness and trickery of Bismarck.[5] The council of ministers met on 6 April to decide

[1] Stanley to Cowley, secret and confidential, 3 Apr. 1867, PRO FO 27/1652, no. 84; ibid., RA I 71/32, Mosse, pp. 264–5. Stanley had just received a telegram from Cowley which reported the emperor having said that possession of the duchy involved his own existence (Cowley to Stanley, private, telegram, Paris, 3 Apr. 1867, PRO FO 27/1672). Stanley still did not think Belgium was in any danger, but he did guess fairly accurately about the Luxemburg business. 'Bismarck has held out hopes to the Emperor, of Prussia giving her consent to the transfer, which hopes will be disappointed by the general feeling of Germany being too strong for any Prussian minister to disregard (Stanley to Grey, private, 3 Apr. 1867, RA I 71/33, Mosse, p. 265). Clarendon felt that this was what occurred and so wrote to Cowley (Clarendon to Cowley, private, Egerton Crescent, 2 Apr. 1867, PRO FO 519/181). Cowley repeated Clarendon's guess to Stanley, which the foreign secretary passed on to Grey (Cowley to Stanley, private, Paris, 2 Apr. 1867, PRO FO 519/233). The original divination was probably Clarendon's and not Stanley's or Cowley's.

[2] Grey to Stanley, private, Windsor Castle, 3 Apr. 1867, RA I 71/34, Mosse, p. 365. The queen might, however, have merely wished to ignite Stanley, for Grey told Bernstorff that she did not think Napoleon would go to war (Bernstorff to William I, London, 3 Apr. 1867, APP viii. 575). Grey also informed the Prussian minister that the queen, as always, was pro-German, and that England would actively intervene if Belgium were menaced (ibid.).

[3] Cowley telegraphed that the 'Prussian Minister saw the Emperor yesterday. Found His Majesty very calm but very determined. Emperor said possession of Luxemburg involved the question of his own existence' (Cowley to Stanley, private, telegram, 3 Apr. 1867, PRO FO 27/1672). Foot has found the above in the Disraeli papers as a note written at 2.40 p.m. from Stanley to Disraeli. It is also in the Foreign Office files. Cowley sent the telegram at 12.40 p.m. and it was received at the Foreign Office at 2 p.m. Disraeli reported that the 'Rothschilds have received information that the Emperor has definitely informed Bismarck that the arrangement between himself & King of Holland is concluded, & that he shall act at once on it' (Disraeli to Stanley, 3 Apr. 1867, Disraeli Pap.).

[4] Cowley to Stanley, private, Paris, 4 Apr. 1867, PRO FO 519/233.

[5] Moustier to Benedetti, private, Paris, 6 Apr. 1867, Orig. xv. 296. Even Werther, the Prussian minister at Vienna, 'says that his govt. are bound to do something by way of compensation to France . . . and he seems to think the cession of Luxemburg

what to do. It was almost unanimously felt, and not only in France, that imperial prestige could barely survive further embarrassment. The choice nevertheless was for retreat, since the army was not ready and France would have to fight alone.[1] Having reached this decision, the council voted on 8 April 'that a pacific declaration should be made to the Chambers'. 'The Emperor will say that Prussia having appealed to the Powers who signed the Treaty of 1839, His Majesty is ready to abide by their decision and has no doubt that the solution will be a peaceable one.'[2]

Two days later Baudin was instructed to drop all negotiations at The Hague.[3]

When questioned in the Commons, Stanley explained the Government's aloofness in terms not unfavourable to France:

I do not think it would be easy to agree . . . that it is the duty of E. to interfere to prevent a transaction which might result in some small aggrandizement on the part of Fr., when the Govt. & the people of this country have seen with entire acquiescence, & even, I believe, with approval, the enormous aggrandizement which has accrued to Germany, or rather to Pr.[4]

The foreign secretary wrote in the same sense to Grey.

Luxemburg would have been a small price to pay for a reconciliation between France and Prussia. As matters stand, the feeling

would be the least she can expect' (Bloomfield to Stanley, private, Vienna, 2 Apr. 1867, PRO FO 356/39).
[1] Rothan, *Souvenirs diplomatiques, L'affaire du Luxembourg* (Paris, 1883), p. 266. Stanley learned on 4 April from Berlin that Holland had dropped all negotiations on Luxemburg. He telegraphed to Cowley asking the French reaction (Stanley to Cowley, telegram, 4 Apr. 1867, PRO FO 27/1652, no. 90). 'I had a long conversation yesterday with La Valette—He had just come from the Council of Ministers. Pacific counsels had, he said, been given by the majority of the ministers present' (Cowley to Stanley, private, 7 Apr. 1867, Stan. Pap. X 6).
[2] Cowley to Stanley, telegram, 8 Apr. 1867, RA I 71/54, Mosse, p. 266. Text in *Orig.* xv. 324. Stanley told La Tour that Prussia had asked England to influence the Dutch against cession of the duchy (La Tour to Moustier, confidential, London, 5 Apr. 1867, *Orig.* xv. 290). William I informed the King of Holland that he was in favour of consulting the powers who signed the Treaty of 1839. On 2 April Goltz made the same suggestion to Napoleon III (Goltz to Bismarck, Paris, 2 Apr. 1867, *APP* viii. 569). The King of Holland, in suspending negotiations, told the French Government that the sale could only take place with consent of Prussia and the powers who signed the Treaty of 1839 (Loftus to Stanley, confidential, Berlin, 6 Apr. 1867, PRO FO 64/619, no. 190).
[3] Moustier to Baudin, telegram, Paris, 10 Apr. 1867, *Orig.* xv. 350.
[4] Hansard, *Parliamentary Debates* (3rd series), clxxxvi. 1255.

of exasperation in France will be aggravated by this fresh failure—
and the prospect of permanent peace seems to me very gloomy.[1]

After a debate of 'little excitement' in the House of Commons,
Stanley reported the predominant sentiment there:

> There is only one feeling as far as I can see, that we are in no way
> bound to interfere. I think this last failure settles the matter. The
> Emperor must fight or abdicate: but he need not fight yet, and may
> try to gain time. . . . My language to La Tour was . . . if that small
> acquisition of territory would remove the feeling of irritation now
> existing, I thought it would be a small price for Europe, and even
> for Prussia to pay for peace. This, if necessary, I would repeat in the
> House: I am sure it is the view of the majority of reasonable men
> here. Your having extracted a fresh declaration about Belgium is a
> good thing done: If we can only make France understand that on
> that subject we are in earnest, there is no danger.[2]

On 6 April Loftus inundated his chief with a barrage of
dispatches, one of which, though admitting the seriousness of
the crisis, minimized any Prussian wish for war.[3]

A more tangible manifestation of the desire to avoid a conflict
was contained in a dispatch from Bismarck which Bernstorff
read to Stanley.

> Count Bismarck urges Her Majesty's government to do what they
> can to prevent a quarrel between Prussia and France on this subject,
> and he throws out a hint that Prussia would not object to go into
> a conference where the whole matter might be discussed.
>
> Count Bernstorff pressed me to use such influence as Her Majesty's
> Government might possess at Paris, to induce the Emperor not to
> press further his demand upon the King of Holland. I said . . . what-
> ever I could do, should be done to avert . . . war between France &
> Prussia, arising out of a cause so inadequate.[4]

---

[1] Stanley to Grey, private, 5 Apr. 1867, RA I 71/40, Mosse, p. 265. Cowley felt
that even the purchase of Luxemburg would little satisfy France or 'calm the
irritation felt against Prussia since the events of last year. Altogether the horizon
looks very black' (Cowley to Bloomfield, private, Paris, 5 Apr. 1867, PRO FO
356/33).

[2] Stanley to Cowley, private, 6 Apr. 1867, PRO FO 356/33.

[3] Loftus to Stanley, confidential, Berlin, 6 Apr. 1867, PRO FO 64/619, no. 190.
The British military attaché likewise reported the French army not prepared for
war (Claremont to Cowley, confidential, Paris, 7 Apr. 1867, PRO FO 27/1659,
no. 10).

[4] Stanley to Cowley, 6 Apr. 1867, PRO FO 27/1652, no. 96. Yet Stanley
cautioned Cowley to avoid being a mediator, judge, or doing anything that
might fetter the freedom of Britain. Bismarck later maintained that he never told

On the same day Napoleon III made his own representation to England in a conversation with Cowley. He told the British minister that Bismarck 'had played him false'. 'He was most desirous to maintain the peace of Europe and if the Great Powers could prevail on Prussia to give him satisfaction, or suggest any mode of settling this question, he would be only too glad to adopt it.'

The emperor favoured one particular mode: 'that Luxemburg should be made over to the Grand Duke, Prussia withdrawing the garrison from the fortress'.

> The object of the Emperor in sending for me was I think to sound how far H.M.'s Govt. . . . might be disposed to propose this arrangement to Prussia. He did not ask me this, but he intimated that I was to tell you what passed between us & you might see whether anything could be done.
>
> If you can do anything in this matter, you will confer a great favour here and I firmly believe will have the satisfaction of preventing a war, tho perhaps only for a time—which is otherwise inevitable.[1]

Cowley's words took effect, for on the following day Stanley saw the French minister and unofficially suggested three possible solutions: the duchy to be ceded to Belgium, the duchy to remain with Holland who would promise never to cede it, the people of Luxemburg to vote to decide their own disposal.[2] What the foreign secretary did not make clear to the French ambassador, though it was probably not necessary to do so, was that he had no intention of taking the initiative on the basis of the proposals which he unofficially offered. On the same day as his conversation with La Tour, he wrote privately to Cowley.

> In such a business as that of Luxemburg to gain time is to gain much—I am not for offering any suggestion as to a settlement as yet,

---

Bernstorff he favoured a conference (Loftus to Stanley, confidential, Berlin, 13 Apr. 1867, PRO FO 64/619, no. 205; ibid., *APP* viii. 649–52).

[1] Cowley to Stanley, private, Paris, 7 Apr. 1867, PRO FO 519/233; ibid., RA I 71/53, Mosse, pp. 265–6; same to same, confidential, Paris, 8 Apr. 1867, PRO FO 27/1659, no. 150. According to Bismarck, Cowley at this meeting with Napoleon suggested a European conference (Bismarck to Bernstorff, confidential, Berlin, *GW* vi, no. 755).

[2] La Tour to Moustier, confidential, London, 8 Apr. 1867, *Orig.* xv. 324. On the same day Beust, the Austrian foreign minister, made similar suggestions with the provision that if the duchy went to Belgium, the latter would cede to France areas of her territory as compensation (Beust to Metternich, Vienna, 8 Apr. 1867, *Rheinpolitik*, ii. 301).

not without being invited to do so, but I am quite willing it should be understood that we will do anything that may be in our power— short of steps which might commit us to armed intervention to bring about a better understanding. Bernstorff has been with me, hinting of course unofficially and as from himself that if we decline to join Prussia, Bismarck is ready to come to an understanding with France on the subject of Belgium.

I told him that . . . I was quite sure England would not sanction its government plunging into a war for an object which did not concern us, merely for a vague apprehension of future contingent dangers.

Bernstorff desired me not to put this into a despatch, but to consider it as private conversation—which I shall do accordingly, but I have no doubt that his question was put by order.[1]

Stanley's involvement was a reflection not of his desire to intervene but of his natural mediatorial position between Paris and Berlin; Napoleon III and Bismarck recognized this fact and therefore sought his support and intervention, particularly as neither at the moment wanted war. He avoided taking the initiative with which France and Prussia presented him, and which England's position as a power entitled her to exercise, because the temper of British opinion coincided with his desire to keep free of continental entanglements. His passion to make foreign policy reflect domestic opinion, in itself not unwise, was not motivated by political expediency.[2] It was sought almost as an end in itself.

Cowley felt that the pacific reaction of France to their failure to obtain Luxemburg was due in part to Niel's[3] influence. In an attempt to arrange an accommodation the British ambassador reported that Goltz thought Bismarck would evacuate the fortress if the duchy were neutralized under the King of Holland.

For my part I shd be very sorry to see Luxemburg in the hands of France, altho I admit that that wd. be preferable to war. . . . You will see what an important post it wd. be for France in the event of her having designs upon Belgium.[4]

[1] Stanley to Cowley, private, 8 Apr. 1867, PRO FO 356/33.
[2] The Reform Bill had so captured public attention that the Luxemburg issue seemed remote (Cowley to Stanley, private, 16 Apr. 1867, Stan. Pap. X 6).
[3] The French minister of war told Napoleon that the army could not be ready for eight months (Cowley to Stanley, private, Paris, 9 Apr. 1867, RA I 71/58).
[4] Cowley to Stanley, private, Paris, 9 Apr. 1867, PRO FO 519/233. Nor was

La Tour expressed as his personal opinion that France must eventually demand the withdrawal of the Prussian garrison.[1] With the immediate threat of war over, solutions to resolve the question of Luxemburg were not wanting. As most of these suggestions entailed Prussian abandonment of the fortress, Moustier's spirits revived with the possibility of balm for French wounds.[2] The French foreign minister preferred uniting Luxemburg to Belgium with territorial compensation to France, and the formation of a customs union between Paris and Brussels.[3] This would have meant an immediate territorial acquisition and possible future control of Belgium for Napoleon. Recognizing that England, Prussia, and Belgium herself would oppose this arrangement, Moustier was prepared to accept any proposal which was consistent with French interests and dignity.[4] One such suggestion offered to Cowley by General Fleury, an intimate of Napoleon III, was the destruction of the fortress and the neutralization of the duchy.[5]

The next day, La Tour, acting on instructions from Paris, asked England to 'do what they could for the preservation of peace'.

Of the various possible combinations by which the matter might

Cowley agreeable to giving the duchy to Belgium as 'it would raise a storm here [France]' (Cowley to Hammond, private, Paris, 9 Apr. 1867, PRO FO 391/6). In a letter to Bernstorff dated 11 April, Bismarck said that German opinion and national feeling would not permit the separation of Luxemburg from Germany or the evacuation of the fortress (Bismarck to Bernstorff, confidential, Berlin, 11 Apr. 1867, *GW* vi, no. 755).

[1] Stanley to Cowley, 10 Apr. 1867, PRO FO 27/1652, no. 109; Great Britain, *Parliamentary Papers*, 1867, 74, 455. Hammond argued that under present conditions it was 'obligatory' to evacuate the fortress (Hammond to Cowley, private, 10 Apr. 1867, PRO FO 391/6).

[2] Moustier to Benedetti, telegram, Paris, 12 Apr. 1867, *Orig.* xv. 387–8. On the day previous, Brunnow, the Russian minister in London, had presented his ideas to La Tour. Luxemburg should go to Belgium and be neutralized by the powers who signed the treaty of 1839, with France obtaining Philippeville and Marienburg. The powers would then renew Belgian neutrality (La Tour to Moustier, confidential, London, 11 Apr. 1867, ibid., pp. 383–4). Moustier telegraphed back that this was acceptable if the powers agreed to it (Moustier to La Tour, telegram, Paris, 13 Apr. 1867, ibid., pp. 400–1).

[3] Moustier to La Tour, private and confidential, Paris, 11 Apr. 1867, ibid., pp. 367–9.

[4] Moustier to La Tour, telegram, Paris, 12 Apr. 1867, ibid., p. 387.

[5] Cowley to Stanley, private, Paris, 11 Apr. 1867, RA I 71/69, Mosse, p. 266. Cowley believed that Fleury spoke to him on orders from Napoleon and that Prussia ought to agree to this (ibid.). As events unfolded the question was not Bismarck's acceptance but Stanley's acquiescence.

be arranged which have been mentioned in conversation . . . the French government absolutely repel none. . . . M. de Moustier must observe . . . its [Luxemburg's] occupation by Prussia, unjustifiable in point of right,[1] is for France a real danger.[2]

In reply, though he inferred a French implication of war, Stanley expressed no opinion, and asked for time to consult the Cabinet. His reaction was not surprising, particularly in the light of a letter from the queen on the previous day:

> She cannot forget how often the expression has been used of coming to the assistance of France, in order to get the Emperor out of some scrape . . . and that we have seldom acted upon this suggestion without having cause to regret it.
> The Queen would urge on Lord Stanley not to allow himself to be easily diverted from the policy . . . of refusing to allow E. to be made a party to the personal (for such they are) differences between Fr. & Pr.
> We may well pause now, before we concur in recommending the cession of that fortress to Fr (for to surrender it to the safe keeping of the Grand Ducal Troops is the same thing as giving it to France). . . . We must not either lose sight of the danger to Belgian independence which E. is bound to maintain, which would necessarily follow the possession of Lux. by France. . . . The Queen must again urge Lord Stanley to take no new step . . . without the full consideration of the Cabinet, to whom she would wish this letter to be shown.[3]

On 13 April the foreign secretary began to incline towards the evacuation of the fortress. He believed that if this were done France would accept any arrangement, though if Berlin objected there would eventually be war.[4] Bismarck, who had been attempting to gain Britain's support by playing on her concern for Belgium,[5] was trying to impress upon Stanley the arguments against evacuation:

> The question was not really that of the possession of Luxemburg. The question was whether the internal position of France did not

---

[1] Hammond, who studied all the relevant treaties, was of the same opinion (Hammond to Cowley, private, 11 Apr. 1867, PRO FO 391/6).

[2] Stanley to Cowley, most confidential, 12 Apr. 1867, PRO FO 27/1652, no. 111.

[3] Victoria to Stanley, Windsor, 11 Apr. 1867, QVL, 2nd ser., i. 416–17.

[4] Stanley to Grey, private, 13 Apr. 1867, RA, I 71/76, Mosse, p. 267.

[5] In his talks with Loftus, as well as in articles in the official press, Bismarck harped on his Belgian concerto (Loftus to Stanley, Berlin, 13 Apr. 1867, PRO FO 64/619, no. 203).

render it necessary to the Emperor Napoleon to seek a war; Luxemburg therefore was but the pretext.

Prussia he [Bismarck] said attributed no great value or importance either to the Grand Duchy or to the fortress, but it was now a question of national honour. . . . He could not take into consideration the question of right, when a higher motive, that of the national honour was at stake.[1]

As to Belgium, Loftus was told 'that a guarantee was in these days of little value'.

If the position of Luxemburg [Bismarck continued] has no interest for you to defend it, neither has Belgium the smallest interest for us. It would not concern us if France were to annex the southern portions of Belgium.

It was evident to me [Loftus] that Count Bismarck would equally engage to defend the existence of Belgium under all circumstances if on return Great Britain should make common cause with Germany in a defensive war against France.[2]

On 15 April war again became probable as Moustier, in a circular note to his ministers in England, Austria, Russia, and Italy, explained that French dignity and honour would be satisfied by Prussian evacuation of the fortress.[3] On this same day Bernstorff communicated to Stanley a dispatch from Bismarck, who maintained that 'Prussia is not in a position to consent to the separation under any form of Luxemburg from Germany, or to the evacuation of the fortress'.[4] German nationalism was given as the reason for this stand. Acting on his own earlier suggestion, Beust of Austria now proposed that Luxemburg should be ceded to Belgium, and the latter would give over to France Philippeville and Marienburg.[5] From Bismarck's

---

[1] Loftus to Stanley, confidential, Berlin, 13 Apr. 1867, PRO FO 64/619, no. 205; ibid., *APP* 649–52. No doubt for the effect it would have on London, Bismarck informed Bernstorff that the Cabinet should not deceive itself, and that a break between the Prussian and German Governments with German national feeling would shake Europe much more than a Franco-Prussian war (Bismarck to Bernstorff, Berlin, confidential, 11 Apr. 1867, *GW* vi. no. 755; Stanley to Cowley, 15 Apr. 1867, RA I 71/82).   [2] Ibid.

[3] Moustier to French diplomatic agents at London, Vienna, St. Petersburg, and Florence, confidential, Paris, 15 Apr. 1867, *Orig.* xvi. 9–11.

[4] Stanley to Cowley, 15 Apr. 1867, PRO FO 27/1652, no. 122.

[5] Bloomfield to Stanley, Vienna, 15 Apr. 1867, PRO FO 120/452, no. 63, no. 67. Belgium opposed Beust's scheme (Cowley to Stanley, telegram, Paris, 16 Apr. 1867, PRO FO 27/1660, no. 143; Stanley to Cowley, 18 Apr. 1867, ibid. 1652, no. 143). Hammond also opposed it out of fear for Belgian integrity. This was the

point of view this was putting the cart before the horse, even allowing for the fact that the minister president was probably exaggerating his claims with an eye to effect.

Stanley was perplexed, yet felt in view of French moderation that Prussia was responsible for the crisis:

I shall wait as long as possible before taking any step, and then do no more than I can help. The real decision rests at Berlin. Once let Bismarck say 'we might consent to evacuate the fortress on certain conditions' and all is plain and easy. Let him on the other hand say 'we will not do this on any terms' [as he just had] and we are landed in a war.

The Prussians are evidently very anxious to drag England into the affair by creating an alarm about Belgium.[1]

He told La Tour of the unsatisfactory news from Berlin. The French ambassador replied that the emperor could only renounce Luxemburg if Prussia evacuated the fortress.[2] Sensing the justice in France's position, the foreign secretary sought to deter Bismarck:

She [Prussia] has a long sea-coast and ports to defend. . . . She has no means of resisting naval pressure by France on her own coasts, and the . . . naval superiority of France . . . in Europe . . . [and] in other ports . . . might produce a very serious financial crisis in Germany, and as a consequence weaken the . . . influence of Prussia over her confederates and tend to loosen the union so lately formed among the states of Northern Germany.[3]

Contrast this with Stanley's telegram to Cowley, who was asking for instructions before seeing Napoleon: 'If he [Napoleon] can suggest any course by which it [war] may be avoided, H.M.'s Govt. would gladly assist in promoting so desirable a result by their good offices, with the understanding of course

official British view (Hammond to Cowley, 18 Apr. 1867, Foot, p. 367). Victoria, on the contrary, thought 'that the most satisfactory settlement of the question would be the transfer of Luxemburg to Belgium' (Grey to Derby, private, 16 Apr. 1867, Stan. Pap., Derby). For a brief period Stanley and Disraeli favoured the cession, but the foreign secretary demurred when Belgium objected to the transfer (Disraeli to Stanley, 17 Apr. 1867, Stan. Pap., Disraeli; Stanley to Disraeli, ibid.; Stanley to Derby, private, 17 Apr. 1867, Derby Pap. 161/3; Stanley to Cowley, confidential, 20 Apr. 1867, PRO FO 27/1652, no. 149).
[1] Stanley to Cowley, private, 16 Apr. 1867, PRO FO 356/33. The foreign secretary told Bernstorff that peace depended upon Prussia moving out of Luxemburg (Bernstorff to Bismarck, 15 Apr. 1867, APP viii. 673).
[2] La Tour to Moustier, London, 17 Apr. 1867, Orig. xvi. 33.
[3] Stanley to Loftus, 17 Apr. 1867, PRO FO 64/615, no. 116.

that Belgium is not interfered with.'[1] The problem for the foreign secretary was avoiding war without sacrificing Belgium or commiting Britain. His perplexity was due to the apparently growing incompatibility of preserving peace and Belgian integrity at the same time.

The urgent necessity of doing both was presented to Stanley after Cowley had seen both Napoleon and the King of Belgium on 18 April. The latter first told the British ambassador of his talk with the emperor:

The Empr said [to the King of Belgium] that he was sincerely desirous for the maintenance of peace and that provided some satisfaction was given him, he was ready to make every possible concession to preserve it. He had abandoned all idea of acquiring Luxemburg . . . his honour however required that the Prussians shd consent to evacuate the fortress of Luxemburg—that must be done or war was inevitable. . . . The Emperor said further, that altho he hoped for peace, he was making every possible preparation for war.

The King [of Belgium] . . . observed to me that . . . he thought that their [neutral powers'] exertions & particularly those of England might be used with effect today. He begged of me to tell you this and to ask you to lose no time in employing y. good offices at Berlin. . . . The King still maintains the opinion that H.M.G. would alone be listened to at Berlin.[2]

Cowley then saw Napoleon:

I am now willing [Napoleon said] to abandon everything but the departure of the Prussians. Do what you like with the fortress . . . but do what you can to obtain this concession from Prussia, or I become powerless and war is inevitable.

When the Emperor dismissed me he again recommended me to write without loss of time to you and to press upon you the necessity of action.

I will only add that the general opinion among my colleagues seems to be that H.M.G. can avert a war. . . . Surely it must be worth while to make the attempt.[3]

The queen saw the crisis almost completely as a threat to the independence of Belgium:

[1] Stanley to Cowley, telegram, 18 Apr. 1867, PRO FO 27/165, no. 141.
[2] Cowley to Stanley, private, Paris, 18 Apr. 1867, PRO FO 519/233.
[3] Ibid. Two days before this appeal to Stanley, Cowley wrote to Hammond, 'I wish that Lord Stanley could be induced to propose some scheme for neutralizing or razing the fortress' (Cowley to Hammond, 16 Apr. 1867, Foot, p. 368).

The Queen is now most anxious at the danger which appears to be impending over Belgium.

E... must not stand aloof. She is bound by every tie that can bind a nation to assist another, to stand by Belgium in the hour of need.
... E. must show the world that she is not prepared to abdicate her position as a great Power ... & that ... she is determined to fulfil her obligations, & (even single-handed if need be) to defend the Independence of Belgium with the whole strength of the British Empire.

But the necessity will not arise if our language at Paris & Berlin is firm & unequivocal.

She feels very strongly on the subject, & will not, if she can help it, be a part to the national disgrace that E. would incur, if she stood by passively, while such an act of violence as the seizure of Belgium territory by Fr. was perpetrated.[1]

Disraeli underlined the queen's letter with one of his own in an attempt to arouse the foreign secretary.

Two things seem to me clear: that France is not prepared, & that Bismarck lies to everyone—his explanations prove his perfidy.

I think myself, as old Brunnow says, 'it is time for a little re-action', & that we might begin to dictate a little to Europe—Gladstonism is at a discount.[2]

Napoleon III's reasonableness[3] and the possibility of war[4] induced Stanley to telegraph his views to Bismarck.

[1] Victoria to Derby, Windsor, 19 Apr. 1867, QVL, 2nd ser., i. 419–20. Malmesbury was anxious about the possible 'absorption of Holland or Belgium ... [because they are] indispensable to our future safety; & I know that this was the decided opinion of both the Duke & Palmerston who urged it upon me over & over again as an axiom when I took the F.O. in 1852' (Malmesbury to Stanley, private, 23 Apr. 1867, Stan. Pap. X 6, cabinet). Stanley had another fear and was not as ready as the queen to defend Belgium. 'I am ready to go so far as may be necessary in support of Belgium, short of giving an absolute pledge to fight for its independence. Suppose we gave such a pledge, that France and Prussia came to an understanding ... where should we be. But I say nothing in an opposite sense, lest we should lose our influence' (Stanley to Disraeli, private, 23 Apr. 1867, Stan. Pap., Disraeli).

[2] Disraeli to Stanley, 22 Apr. 1867, Stan. Pap., Disraeli.

[3] Cowley wrote to Stanley that 'I cannot but express the opinion that the Emperor is not unreasonable in his present demands ... a calm & solemn representation at Berlin of facts as they exist ... has become a duty, even if the appeal is to be unsuccessful. It is perhaps the last chance for the preservation of peace' (Cowley to Stanley, most confidential, Paris, 19 Apr. 1867, PRO FO 27/1660, no. 200).

[4] Delane, editor of The Times, thought war imminent and felt Stanley should act to get Prussia to withdraw her garrison (Delane to Dasent, Paris, 25 Apr. 1867, A. I. Dasent, John Delane, Editor of the Times, 2 vols. [New York, 1928], ii. 201).

As far as H.M. Govt. understand the present state of the Luxemburg question, its solution without war depends on the withdrawal of the Prussian garrison. . . . It is deserving of the consideration of Prussia whether she should not make so small a sacrifice.

Speak in this sense to Ct. Bismarck and ascertain his views— H.M. Govt. would see with deep regret the breaking out of a war, for an object apparently so trifling, which could not but retard the consolidation of Germany.[1]

The foreign secretary's appeal was reinforced by Victoria's letter to the King of Prussia.[2] The queen wrote that the withdrawal of the Prussian garrison was a 'very small thing' for the sake of preserving peace, and if Prussia objected to such a withdrawal the ensuing war would be that country's responsibility. Victoria appealed to William to maintain the peace.[3] Stanley viewed the queen's letter with 'extreme satisfaction', particularly since it would not commit the Cabinet.[4] At this moment the queen wrote to her daughter a very prophetic letter.

In the present instance it is not France or the Emperor who wish for war. . . . It is Bismarck who has for the last 8 months encouraged the Emperor to believe he cd get Luxemburg without difficulty. . . .

[1] Stanley to Loftus, telegram, 19 Apr. 1867, PRO FO 64/615, no. 120. Bismarck was, as he would be again during July 1870, absent from Berlin. Loftus communicated Stanley's telegram to Thile, Bismarck's stooge at the foreign ministry. The under-secretary promised to give the message to William (Loftus to Stanley, Berlin, 20 Apr. 1867, PRO FO 64/620, no. 224, no. 235). Stanley was astonished at Bismarck's absence during the crisis (La Tour to Moustier, London, 23 Apr. 1867, *Orig.* xvi. 141).

[2] Both Prince Napoleon and the King of Belgium thought England could save the peace by pressing Berlin to recede (extract from queen's journal, 17 Apr. 1867, *QVL*, 2nd ser., i. 418–19). Grey and Derby both suggested to Victoria that she intercede with William. Stanley told La Tour in 'absolute secrecy' that he had persuaded the queen to do so (La Tour to Moustier, confidential, Paris, 22 Apr. 1867, *Orig.* viii. 129–30). This was probably not true, as the situation was quite the opposite. Both Victoria and Grey, her secretary, enlightened Disraeli in order to get him to influence Stanley to act, particularly as Belgium was involved. Disraeli wrote in this sense to Stanley (Disraeli to Stanley, Windsor, 22 Apr. 1867, Buckle, iv. 470–1).

[3] Victoria to William I, Windsor, 22 Apr. 1867, RA I 71/122, Mosse, pp. 267–8; ibid., *Letters of Queen Victoria from the Archives of Brandenburg—Prussia.* ed. by H. Bolitho (New Haven, 1938), pp. 161–2. Stanley felt war was still probable (Stanley to Malmesbury, 23 Apr. 1867, Earl of Malmesbury, *Memoirs of an Ex-minister*, 2 vols. [London, 1884], ii. 369).

[4] Stanley to Grey, private, 23 Apr. 1867, Stan. Pap., the Queen. This seemed to be his main consideration as he admitted to Clarendon that 'whatever this government can do to preserve it [peace], without risk of being itself involved in the quarrel, ought to be, and shall be done' (Stanley to Clarendon, 23 Apr. 1867, Stan. Pap., official).

I fear the time may come when Europe will wish France to be strong to keep the ambition of Germany in check.[1]

The Russian Government, which had recognized the doubtful legality of Prussia's right of garrison,[2] began to use its influence in Berlin. The Tsar wrote to William I espousing the evacuation of the fortress,[3] and Gorchakoff suggested a conference in London which would neutralize the duchy.[4] Stanley doubted the efficacy of a conference unless France and Prussia agreed beforehand to abide by its decision.[5] Since Bismarck was in Varzin nothing could be done in Berlin[6] for the time being.

Having kept Europe in suspense Bismarck returned to Berlin on 24 April to consider the Russian proposal for a conference in London.[7] At an interview with Loftus the Prussian leader spoke for peace, and suggested that Holland should ask the powers to arrange a conference so that Prussia could 'then make concessions to Europe and to Holland in behalf of peace which she could not make to France'. Loftus stated confidentially that Prussia would accept neutralization of Luxemburg and withdraw the garrison if the duchy were placed under a European guarantee.[8] With French acceptance of the conference

---

[1] Victoria to Crown Princess of Prussia, Windsor, 24 Apr. 1867, RA U/32.

[2] Talleyrand to Moustier, telegram, St. Petersburg, 20 Apr. 1867, *Orig.* xvi. 90; Bismarck to Bernstorff, confidential, Berlin, 26 Apr. 1867, *GW* vi, no. 764.

[3] Cowley to Stanley, most confidential, Paris, 23 Apr. 1867, PRO FO 27/1660, no. 216.

[4] Stanley to Cowley, 24 Apr. 1867, PRO FO 27/1652, no. 165. Austria was also influencing Berlin towards mediation (Bismarck to Bernstorff, confidential, Berlin, 26 Apr. 1867, *GW* vi. no. 764). The queen urged Stanley to accept the conference and 'press the other Govts. to accept' (Grey to Stanley, 24 Apr. 1867, RA I 71/131).

[5] Ibid. The foreign secretary inquired of both governments whether they would be willing to do this (ibid.; Stanley to Loftus, telegram, 24 Apr. 1867, PRO FO 64/615, no. 130; same to same, 24 Apr. 1867, RA I 71/137; Stanley to Cowley, 24 Apr. 1867, ibid., no. 136).

[6] Loftus to Stanley, Berlin, 25 Apr. 1867, PRO FO 64/620, no. 232. Thile told Loftus that he communicated Stanley's telegram of 19 April to the king who ordered it to be forwarded to Bismarck (Loftus to Stanley, Berlin, 25 Apr. 1867, PRO FO 64/620, no. 233).

[7] Talleyrand to Moustier, telegram, 26 Apr. 1867, *Orig.* xvi. 183; Benedetti to Moustier, telegram, Berlin, 26 Apr. 1867, ibid., p. 184. He intimated that if the duchy were neutralized, Prussia would evacuate the fortress (Talleyrand to Moustier, telegram, Vienna, 29 Apr. 1867, ibid., p. 236). Beust claimed that a conference was his idea, which Russia supported at Berlin (Stanley to Cowley, 26 Apr. 1867, PRO FO 27/1652, no. 177).

[8] Loftus to Stanley, telegram, Berlin, 26 Apr. 1867, PRO FO 64/620, no. 236. The King of Prussia told the King of Belgium that a European guarantee would

proposal on the basis of neutralization,[1] Bismarck publicly
declared his agreement on the same basis, again stipulating a
guarantee by the powers.[2]

Though still wary,[3] Stanley was relieved that both Prussia
and France seemed agreed to accept beforehand any decision
of the conference. Hammond, the under-secretary, was a
dominant influence on Stanley throughout the Luxemburg
crisis and the two men were at one on the importance of this:

As to Gorchakoff's idea of a conference on the Luxemburg affair,
I conclude you would not consent to take part in it, unless both
France and Prussia would declare beforehand that they are willing
to accept any solution that may be recommended. . . . Without such
previous understanding on the part of the litigants a conference
would not only not tend to settle the dispute, but might involve
other parties in it. I believe your opinion on the subject to be in
conformity with what I have written.[4]

enable him to evacuate the fortress (Loftus to Stanley, telegram, confidential,
Berlin, 27 Apr. 1867, PRO FO 64/620, no. 248). Bismarck also wrote this to
Bernstorff (Bismarck to Bernstorff, confidential, Berlin, 26 Apr. 1867, *GW* vi, no.
764).

[1] Moustier to French diplomatic agents at Vienna, London, and St. Petersburg,
telegram, Paris, 27 Apr. 1867, *Orig.* xvi. 207–8.

[2] Stanley to Loftus, 27 Apr. 1867, PRO FO 64/615, no. 133; Bismarck to Bernstorff, Berlin, telegram, 26 Apr. 1867, *GW* vi, no. 765, no. 767.

[3] Stanley felt France wanted peace but distrusted Bismarck and the King of
Prussia. 'The fact is, one cannot trust Bismarck, even if he had given a promise,
unless it were in a form which could be made public' (Stanley to Grey, private,
27 Apr. 1867, RA I 71/175, Mosse, p. 269).

[4] Hammond memorandum, 24 Apr. 1867, Stan. Pap., Luxemburg. Many
times the foreign secretary merely mouthed Hammond's words. Stanley's letter to
Grey of 27 April is a rephrasing of a memorandum of the same date by the under-
secretary. Both the letter and the memorandum mention Bismarck's insincerity and
his refusal to abide by any decision the conference might give (Hammond memorandum to Stanley, 27 Apr. 1867, Stan. Pap., Luxemburg). 'You asked me on
Saturday what you should say about Luxemburg today. I think you had better
give no details, but merely say that communications are going on between the
various powers, and that you have a well assured hope that they will have a satisfactory result' (Hammond memorandum to Stanley, 29 Apr. 1867, Stan. Pap.,
Luxemburg). At the beginning of the Luxemburg crisis Hammond had been
opposed to a European conference fearing that England 'would . . . be left in the
lurch if a question arose of enforcing our pacific counsels' (Hammond to Cowley,
24 Apr. 1867, PRO FO 519/193, Mary Anderson, 'Edmund Hammond, permanent undersecretary of state for foreign affairs, 1854–73' [University of London
dissertation, 1956], pp. 95–96). When the conference became a reality, Hammond
wished to avoid a guarantee as much as Stanley, but he too gave way before the
pressure of Derby, Disraeli, and the queen. 'I see nothing to object to in Bernstorff's proposed form [of guarantee]' (Hammond to Stanley, 9 May 1867, Stan.
Pap., Luxemburg).

Stanley informed Bernstorff that without such an assurance England herself could not take part in the conference.[1] The circumspection of the foreign secretary was compounded of natural reserve, the third reading of the Reform Bill, the afore-mentioned distrust of Prussia, public feeling in Britain, and the influence of Hammond. Stanley expressed his uneasiness to Grey.

We have a difficult part to play: there never was a time when the E. public was more thoroughly bent on incurring no fresh responsibilities for Continental objects; yet it is expected, & reasonably, that we shall do what is in our power to preserve peace. The difficulty is increased by the impossibility of placing confidence in the Prussian Govt. That Fr. desires peace, is, I think, as certain as anything can be in the actual condition of the world. I do not feel the same conviction as to B. [Bismarck]; & still less as to the K. of Pr.[2]

On the twenty-ninth the crisis passed and the possibility of war became remote. France and Prussia agreed to suspend further armaments, and Rouher and Goltz, Moustier having been by-passed, arranged 'the details . . . to be sanctioned by a conference'.[3] Stanley, acting upon Bismarck's preference as well as his own, advised the Dutch king to issue invitations to the powers who signed the treaty of 1839 to meet at a conference in London on 7 May.[4]

Having taken the lamb by the tail, Stanley was the man of the hour. Clarendon referred to his intervention ungraciously to Cowley,[5] but Napoleon III was more courteous.[6] The *Revue*

[1] Stanley to Cowley, 27 Apr. 1867, PRO FO 27/1652, no. 189. Stanley actually assented to a conference without France and Prussia categorically agreeing to abide by its decision (Cowley to Stanley, telegram, Paris, 30 Apr. 1867, PRO FO 27/1652; Bismarck to Bernstorff, Berlin, telegram, 28 Apr. 1867, *GW* vi, no. 770).

[2] Stanley to Grey, 27 Apr. 1867, *QVL*, 2nd ser., i. 423. Cowley negated in part the impress of Hammond. 'I fear that if we are not prepared to run some risk in this way, [neutralization of Luxemburg] no arrangement will be possible. War sooner or later will be the consequence' (Cowley to Stanley, private, 28 Apr. 1867, Stan. Pap. X 6).

[3] Cowley to Stanley, telegram, Paris, 29 Apr. 1867, PRO FO 27/1660, no. 247, no. 248; Bismarck to the missions in Paris, London, Vienna, and St. Petersburg, telegram, 27 Apr. 1867, *GW* vi, no. 767.

[4] La Tour to Moustier, telegram, London, 29 Apr. 1867, *Orig.* xvi. 234; Stanley to Cowley, telegram, 29 Apr. 1867, PRO FO 27/1652, no. 194; Stanley to British diplomatic agents at Paris, Berlin, Vienna, St. Petersburg, and Brussels, telegram, 30 Apr. 1867, PRO FO 27/1652, no. 197.

[5] Clarendon to Cowley, private, Watford, 1 May 1867, PRO FO 519/181.

[6] 'Mon cher Lord Cowley,

Je vous remercie des bonnes nouvelles que vous me donnez. Je suis heureux de

des deux mondes saw England as the preserver of the peace and characterized Stanley's action as a repudiation of the line of non-intervention.[1] At the very time this was written Stanley was considering the limitations which would severely alter the policy that had evoked praise.

> I think the European guarantee will be made a strong point of, and that it will not be easy to escape giving one in some shape; but I will certainly give none that amounts to a pledge to take up arms in defence of the arrangements to be made, should they be attacked. Such a pledge would be useless, for opinion here would not allow of its being made good: unless we change more in the next few years than I think likely, and in a direction opposite to that in which we are now tending.[2]

While the foreign secretary was worrying about the 'very stringent guarantee' upon which Prussia would insist,[3] the French and Russian ambassadors suggested that he submit an arrangement to the powers prior to the conference.[4] In order to avoid giving a new guarantee, Stanley proposed to the powers a treaty on Luxemburg with three main points—withdrawal of the Prussian garrison, dismantlement of the fortress, promise by the King of Holland that he would not alienate the duchy without the consent of the powers.[5] His reluctance to give a new

penser que si une paix honorable pour nous est maintenue, je la devrai en partie aux bons offices du gouvernement Anglais.

Je vous prie d'exprimer mes remerciments à Lord Stanley et de recevoir pour vous l'assurance de mon ancienne amitié' (Napoleon to Cowley, copy, 30 Apr. 1867, Stan. Pap. X 6).

[1] *Revue des deux mondes*, lxix. 239 ff., 1 May 1867, Gordon A. Craig, 'Britain and Europe 1866–1869' (dissertation, Princeton University, 1941, p. 97).

[2] Stanley to Cowley, private, 2 May 1867, PRO FO 519/182. Cowley had anticipated this problem. 'It seems to me however, that if you have a repugnance to join in any such act, the difficulty may be turned by a solemn declaration on the part of France and Prussia that they will respect the neutrality of Luxemburg, which declaration may be consigned to a protocol which all members of the conference would sign' (Cowley to Stanley, private, 30 Apr. 1867, Stan. Pap. X 6).

[3] Stanley to Grey, private, 3 May 1867, RA I 71/227, Mosse, p. 269.

[4] La Tour to Moustier, telegram, confidential, London, 3 May 1867, *Orig.* xvi. 308. Bernstorff suggested a Luxemburg guarantee identical with Belgium's. Brunnow offered the phrase 'sous la garantie des hautes parties contractantes', and proposed that neutralization ought to come first, followed by the evacuation and dismantling of the fortress. On 3 May, Hammond drew up a draft containing Brunnow's corrections, but still avoiding a firm guarantee. 'The Grand Duchy of Luxemburg shall enjoy the advantages of a perpetual neutrality; and the high contracting parties engage to respect that neutrality' (Bernstorff to Stanley, private, 2 May 1867, Stan. Pap., Luxemburg).

[5] Stanley to Cowley, telegram, 3 May 1867, PRO FO 27/1653, no. 223.

guarantee had been previously made clear.[1] Both La Tour and
Bentinck, the Dutch ambassador, felt Prussia would not leave the
fortress without a European guarantee.[2] Bismarck was not happy
with Stanley's Luxemburg proposals and told Loftus that
the removal of the Prussian garrison must proceed from the
neutralization of the duchy under a European guarantee.[3] The
foreign secretary refused to 'contract a new guarantee'. He was
only willing to state 'that the Grand Duchy of Luxemburg shall
enjoy the advantages of a perpetual neutrality and that the
high contracting parties engage to respect that neutrality'.[4]

The French Government agreed to Stanley's proposals but
questioned their efficacy in the light of Bismarck's objections.[5]
Moustier did not object to a formal guarantee, particularly if
its acceptance would result in an end of the whole affair.[6] The
pressure put upon Stanley to agree to a guarantee became
overwhelming. On 5 May Loftus wrote that he feared 'that
Prussia will not withdraw from the fortress unless the Grand
Duchy is neutralized and placed under an European guarantee'.[7]
Victoria urged the foreign secretary to give way in order to

[1] On 20 April Stanley had suggested that if the duchy were given to Belgium the
guarantee of 1839 would then include Luxemburg (Stanley to Cowley, confidential,
20 Apr. 1867, PRO FO 27/162, no. 149).

[2] La Tour to Moustier, confidential, London, 3 May 1867, *Orig.* xvi. 309;
Stanley to Cowley, 3 May 1867, PRO FO 27/1653, no. 277.

[3] Loftus to Stanley, Berlin, 4 May 1867, *APP* viii. 794-5; ibid., **Great Britain,
Parliamentary Papers**, 1867, 74, 479; ibid., telegram, 4 May 1867, PRO FO 64/620,
no. 272, no. 273. This is what Brunnow had suggested. Bernstorff, as instructed, told Stanley that the latter's draft treaty on Luxemburg was unacceptable.
To the ambassador's request for a European guarantee, the foreign secretary did
not see how this was possible since Parliament would never agree to a guarantee
that might obligate England to go to war (Bernstorff to Bismarck, telegram, 4 May
1867, *APP* viii. 792-3).

[4] Stanley to Loftus, telegram, 4 May 1867, PRO FO 64/615, no. 148.

[5] Cowley to Stanley, telegram, Paris, 4 May 1867, PRO FO 27/1661, no. 273; La
Tour to Moustier, telegram, London, 4 May 1867, *Orig.* xvi. 326; Cowley to
Stanley, Paris, 5 May 1867, PRO FO 27/1661, no. 280. 'Bismarck seemed rather
put out by your articles—and said to me that . . . they would not even . . . [please
France] for France would likewise require the neutralization under the guarantee
of Europe. He added that Prussia could have made more suitable terms with
France directly' (Loftus to Stanley, Berlin, 4 May 1867, RA I 71/241).

[6] Moustier to La Tour, telegram, Paris, 5 May 1867, *Orig.* xvi. 328-9.

[7] Loftus to Stanley, telegram, confidential, Berlin, 5 May 1867, PRO FO 64/620,
no. 276. In a long essay to Bernstorff, Bismarck emphasized that Prussia could only
make the 'concession' of evacuating the fortress after it had been placed under
a European guarantee (Bismarck to Bernstorff, Berlin, 3 May 1867, *GW* vi, no.
782, no. 783).

avoid a war for which the responsibility would be England's.[1] Disraeli, who more than once was asked to intercede with Stanley, assured the foreign secretary that public opinion would support him on a general guarantee as an alternative preferable to bloodshed.[2]

As Stanley was being dragged from his uncompromising objection to a new commitment talk of war and armaments again floated through official corridors in Paris and Berlin. But diplomacy averted any further complications. Brunnow, the Russian ambassador in London, with the authorization of his Government, proposed a compromise between what Stanley was disposed to grant and Prussia willing to accept. He suggested that Luxemburg's neutrality would be perpetual under the sanction of a 'collective guarantee' of the powers.[3] With the opening of the London conference one day off, La Tour reported that the Austrian and Prussian ministers agreed to Brunnow's plan, and that Stanley, though hesitant, would probably agree also.[4] Moustier wired back at once that as Prussia and England had accepted France would not object to the Russian proposal.[5]

Stanley wished to avoid the mistake of Palmerston and Russell in 1863 and 1864. 'Their fault was to treat words, unbacked by a reasonable prospect of deeds, as being good international currency in a Europe where, in the prevailing state of international anarchy, force alone, either actual or plainly foreshadowed, could count effectively.'[6] The foreign secretary knew that he could contemplate using force only

---

[1] Victoria to Stanley, Osborne, 5 May 1867, RA, I 71/248, Mosse, p. 269; extract from queen's journal, 5 May 1867, *QVL*, 2nd ser., i. 424. At the queen's behest Grey wrote to Disraeli that 'H.M. cannot understand the hestitation on this point [the guarantee]. We are already parties to the guarantee of Belgian neutrality & independence, & to extend the guarantee of neutrality to Luxemburg does not seem to entail upon us any great additional responsibility' (Grey to Disraeli, private, 5 May 1867, Disraeli Papers, 85).

[2] Disraeli to Victoria, Commons, 6 May 1867, *QVL*, 2nd ser., i. 424. 'I think the settlement of the European question now hangs on the course we are prepared to take. If the "European guarantee" can be accepted in the sense in which Prussia is willing to accept it, I do not see that it need interpose an insuperable obstacle to a settlement' (Derby to Stanley, 5 May 1867, Stan. Pap., Derby).

[3] La Tour to Moustier, confidential, London, 5 May 1867, *Orig.* xvi. 335–8. He had suggested this earlier to Stanley.

[4] La Tour to Moustier, telegram, London, 6 May 1867, *Orig.* xvi. 341–2.

[5] Moustier to La Tour, telegram, Paris, 6 May 1867, *Orig.* xvi. 342.

[6] Lord William Strang, *Britain in World Affairs* (New York, 1961), p. 183.

where its use would be warranted by success. The waning prestige of Britain made unsuccessful intervention an exorbitant luxury.

Stanley's timidity weakened the very prestige he wished to secure. Lord Strang has pointed out:

Influence can be, and is indeed often, exercised on the strength of what is called prestige. Influence can be powerful, even in the absence of strong and immediately available armed forces, if there has been recent successful assembling, deployment and use of such forces in war. Influence can persist if the required resources in manpower and finance are present, and if there is a manifest national will to recreate and use those forces if occasion should arise.

But prestige is a wasting asset. It is the product of expectation about future conduct based upon present or remembered performance. It has to be constantly renewed.[1]

Such a renewal in the 1860's was almost impossible. Cobden, Bright, and the middle-class had temporarily captured opinion, which had already begun to turn away from a policy of commitment as a result of the Crimean war, and the influence of British governments in the 1860's was impaired. An active policy in Europe would have had a hollow basis of support and would have probably been repudiated. The foreign secretary was himself a contributor to this mood of alienation from the continent. His popularity at home resulted from the fact that he so closely mirrored the public mood and to have flown in the face of it was beyond his capacity and repugnant to his character.

In the avoidance of commitment and the pursuit of effacement there was no difference between the policies of Stanley and Clarendon. But the austere carefulness of the former as compared with the diplomatic finesse of the latter led to a significant depreciation of Britain's image in Europe.

The conduct of foreign relations [following Lord Strang] consists not merely in the formulation of general lines of action. It involves the application of general policies to the problems that present themselves from day to day. Indeed the substance and colour of a foreign policy are determined as much, if not more so, by the details of its application as by the direction of its general drift.[2]

Stanley attributed England's unwillingness to commit herself

---

[1] Ibid., pp. 116–17.   [2] Ibid., p. 108.

in Europe to the state of public opinion, but this was not the only reason. Just as important was the lack of a reliable continental ally to make intervention effective. This had been a prerequisite for England when she was stronger and more respected than she was in the 1860's. Napoleon III evoked unpleasant memories of his uncle, and Bismarck achieved a reputation for untrustworthiness in official British circles: neither could be relied upon. Nor was British distrust of Napoleon III and Bismarck excessive in the circumstances. On the contrary England's willingness to be reassured about Belgium was somewhat naïve. Franco-Prussian complaints of the selfish isolation of Britain carry little weight when it is considered that both were conspiring together to do the one thing that might cause English intervention—interfere with Belgian integrity. Stanley's reluctance to bind England at the London conference was domestically wise therefore, and in view of the amorality of Bismarck's policy and Napoleon's thirst for compensation not unrealistic.

V

THE LONDON CONFERENCE AND AFTER

THE day before the conference was to meet Stanley received a long note of instruction from Hammond, the under-secretary for foreign affairs.

If Lord Derby and Mr. Disraeli, backed by the Queen, press you to give way on the guarantee point, there can be no question, I think, but that you should give in, but not till after a decent fight recorded on the protoco .

In the meanwhile I should not breathe a syllable to any foreign diplomat as to the possibility of your giving way.

I think too as you brought the matter before the cabinet on Saturday, you ought to have a cabinet to sanction a different course to what they agreed to.

When you have made the proposal of the draft for deliberation which I should do without attending to the question of guarantee, you will invite the plenipotentiaries in succession to express their opinion.

If Bernstorff holds out for guarantee and presses for immediate decision, you will say that on so important a measure . . . you must before you give a definite answer consult the cabinet and take the Queen's pleasure and therefore you propose that the conference should adjourn till Thursday.

You could then get on record your objections, and show to Parliament and the country that you consented to guarantee only under the sanction of your colleagues and of the Queen.[1]

Hammond's shrewd campaign brought almost total success for the foreign secretary. Stanley, as planned, was reluctantly ready to accept the Russian compromise of a 'collective guarantee' before Loftus telegraphed from Berlin at 4 p.m. on 7 May that Bismarck would mobilize the Prussian army if 'peace were not assured' within three days.[2] Before he received this telegram,

[1] Hammond to Stanley, 6 May 1867, Stan. Pap., Luxemburg.
[2] Loftus to Stanley, telegram, Berlin, 7 May 1867, PRO FO 64/620, no. 278. Stanley received this telegram between 4 p.m., when Loftus sent it, and 6 p.m.,

the conference met with Stanley acting as president. Bernstorff objected to the absence of a European guarantee in the foreign secretary's draft treaty and was supported by the other plenipotentiaries.[1] Stanley stated his objections to a guarantee and promised to refer this point to the cabinet, returning with an answer at the next session two days hence.[2]

The only effect of Bismarck's demand for an assurance of peace within three days on Stanley was to cause the foreign secretary to call the second sitting of the conference two days after the first 'lest the Prussians break away'.[3] Convinced of Bismarck's duplicity, Stanley was probably more influenced in his decision to give way by Hammond, Cowley, Derby, Disraeli, and Victoria and by his private talks with Brunnow, La Tour, and Bernstorff.[4] By the evening of 7 May he had decided if 'absolutely pressed' to guarantee the neutralization of the

when the foreign secretary telegraphed it to Cowley (Stanley to Cowley, telegram, 7 May 1867, PRO FO 27/1653, no. 239). According to Hammond, Stanley gave way 'in consequence of something that passed' prior to 6 p.m. on 6 May when the foreign secretary had just come back from the Commons (Hammond to Cowley, private, 22 June 1867, PRO FO 519/193; Hammond to Stanley, 21 June 1867, Stan. Pap., Luxemburg). According to Bernstorff, Stanley told him prior to 3.25 p.m. on 7 May that if the other powers wanted the guarantee he would not object though he thought Parliament would. The foreign secretary asked the ambassador to say nothing of this for the moment (Bernstorff to Bismarck, telegram, 3.25 p.m., 7 May 1867, APP viii. 805).

[1] Hammond to Cowley, private, 7 May 1867, PRO FO 391/6.

[2] Ibid. Stanley's planned withdrawal was being effected exactly as Hammond had envisaged it. The other representatives realized that Stanley's objections were merely for the record, as they all looked 'on the Luxemburg affair as settled' (Stanley to Derby, private, 7 p.m., 7 May 1867, Derby Pap. 161/3). Hammond and Stanley at this point seemed most concerned about the effect that any sort of guarantee would have on Parliament (Hammond to Stanley, 8 May 1867, Stan. Pap., Luxemburg). Stanley informed Bernstorff that he told the conference that Prussia demanded a guarantee so that he would have a weapon to use against Parliament (Bernstorff to Bismarck, 7 May 1867, APP viii. 806–8).

[3] Hammond to Stanley, 21 June 1867, Stan. Pap., Luxemburg. Rouher impressed Cowley with France's war preparations (Cowley to Stanley, Paris, confidential, 7 May 1867, RA I 71/258).

[4] Bernstorff told Clarendon that his pressure on Stanley a few hours before the opening of the conference on 7 May caused the foreign secretary to concede a guarantee (Clarendon to Cowley, private, Egerton Crescent, 18 May 1867, PRO FO 519/181). Cowley wrote, after Stanley had decided to accept a guarantee, that 'it is very desirable that a treaty should be signed as soon as possible' (Cowley to Stanley, private, 9 May 1867, Stan. Pap. X 6). Bismarck continued to put pressure upon Stanley. On 6 July he instructed Bernstorff confidentially to tell the other representatives in London that unless Prussia got her guarantee immediately she would be forced to prepare for war (Bismarck to Bernstorff, Berlin, telegram, 6 May 1867, GW vi, no. 789).

duchy.[1] The possibility of war and his responsibility for it evidently convinced him.[2]

At the second sitting of the conference on 9 May Stanley announced that England assented to a collective guarantee as suggested by Brunnow,[3] and proposed as an amendment by Bernstorff. If there was doubt in the foreign secretary's mind about the obligation he had contracted, Hammond certainly reassured him. 'It was only on your return from the conference that I heard from you that the guarantee was "collective", and my remark to you was that you might very safely undertake [it] . . . as it amounted to nothing.'[4]

With the major obstacle overcome, Stanley announced in the House of Commons that a European war had been averted, and what was more, 'we have not incurred any fresh responsibility'.[5] If it were not a glorious achievement, it was, at least in the foreign secretary's mind, peace without commitment.

The House of Commons cheered loudly the announcement that all was settled, and received with complacency Lord Stanley's explanation about guarantee to the effect that the choice lay between giving it and an European war, while when given, it involved little, if indeed it involved that. . . . There was no further discussion, and so the affair ended with repeated cheering for Lord Stanley.[6]

The foreign secretary's relief at the parliamentary support of his work was immense.[7] It was also, as he wrote to the queen, a pleasant surprise:

I hope I may be allowed to say—though to my own shame—that in the matter of the guarantee Her Majesty has proved that she knows

---

[1] Stanley to Cowley, private, 7 May 1867, PRO FO 519/182. Two days later Hammond wrote that if Stanley refused 'to give the guarantee it is quite clear you could be impeached' (Hammond to Stanley, 9 May 1867, Stan. Pap., Luxemburg).
[2] Such was Cowley's interpretation (Cowley to Bloomfield, private, Paris, 8 May 1867, PRO FO 356/33). As hesitant about giving a guarantee as Stanley, Clarendon approved the decision to do so (Clarendon to Cowley, private, Egerton Crescent, 8 May 1867, PRO FO 519/181).
[3] La Tour to Moustier, telegram, London, 9 May 1867, Orig. xvi. 400–2; Stanley to Cowley, telegram, 9 May 1867, PRO FO 27/1653, no. 241.
[4] Hammond to Stanley, 21 June 1867, Stan. Pap., Luxemburg.
[5] Hansard, Parliamentary Debates (3rd series), clxxxvii. 239–90.
[6] Hammond to Cowley, private, 9 May 1867, PRO FO 519/193. Bernstorff to William I, London, 15 May 1867, APP ix. 51–52.
[7] 'The public has swallowed the guarantee more easily than I thought possible' (Stanley to Bloomfield, private, 14 May 1867, PRO FO 356/33).

the feeling of the House of Commons better than I did, after sitting 18 years in it. Not a word of objection has reached me.[1]

The next day Stanley suggested to the conference that Prussian evacuation should begin immediately after the treaty was ratified. As neither Bernstorff nor La Tour had instructions on this point instantaneous agreement was impossible.[2] Brunnow, who was proving to be a most conciliatory Russian, got together with the French and Prussian ambassadors and a compromise was arranged when Bismarck proved amenable to it.[3] Withdrawal would begin as soon as ratifications were exchanged, and it would be completed as quickly as was feasible.[4]

The Guarantee

On the late afternoon of 11 May the treaty was signed. The repercussions were now to begin. Losing no time, Derby, like his son, minimized the guarantee[5] by the definition he gave of it in the House of Lords:

The former guarantee [of 1839] which was under the collective guarantee of all the Powers of Europe, declared that Luxemburg should continue to form part of the possessions of the King of Holland; whereas the present guarantee, which is also under the guarantee of the collective Powers, declares that the territory shall be neutralized. . . . The guarantee is not a joint and separate guarantee, but it is a collective guarantee, and does not impose upon this country any special and separate duty of enforcing its provisions. It is a collective guarantee of all the Powers of Europe.[6]

For the moment England was congratulated. The *Revue de*

[1] Stanley to Grey, 10 May 1867, RA B 23/60.

[2] Stanley to Cowley, telegram, 10 May 1867, PRO FO 27/1653, no. 243.

[3] Stanley to Cowley, telegram, 11 May 1867, PRO FO 27/1653, no. 247; Loftus to Stanley, telegram, Berlin, 11 May 1867, PRO FO 64/620, no. 290; Bismarck to Bernstorff, Berlin, telegram, 9 May 1867, *GW* vi, no. 794, no. 796.

[4] Ibid.; La Tour to Moustier, telegram, London, 10 May 1867, *Orig.* xvi. 404-5; Bismarck to Bernstorff, Berlin, telegram, 10 May 1867, *GW* vi, no. 797.

[5] Clarendon thought it entailed 'infinitesimal responsibility' (Clarendon to Cowley, private, Egerton Crescent, 29 May 1867, PRO FO 519/181).

[6] Hansard, *Parliamentary Debates* (3rd series), clxxxvii. 379. 'I thought it as well to *volunteer* a statement to the H. of L. as to the signature and purport of the Treaty' (Derby to Stanley, 13 May 1867, Stan. Pap., Derby). Derby must have made the above statement without consulting the Treaty of 1839 which does not contain the word 'collective'.

deux mondes praised her for preventing war,[1] and Stanley became the most popular man in the Government.[2] Nor was there appreciable domestic dissatisfaction with the guarantee a month after the treaty was signed: 'We had Luxemburg brought on last night in a thin House. The result entirely satisfactory; the guarantee went down more easily than I had ventured to expect or even to hope.'[3]

Then almost simultaneously dissatisfaction with Derby's and Stanley's interpretation of the guarantee[4] emanated from both Prussia and Parliament. As late as 17 June, Clarendon wrote to Hammond:

> The so called guarantee given in the Luxg. Treaty is as you said in your note the other day, no guarantee at all because it is collective and no power engages to enforce it individually, but I cannot say that the guarantee of 39 has much more validity or binding force— the words . . . wd. not make it obligatory upon any single power to interfere, & the same obstacles to collective action wd probably arise as those wh. are now thought to render the Luxg. guarantee a nullity.[5]

Three days later a debate in the House of Lords caused the Government some embarrassment.

Russell hoped 'that we have not made too great a sacrifice to maintain the peace, & have not entered into any guarantee involving probable danger'. Derby's reply seemed to make a mockery of the guarantee:

> A guarantee of neutrality is very different from a guarantee of possession. If France and Prussia were to have a quarrel between themselves, & either were to violate the neutrality of Luxemburg by passing their troops through the duchy for the purpose of making war on the other, we might, if the guarantee had been individual as

---

[1] Craig, p. 90.

[2] Clarendon to Cowley, private, 18 May 1867, PRO FO 519/181.

[3] Stanley to Cowley, private, 15 June 1867, PRO FO 519/182. In explaining the guarantee to the Commons Stanley minimized it. 'Such a guarantee has obviously rather the character of a moral sanction to the arrangements which it defends than that of a contingent liability to make war. It would, no doubt, give a right to make war, but it would not necessarily impose the obligation' (Foot, p. 377).

[4] The interpretation was as much Hammond's as Derby's or Stanley's.

[5] Clarendon to Hammond, private, Egerton Crescent, 17 June 1867, PRO FO 391/4. In reply to Granville's request in 1870, a legal opinion was given 'that the refusal or incapacity of one or more of the guaranteeing Powers to act does not . . . liberate the remaining Powers from the obligation to do so'. This opinion referred to the Treaty of 1839 (Temperley and Penson, pp. 340–1).

well as joint, have been under the necessity of preventing that violation, & the same obligation would have rested upon each guarantor;
but . . . the guarantee is only collective . . . it is binding only upon
all the Powers in their collective capacity; they all agree to maintain
the neutrality of Luxemburg, but not one of those Powers is bound
to fulfill the obligation alone. . . . The only two Powers by which the
neutrality of Luxemburg is likely to be infringed are two of the
parties to the collective guarantee; &, therefore, if either of them
violate the neutrality, the obligation on all others would not accrue.[1]

Derby's interpretation was attacked from opposite points of view.
The Duke of Argyll maintained that the prime minister's
analysis meant that the guarantee was meaningless. Granville
argued 'that we may have rendered ourselves liable . . . or
[run] the risk of being considered unfaithful to our agreements'.[2]
Russell felt that if Luxemburg's neutrality were violated England
was committed to action on the duchy's behalf.[3]

On 20 June, the same day as the parliamentary debate, Bismarck expressed to Loftus his 'astonishment and regret' over
Stanley's explanation of the guarantee, an explanation which
according to the Prussian leader made the guarantee 'illusory'.[4]

Count Bismarck said that he could not accept this view of the
collective guarantee. In such case all treaties and solemn engagements would be worthless. He could not imagine that England would
undertake to give a guarantee which should be a mere delusion.[5]

Five days later Bernstorff spoke to Stanley in the same sense.
Stanley replied that it was 'impossible to define with legal
strictness the amount of obligation really incurred, but whatever that might be, I could not see the binding force of the
engagement which we had signed, was in any degree lessened by
comments made in debate upon it, even by its author.'[6] The foreign

---

[1] Hansard, *Parliamentary Debates* (3rd series), clxxxvii. 144–51.

[2] Ibid., pp. 154–7. When Stanley told Hammond that the guarantee was to be
collective, the under-secretary 'wished him joy as it was no guarantee at all'
(Hammond to Cowley, private, 22 June 1867, PRO FO 519/193).

[3] Hansard, *Parliamentary Debates* (3rd series), clxxxviii. 157–8. Clarendon supported Derby and Stanley in their definition of a collective guarantee (ibid.).

[4] Loftus to Stanley, Berlin, 22 June 1867, PRO FO 64/621, no. 363. Thile wired
Bernstorff that Stanley's and Derby's interpretation of the guarantee caused
'extreme consternation' and the 'worst impression' in Berlin (Thile to Bernstorff,
Berlin, telegram, 24 June 1867, *APP* ix. 116).   [5] Ibid.

[6] Stanley to Loftus, 25 June 1867, PRO FO 64/215, no. 200. Hammond observed to Stanley 'that under the construction which Ct. Bernstorff now would
seem to give to the term "collective guarantee", there would seem to be some

secretary added that if he 'had regarded the guarantee which he had given as purely illusory, neither I nor my colleagues would have had anything to do with it'.[1] In the light of this, Stanley was not so much privy to a scheme that would satisfy German opinion as uncertain over the legal obligation contracted, which for domestic consumption he interpreted as no obligation at all. Ironically it was British, not German opinion, that was beguiled. Stanley undeceived Grey, the queen's private secretary. 'I however held back so far as to make it appear on the protocols that we only yielded to the unanimous opinion of all the powers, and to the conviction that the step we were taking was necessary for the maintenance of peace.'[2]

Bismarck did not make things easy for Stanley. An article in the *Norddeutsche Allgemeine Zeitung* referrred to the Stanley and Derby guarantee with some derision:

Was it intended to guarantee the neutrality of Luxemburg only against Lichtenstein, Greece or Mexico?

It seems to us that the object Lord Stanley had more particularly in view was to reconcile parliament as much as possible with this breach of the principle of nonintervention to which they are wedded.[3]

There was further debate in Paliament concerning the extent of British commitment. Derby and his son insisted on the collective nature of the Luxemburg guarantee as distinct from the individual obligations imposed by the guarantee of 1839.[4]

difficulty in reconciling the present insistence of Prussia with the Porte to cede Candia, with the obligation which Prussia would have contracted singly to maintain the independence & integrity of the Ottoman Empire' (Hammond to Stanley, 25 June 1867, Stan. Pap., Luxemburg).

[1] Ibid. Stanley admitted privately to Loftus that 'Lord Derby's language about the guarantee was, I suspect, not quite accurately reported: but I have admitted to Bernstorff that if he said what appears in the newspapers, he went rather further than I should have done in denying the existence of any obligation—I think I satisfied him; but considering Bismarck's own language on the subject of guarantees, his indignation, if real, is curious' (Stanley to Loftus, private, 25 June 1867, Stan. Pap., Prussia).

[2] Stanley to Grey, private, 12 May 1867, RA I 71/268.

[3] Enclosure in Loftus to Stanley, Berlin, 29 June 1867, PRO FO 64/621, no. 373.

[4] Hansard, *Parliamentary Debates* (3rd series), clxxxviii. 967–76. According to the *Cambridge History of British Foreign Policy* there is no distinction of the kind Stanley and Derby were drawing between the treaties of 1839 and 1867. Neither treaty has the word collective in it, therefore legally the guarantee of 1867 was the same as the guarantee of 1839 (*Cambridge History of British Foreign Policy 1783–1919*, 3 vols. [Cambridge, 1923], ii. 14–15). This does not seem to be the case, since the treaty

As a result of this discussion, the *Norddeutsche Allgemeine Zeitung* commented that 'Lord Derby has again expressed his opinion upon the guarantee in such a manner that . . . [it] will effectually prevent any treaties being concluded with England in the future'.[1]

On 12 July, Bernstorff called on Stanley and expressed Bismarck's surprise and anxiety. He reported that Prussia refused to accept the English interpretation of a collective guarantee, and his Government was sure that if the guarantee were violated Britain would act to uphold it. Further discussion, Bernstorff concluded, was unnecessary 'as no practical result can follow'.[2] Victoria wrote to the foreign secretary that she thought 'regard for our character for fidelity to our engagements, imperatively demands some official notice'.[3] In view of Prussian acquiescence Stanley did not think so, and he told the queen that Luxemburg's neutrality was safe. 'No great Power could, without utter discredit, violate a solemn pact lately made in the face of Europe.'[4] This is what the foreign secretary hoped, but

---

of 1839 was 'placed under the Guarantee of their said majesties', and the treaty of 1867 was 'placed under the sanction of the collective Guarantee of the Powers' (Edward Hertslet, *The Map of Europe by Treaty* [London, 1875–91], ii, pp. 996–7, 1803). Without going into the question of the legal issues involved and their applicability to international politics, the fact that the guarantee of 1867 was qualified by the word 'collective' and the guarantee of 1839 was not would seem to support Stanley and Derby in their contention that the Luxemburg guarantee placed a less onerous obligation upon the powers which undertook it than the Belgian guarantee. The plausibility of their case was weakened, not because of the distinction they drew between the two guarantees, but because of the drastic and public way in which they minimized the responsibility involved in the Luxemburg Treaty. The argument that the other powers made no distinction between the two guarantees is not true if Hammond is to be believed. 'I know Van der Weyer [the Belgian ambassador], and I think one or more besides of the foreign ministers who took part in the conference consider that the guarantee of 1867 is quite a different thing from that of 1839' (Hammond to Stanley, 21 June 1867, Stan. Pap., Luxemburg). Bernstorff, Bismarck, and the conference knew the guarantee was 'moonshine' (Hammond to Cowley, private, 22 and 25 June 1867, PRO FO 519/193). Speaking in the Commons on 1 August 1870, Disraeli said that the Luxemburg 'treaty is not so large as the scope of the treaty which secures the neutrality of Belgium' (Hansard, *Parliamentary Debates* [3rd series], cciii. 1289–91).

[1] Enclosure in Loftus to Stanley, Berlin, 13 July 1867, PRO FO 64/622, no. 393.

[2] Stanley to Loftus, 12 July 1867, PRO FO 64/616, no. 209.

[3] Victoria to Stanley, Osborne, 18 July 1867, *QVL*, 2nd ser., i. 447. Victoria's letter was in part motivated by one from the King of Prussia to the Queen of Prussia who was then in England (King of Prussia to Queen of Prussia, 26 June 1867, *QVL*, 2nd ser., i. 437–40). See p. 101.

[4] Stanley to Victoria, 20 July 1867, *QVL*, 2nd ser., i. 448.

minimizing the obligation involved in the treaty was hardly the way to create respect for it.

Stanley's equivocation was no match for Bismarck's, but whereas the English minister publicly appeared to negate the sanctity of a European treaty his German counterpart took the opposite position except in private. Hammond wrote to Cowley that 'the Prussians [and] the members of the conference . . . know and admit . . . the collective guarantee . . . has no value'.[1] La Tour told the under-secretary 'that Bernstorff and Bismarck were fully aware that the collective guarantee was moonshine if it was supposed to mean more than the previous words as to respect of neutrality; but they held that the term "guarantee" must appear to satisfy the susceptibilities of the Fatherland'.[2] The requirements of British and German opinion differed, and Bismarck did not wish to admit openly what Stanley felt obliged to proclaim.

The inexperience of the foreign secretary was a handicap. His reserve, caution, and circumspection were the natural reactions of one who, for the first time, is forced to play for big stakes. The wish to avoid a blunder[3] was subordinate only to the desire to keep England out of war. Stanley could not feel comfortable with Bismarck's trickery and Napoleon III's moods. His lack of assurance caused the smallest step to be taken grudgingly. To assert Britain's position was impossible, as he only felt safe when he was not in the game. His self-acknowledged good fortune in the Luxemburg affair was due largely to Napoleon's moderation and to Bismarck, who felt that the propitious moment for conflict was not yet come.[4] Stanley was

---

[1] Hammond to Cowley, private, 22 June 1867, PRO FO 519/193.
[2] Hammond to Cowley, private, 25 June 1867, ibid.
[3] Monypenny and Buckle refer to Stanley's 'shrinking from risk and responsibility . . . so markedly shown' (Monypenny and Buckle, iv. 429).
[4] Not only was Bismarck not certain that he would have all Germany with him in a war against France, but he was not sure that the military support of the other German states would amount to anything. 'The second inquiry of the Prussian government related to the state of preparation of the Bavarian army—it is the answer to it . . . which is not likely to be very satisfactory' (Howard to Stanley, Munich, confidential, 30 Apr. 1867, PRO FO 9/181, no. 102). Holstein, Bismarck's subordinate at the foreign office, felt that his chief was wise in postponing a decision because 'Hanover was still in the throes of internal unrest & . . . in the event of war there would be an outbreak of "murder & violence"' (Holstein Papers, ed. N. Rich and M. H. Fisher [Cambridge, 1955], i. 35). In April the south German states were asked about their readiness and 'willingness' to go to war. Loder, the

well aware that 'We have been lucky in our foreign policy; for what we did involved no risk and cost no trouble, while it has given us an appearance of having helped, more than we really did, to bring about the result.'[1]

Crete

Stanley's apprehension concerning involvement was not limited to the West. The Cretan revolt had continued throughout the Luxemburg crisis, and the powers were no nearer a solution. Since the Sultan realized that Britain wished to preserve his sovereignty in Crete he was not receptive to Franco-Russian proposals that might limit it. The foreign secretary's reluctance to associate England with France and Russia in the East tended to prolong the crisis, as Turkey remained adamant to anything that would not lead to a complete suppression of the revolt.[2]

At the beginning of April French flirtations with Russia resulted in a joint suggestion for the formation of an international commission to inquire into Cretan affairs. These two powers requested Austria, Prussia, England, and Italy to support their suggestion at Constantinople.[3] Moustier went further and urged Turkey to 'suspend hostilities', a proposal which, like the one for an international commission, the Turkish Government refused to consider.[4] Stanley was cool to Beust's request that England should propose that commissioners should be sent to Crete,[5] and was no more favourable towards the French solicitation of support. He told La Tour that 'in principle he

Württemberg minister to Bavaria, told Howard, the British minister, this in 1870 (Howard to Clarendon, Munich, 4 Mar. 1870, RA I 48/159). Bismarck also knew that Prussia could not count on England in case of war with France over Luxemburg (Bernstorff to Bismarck, confidential, 3 Apr. 1867, APP viii. 575–6).

[1] Stanley to Disraeli, Knowsley, 20 May [no year, but probably 1867], Disraeli Pap., 113. The biographers of Disraeli date the letter 1875 (Monypenny and Buckle, v. 424).

[2] Loftus to Stanley, Berlin, 6 Apr. 1867, PRO FO 64/619, no. 181; Stanley to Cowley, 27 Apr. 1867, PRO FO 146/1294, no. 180; Moustier to La Tour, 16 May 1867, Orig. xvii. 34.

[3] Ibid.

[4] Lyons to Stanley, Constantinople, 29 Apr. 1867, PRO FO 146/1294.

[5] Stanley to Cowley, 13 May 1867, PRO FO 146/1295, no. 250. Beust attempted to draw England out of isolation by allusion to the 'steady policy of Russia and the vacillating policy of France' in the East (ibid.).

did not believe in the right of intervention in the struggles of the Porte with his [*sic*] subjects'.[1]
Stanley privately explained his position to Bloomfield.

My answer to enquiries on the eastern question, is that we should gladly see a settlement come to as to Crete, will advise administrative reforms but do not exactly see what are to be the functions of the proposed commission—whether enquiry only, or mediation. Nor can we send it except with the consent of the Porte. I wish to gain time: if Omar Pacha [who was trying to stamp out the rebellion] fails, the Porte will be ready to yield: if he succeeds, large concessions may be made after a victory which could not well be made before.[2]

While Stanley was waiting and hoping for a Turkish victory to obviate the necessity for European intervention, the Sultan hoped to forestall the interference of the powers by appointing his own commissioners to meet a delegation from Crete.[3]

Moustier now returned to the idea of local autonomy for Crete,[4] but the foreign secretary hoped that reforms taken at the Sultan's initiative would make this unnecessary.[5] At the beginning of June, Stanley agreed to instruct Lyons to recommend to the Sultan a commission of inquiry.[6] His change of mind was calculated to frustrate any Russo-French entente in the East, a possibility made more real by the arrival in Paris of Alexander and Gorchakov.[7] At the same time Stanley advised 'the Porte quietly to take the initiative in making the reforms desired, & thereby supersede the necessity for the proposed enquiry'.[7]

I have [he wrote to Bloomfield]—while declining all collective representations, joint notes, or identic notes—consented to recommend the Porte separately to give way if urged on the point of having

---

[1] La Tour to Moustier, London, 18 May 1867, *Orig.* xvii. 59.
[2] Stanley to Bloomfield, private, 20 May 1867, PRO FO 356/33.
[3] Lyons to Stanley, Constantinople, 22 May 1867, PRO FO 244/218, no. 205. This step did not reassure either France or Russia (Stanley to Cowley, 23 May 1867, PRO FO 146/1296, no. 272).
[4] Cowley to Bloomfield, private, Paris, 29 May 1867, PRO FO 356/33. Stanley was not opposed to this idea, especially as it was preferable to cession of Crete to Greece (Stanley to Bloomfield, private, 28 May 1867, PRO FO 356/33; Stanley to Lyons, 1 June 1867, PRO FO 146/1296, no. 157).
[5] Ibid.; Stanley to Cowley, private, 3 June 1867, PRO FO 519/182.
[6] Stanley to Cowley, 3 June 1867, PRO FO 244/218, no. 297.
[7] Stanley to Cowley, private, 3 June 1867, PRO FO 519/182.

H

a commission to enquire as to the wants of the islanders; it being well understood that the question of cession is not raised. . . . I do not think much will come of this nor do I altogether like it; but the danger of throwing France entirely into the hands of Russia is not to be lost sight of.[1]

Stanley's avoidance of close co-operation with France was done in the face of French threats to concert with Russia.[2] His support of the proposed commission of inquiry was not even half-hearted, as he hoped the Sultan would 'accept it in principle, and break it down by impossible conditions'.[3] He evidently feared, all protestations to the contrary, that the commission would be a step leading to the separation of Crete from the Ottoman Empire.[4] It was believed that this was Russia's only object.

I can do nothing with the Turks about Crete, because they mistrust the intentions of France. The Russian ambassador tells them plainly that Russia is determined that Crete shall be annexed to Greece and declares that France has given Russia assurances that the object of all the steps taken by France is to place the Porte in a position, in which it cannot escape from this.[5]

Even Prussia seemed to be playing Russia's game in the East: Bismarck told Loftus 'that if England would assist in obtaining the cession of Candia to Greece, all present difficulties in the East would be at once arranged'.[6]

Stanley's natural hesitation to concert with the powers on Crete was reinforced by the fear that his co-operation would be twisted into supporting Greek annexation of the island. Yet to have remained completely aloof might have thrown France and Prussia into the hands of Russia and resulted in a solution damaging to British interests. The foreign secretary's decision

---

[1] Stanley to Bloomfield, private, 4 June 1867, PRO FO 356/33.

[2] Cowley to Stanley, Paris, private, 6 June 1867, Stan. Pap. X 6. 'Moustier tells me that he [Gorchakov] presses him hard upon the Cretan question, and wants him to go on without any reference to the opinions or hesitations of H.M.'s govt' (ibid.).

[3] Stanley to Cowley, private, 15 June 1867, PRO FO 519/182.

[4] Cowley thought so. 'The enquiry is a mere cloak to cover the scheme of separation and if I were in the Sultan's place, I would refuse it, but grant at the same time a large measure of administrative reform' (Cowley to Stanley, Paris, private, 16 June 1867, PRO FO 519/233).

[5] Lyons to Cowley, private, 19 June 1867, Lyons Pap. RD I.

[6] Loftus to Stanley, Berlin, 22 June 1867, PRO FO 146/1297.

was to support the proposed commission of inquiry by a British representation through Lyons, distinct from the joint démarche of Russia, France, Prussia, and Italy.[1] As Stanley hoped, the Sultan accepted the commission in principle but so qualified his acceptance as to make it worthless.[2]

France had seemed willing to humour Russia in the East in the hope of receiving active support in the West. But Russia's mediation in the Luxemburg dispute brought no large gains to France, and the visit of the Tsar and Gorchakov to Paris in June led to coolness between the two powers. No wonder then that in July Moustier seemed more anxious to co-operate with Britain on the Cretan question. 'He heartily wished for the support of Her Majesty's Government on this question, because the joint influence of England and France might . . . check . . . the action of other powers who might be disposed to be less moderate than they in regard to Turkish affairs.'[2] The foreign minister's attitude was no doubt a reflection of his master's. 'La Valette told me last night that there was a change coming over the Imperial mind in respect to the East and a desire to come together with England.'[3]

The warm reception of the Sultan in Paris and London in July confirmed the Turkish Government in its refusal to admit a commission of inquiry. The absence of Austria-Hungary and Britain from the collective pressure of the other four powers made the Sultan's refusal a safe one. The failure to gain compensation in the West checked Paris's Russian ardour and forced St. Petersburg to temporize until active French or Prussian support in the East would allow her to set aside the Treaty of Paris. The Cretan revolt, therefore, lingered on, and the focus of European diplomatic activity returned to the West.

Franco-Prussian Tension

In August, at Salzburg, the French failed to obtain Austro-Hungarian support along the Rhine, though the two powers came closer together. The Russo-Prussian understanding of

---

[1] Lyons to Ellis, private, 19 June 1867, Lyons Pap. RD I.

[2] Lyons to Stanley, Constantinople, 23 June 1867, PRO FO 244/218, no. 286; Lyons to Ellis, private, 3 July 1867, Lyons Pap. RD I; Fane to Stanley, Paris, 10 July 1867, PRO FO 27/1663, no. 308.

[3] Cowley to Stanley, Paris, private, 11 July 1867, Stan. Pap. X 6.

March 1868, though it was more definite, did not commit Russia to fight in the West.[1] In these circumstances the attitude of England might have been crucial in Franco-Prussian relations. It was not, because both Prussia and France felt that Britain would not act, a fact indeed which Stanley never tired of reiterating. Both powers, however, tried to gain English sympathy, and not merely for moral support. There was always the possibility, however presently remote, that Britain would intervene in western Europe with Prussia or France. Neither Paris nor Berlin wanted the other to gain an ally, even a cautious one, in the tense atmosphere that existed after the London conference.[2]

The tension manifested itself in French irritability over the proposed German customs parliament, the position of Luxemburg in the Zollverein,[3] and Prussia's failure to fulfil article five of the treaty of Prague regarding the retrocession of part of Schleswig to Denmark.[4] Stanley refused to get involved and told La Tour that Denmark would be better off dropping the question of Schleswig.[5]

French concern about northern Schleswig reflected the larger anxiety over the extension of the North German Confederation into south Germany.

I [Cowley] added ... [to Bismarck that] if any attempt was made to force the southern states to join the northern confederation or if any overt act of hostility towards France whether for offensive or defensive purposes ... I wd. not answer for the consequences.

M. de Bismarck replied that the F[rench] G[overnment] need fear nothing of the king.[6]

Bismarck's assurance lacked conviction as he readily admitted

---

[1] Mosse, pp. 282–90.

[2] Fane to Stanley, Paris, confidential, 18 June 1867, PRO FO 27/1664, no. 346. In June of 1868 Bernstorff was instructed to send £200 to the Prussian consul at Liverpool in order to influence the English provincial press in a Prussian sense. It was felt that the best results would be obtained with the Free Trade and Manchester journals (Thile to Bernstorff, Berlin, confidential, 19 June 1868, *APP* ix. 85–86; same to same, 6 Feb. 1869, *APP* x. 527–8).

[3] Cowley to Stanley, 17 May 1867, PRO FO 27/1661, no. 317; same to same, Paris, confidential, 14 June 1867, PRO FO 27/1662, no. 399.

[4] Fane to Stanley, Paris, confidential, 18 June 1867, PRO FO 27/1664, no. 346.

[5] La Tour to Moustier, London, 19 May 1867, *Orig.* xvii. 73. La Tour characterized the attitude of the British Government to this question as one of 'almost complete indifference' (same to same, London, 14 June 1867, *Orig.* xvii. 227).

[6] Cowley to Stanley, Paris, private, 7 June 1867, PRO FO 519/234.

that he could not 'withstand public opinion if the States [of south Germany] themselves ask for annexation'.[1] The Prussian minister, in conversation with Napoleon III, paraded the pressure of the southern populations for association with the northern confederation, but said he would do everything to prevent its realization.[2]

At the same time that France was seeking English support in upholding the Treaty of Prague, article five of that treaty being for the moment in question, Prussia was playing for the same support. The King of Prussia wrote a letter to Augusta to show to Victoria, whom she was visiting:

> Whoever could induce the unfortunate K.[ing George of Hanover] to consent to such a transaction as would compensate him . . . for the loss of his rights, would do a great service. . . . To these difficulties . . . are to be added those produced by the peculiar steps taken by Fr. before & after the Treaty of Prague.
>
> If E.[ngland] together with the 30 millions of the N. Ger. Confederation sincerely wishes for peace, & in proper time removes all causes which eventually might lead to war, that is to say, if she keeps a watchful eye on Fr., & if she does not desert Ger. whenever that country has a natural right to expect at least the moral support of E.[ngland], then Fr. . . . will [not] be able to provoke a conflict.[3]

Victoria showed the letter to Stanley,[4] who felt that any official tendency to incline towards either Prussia or France would only add to the risk of war. He told La Tour that 'if the peace of Europe were menaced . . . he would not hesitate to intervene diplomatically with the other powers',[5] but this intervention would be most effective if the British Government observed an attitude of 'strict & impartial neutrality'.[6] The queen was not satisfied with Stanley's justification and wrote to Disraeli.

---

[1] Cowley to Clarendon, Paris, 12 June 1867, Maxwell, ii. 336.

[2] Cowley to Stanley, Paris, confidential, 14 June 1867, PRO FO 27/1662, no. 398. Certainly Moustier was not fooled (same to same, Paris, confidential, 28 June 1867, PRO FO 27/1662, no. 467).

[3] King of Prussia to Queen of Prussia, 26 June 1867, QVL, 2nd ser., i. 437–40.

[4] The foreign secretary was unmoved: 'I return . . . letter of the King of Prussia. . . . We shall continue to do what is in our power for that object [peace]; without leaning (in the event of future disputes) to either side, but endeavoring to hold fairly and impartially the balance between them' (Stanley to Grey, 5 July 1867, RA I 48/18).

[5] La Tour to Moustier, London, 7 July 1867, Orig. xvii. 376.

[6] Stanley to Victoria, 20 July 1867, QVL, 2nd ser., i. 448.

You will easily understand why H.M. wishes you to consider this expression of her views to be considered or meant exclusively for yourself. Not that she has any reason for concealing her opinion, but she wd. be sorry Ld Stanley shd think she has so little confidence in him, as to make it necessary for her to appeal to his leader in the H. of Commons. Without going quite that length, she cannot shut her eyes to the fact that it does require some shoving to get him out of a somewhat ignoble groove.[1]

Shortly after this letter another much more specific one went off to Disraeli echoing the sentiments of the King of Prussia.

The Queen cannot see such a state of things without asking herself seriously whether E[ngland], adhering to a cold policy of non-interference or rather to one of total abstention from all concern in the affairs of the Continent, is to continue in her passive attitude, nor make any attempt to avert such a calamity? Yet she fears that such may be the course which Lord Stanley, unless some pressure is exercised upon him, may be inclined to pursue.

Lord Stanley, is quite right in saying . . . that we should hold the balance even between the 2 countries [France and Prussia] . . . yet our interests are very differently affected by the 2 countries. . . . The principle of our Foreign Policy . . . should be a thorough understanding for mutual support, in the interest of peace, with North Germany.

She [France] can have no right to interfere in the internal organization of Germany. . . . The result of the war between A[ustria] & P[russia] gave her no legitimate pretense for demanding territorial compensation from the latter. . . . Were France, therefore, to provoke a quarrel with Pr. . . . she would clearly be the aggressor, but she will never venture to do so if she knows that such was our opinion.[2]

Disraeli defended his foreign secretary by maintaining that Stanley was pro-German, which was true, and that he, Disraeli, had always encouraged this tendency,[3] which probably was not. Court pressure on Disraeli and Stanley for a closer relationship with Prussia continued, especially as General Grey, Victoria's

---

[1] Grey to Disraeli, confidential, 20 July 1867, Disraeli Pap. 85. Disraeli, for some time, had flattered Stanley with the hope that increased confidence would loosen his granite reserve. 'In such a balanced state of circumstances, you will be master. I expect you to become the greatest foreign minister since Chatham' (Disraeli to Stanley, private, 1 Sept. 1867, Stan. Pap., Disraeli 1866–8). 'Gladstonism is at a discount . . . I begin to believe you will turn out a regular Chatham' (same to same, Windsor, 22 Apr. 1867, Stan. Pap., Disraeli).

[2] Grey to Disraeli, 29 July 1867, QVL, 2nd ser., i. 451–5; ibid., Disraeli Pap. 85.

[3] Disraeli to Grey, confidential, 31 July 1867, QVL, 2nd ser., i. 455–6.

secretary, was more German than the queen.[1] According to the queen, the possibility of English intervention on the Continent, particularly to preserve Belgian independence, should be made known. As its violation would probably be accomplished by France, a German alliance was an ineluctable conclusion.[2] Ironically, it was at this moment that Stanley expressed some irritation at the extreme sensitivity of the Prussian Government. Berlin had opted to create an incident over a French representation about Schleswig, a representation which the French Government subsequently disavowed.

> I asked him [the Prussian chargé d'affaires] whether, what I must be allowed to call, the extreme sensitiveness and suspicion with which the Prussian government appeared disposed to regard every act and word proceeding from France, was not itself quite as much calculated to increase the danger of war as any part of the conduct of which they now complained. There was, I said, no surer way of bringing about a quarrel than by seizing every occasion to declare it inevitable.[3]

Victoria and Grey were convinced that France was the complete villain because they were both so pro-German in feeling. Stanley's Prussian leanings derived less from sentiment than from apparent interest. His holding the 'balance even' was a justification for not acting, and his Prussian tendency, a reflection of his fear of France and Russia, was highly tempered by his abhorrence of war.

> I fear there is no resisting the evidence of a growing expectation of war, both in France and Prussia. . . . I really think we are experiencing as much inconvenience in the way of disturbed trade and so forth, as we should if the fighting had actually begun. The expectation of it paralyzes everything.
>
> If war does break out, we have only one course; that of a rigidly impartial neutrality.[4]

This was the man who Disraeli hoped would 'destroy & shatter to pieces the decaying theory of non-interference'.[5] But

---

[1] Grey to Victoria, 28 July 1867, RA I 48/27; Grey to Disraeli, private, 29 July 1867, ibid., no. 28; Grey to Victoria, 31 July 1867, ibid., no. 16.

[2] General Grey to Disraeli, private, 5 Aug. 1867, QVL, 2nd ser., i. 456–8.

[3] Stanley to Loftus, 5 Aug. 1867, PRO FO 64/616, no. 221.

[4] Stanley to Grey, private, 9 Aug. 1867, Stan. Pap., queen; ibid., QVL, 2nd ser., i. 458.

[5] Disraeli to Victoria, 16 Aug. 1867, Buckle, iv. 473–4. On the same day that

whereas Disraeli hoped that an even balance of force on the Continent would make England's position decisive,[1] Stanley talked about holding the 'balance even' so that no intervention would be necessary.

In September of 1867 Franco-Prussian relations were further disturbed by the desire of Baden and its grand duke to be united with northern Germany.[2] Bismarck took this opportunity to react to the Salzburg meeting of Napoleon III and Francis-Joseph, and published a circular warning against any foreign meddling in German affairs.[3] France looked upon the circular as an 'uncalled for defiance'.[4]

The general tendency of the public mind [in France] is to view not only with jealousy but with fear the partly accomplished and clearly foreshadowed unity of Germany, and it would require very slight provocation from abroad to inflame this sentiment into one of national desire for war . . . war which would unite against her every fraction of the population of Germany.[5]

Bismarck realized this but was willing to allow the existing momentum for unification to accomplish what it could before doing anything more to build it up.[6]

In October 1867 Garibaldi was active once again in the Papal States. The intention of Napoleon III to send French troops back to Italy met with strenuous opposition from the Italian Government and Bismarck lost no time in attempting to promote French embarrassment.[7] The Prussian chargé d'affaires asked Stanley what England would do in the event of a Franco-Italian war. The foreign secretary replied that he

Disraeli sent this letter, the Government decided upon a declaration of war against the Emperor of Abyssinia. This ruler was charged with unjustly making Europeans captives. British troops sent to Abyssinia were completely successful in defeating the African forces.

[1] Disraeli to Stanley, private, 1 Sept. 1867, Stan. Pap., Disraeli; ibid., Buckle, v. 82–84.

[2] Gordon to Stanley, Stuttgart, 10 Sept. 1867, PRO FO 82/129, no. 75; Fane to Stanley, Paris, 17 Sept. 1867, PRO FO 27/1667, no. 593.

[3] Baude to Moustier, London, 21 Sept. 1867, *Orig.* xviii. 324; Fane to Stanley, Paris, 24 Sept. 1867, PRO FO 27/1667, no. 612.   [4] Ibid.

[5] Fane to Stanley, Paris, confidential, 8 Oct. 1867, PRO FO 27/1668, no. 658.

[6] Loftus to Stanley, Berlin, 18 Oct. 1867, *APP* ix. 301–2.

[7] Bismarck did not want a Franco-Italian war because he did not wish Italy crushed nor did he wish to have to justify protecting the Pope to German Protestant opinion (Bismarck to Bernstorff, Berlin, secret, 19 Oct. 1867, *GW* vi A, no. 895).

believed Prussian fears to be premature, but that if war did occur the sympathies of Britain would be with the Italians.[1] Stanley refused to be drawn further and instructed Lyons, who had replaced Cowley at Paris, to say, if he thought it necessary, that a French war on Italy would be viewed with deep regret in London.[2] To the French, Stanley seemed to be playing Bismarck's game, for neither Prussia nor England were inclined to join a conference suggested by the French in order to settle the Roman question.[3] Lyons, however, hoped to avoid giving this impression.

I am anxious [that] we should keep clear of all suspicion of conspiring with Prussia against the conference, and that we should do all we can to avoid damaging the Emperor's position with his own people. For the present we may perhaps remain quiet.[4]

The foreign secretary maintained his usual reserve, and Lyons explained to Moustier that 'no special concert existed between Her Majesty's government and Prussia either on the Roman or the Eastern question'.[5]

By the summer of 1868 the politically conscious in Europe recognized the high probability of a war between France and Prussia. Apart from reasons of humanity, it was in the interest of Britain to prevent such a war. Lyons was sure that 'if France is ever hard pressed by Prussia, the Italians will go to Rome and the Russians to Constantinople'.[6] Prince Napoleon pointed out that if Prussia defeated France there would be no one to

---

[1] Stanley to Loftus, 23 Oct. 1867, PRO FO 64/616, no. 233. Bismarck was fishing for an understanding with England. 'Count Bismarck . . . informed the Italian government . . . [that] in the event of any attack being made upon the Italian kingdom, such an attack would not be seen with indifference by Prussia and he wished to know what view her Majesty's government would take on it' (ibid.).

[2] Stanley to Lyons, telegram, 28 Oct. 1867, PRO FO 27/1655, no. 2.

[3] Baude to Moustier, London, 10 Nov. 1867, Orig. xix. 213; same to same, 12 Nov. 1867, ibid., p. 233; Lyons to Stanley, private, 16 Nov. 1867, Lyons Pap. RC 2; Stanley to Lyons, 18 Nov. 1867, ibid., pp. 270–1. 'Moustier is confirmed in his suspicion that Prussia wishes to keep France in hot water with Italy, and therefore works against the conference, while seeking to throw the blame of its failure on England or some other power' (Lyons to Stanley, private, 26 Nov. 1867, Lyons Pap. RC 2).

[4] Lyons to Stanley, private, 6 Dec. 1867, Lyons Pap. RC 2.

[5] Stanley to Bloomfield, private, 10 Dec. 1867, PRO FO 356/33; Lyons to Stanley, confidential, 2 Jan. 1868, PRO FO 27/1700, no. 8.

[6] Lyons to Stanley, Paris, confidential, 14 Jan. 1868, Lyons Pap., RC 2.

stop Russia in the East, and if France were victorious territorial compensation would be obtained.[1]

Stanley did not take the probability of war as seriously as he might have. He was optimistically convinced that Bismarck was wise enough not to provoke France. 'Bismarck, I fully believe, is as well aware as anyone of the danger of precipitating matters. Time works many changes: and France may accept as inevitable, two or three years hence, what she now would resent as an insult.'[2] The foreign secretary was even more convinced that Napoleon III did not want war. In November 1867 the emperor delivered a verbal La Valette circular. In a speech at the opening of the legislature he proclaimed that French interests and dignity were not menaced by the recent changes in Germany, and therefore the Government would not interfere across the Rhine.[3] Lyons, at Paris, confirmed the emperor's aversion to war:

I have heard on excellent authority that there can be no doubt whatever that the Emperor is personally very averse to war.

I had a conversation with General Fleury the day before yesterday. . . . He spoke very positively of the determination of the Emperor to preserve peace, but he dwelt a great deal more than I liked upon the necessity of some satisfaction being given to the amour propre of France.[4]

It has been argued by Raymond that 'the task of England was either to preserve the status quo or to convince France that a united Germany would oppose no real danger to her freedom and prestige'.[5] A united Germany was a 'real danger' to France, though some attempt was made by Britain to convince her that it was not. It was a half-hearted attempt because Stanley desired a united Germany precisely because it would counteract and limit French power and prestige. 'My personal opinion',

---

[1] Loftus to Stanley, Berlin, 7 Mar. 1868, PRO FO 64/640, no. 147; ibid., *APP* ix. 781–4; Lyons to Stanley, Paris, private, 31 Mar. 1868, Stan. Pap. X 6, France.
[2] Stanley to Loftus, private, 15 Apr. 1868, Stan. Pap., Prussia.
[3] Baude to Moustier, London, 19 Nov. 1867, *Orig.* xix. 288. *The Times* referred to this speech as the most liberal, peaceful, and rational the emperor ever made (ibid.).
[4] Lyons to Stanley, Paris, private, 28 May 1868, Stan. Pap. X 6, France.
[5] Dora N. Raymond, *British Policy and Opinion during the Franco-Prussian War* (New York, 1921), p. 24.

he wrote, 'is for Prussia rather than Germany—for a compact unity as preferable to a loose federation'.[1]

Stanley consequently had no wish to preserve the *status quo*, and though he would not admit it publicly he much preferred a strong and solid German state.

All that Germany can do for us is to act as a counterpoise to France and Russia; and for that purpose she cannot be too closely united. I could wish, if it had been possible, that the mediatisation of the small sovereigns had been complete. . . . I only hope Bismarck's health may not so break down that he will be unable to control his Parliament—That would be a misfortune for all the world—These people would fail in 1867 as they failed in 1849.[1]

When Victoria attempted to obtain for Morier, an English diplomat and also a severe critic of Bismarck, a position in the British embassy at Berlin, Stanley successfully objected.

I am really indebted to you for the support you [Derby] have given me with H.M. in the matter of Morier's claim to go to Berlin. My letter to the Queen did not state the whole case, nor was it possible to do so: but you may as well know it. The Crown Prince and Princess [of Prussia] are on bad terms with Bismarck, and trying to displace him, or at least to lessen his hold on the King's [of Prussia] mind.

The fact is, the Queen and her daughter agree in disliking Bismarck, and think that Morier's presence will be at least a check upon him, possibly a means to his removal.[2]

The foreign secretary wanted Bismarck to stay in power because 'with all his faults, he was and is fitter to guide his country through the present difficulties than any minister who is likely to replace him'.[3] Stanley was convinced that Bismarck recognized the necessity of peace in order to consolidate Germany, and therefore considered 'his tenure of power as one of the surest guarantees for peace that we have'.[4]

The shrewdness and purposefulness of Stanley was masked behind a reserve that fooled everyone, including his own queen, who thought him insufficiently pro-German in policy. In fact he was more German or Prussian than Victoria. He perceived

1 Stanley to Loftus, private, 26 Dec. 1866, Stan. Pap., Prussia.
2 Stanley to Derby, private, 3 Oct. 1867, Derby Pap. 161/3.
3 Stanley to Loftus, private, 15 Apr. 1868, Stan. Pap., Prussia.
4 Stanley to Loftus, private, 17 June 1868, Stan. Pap., Prussia.

that a powerful Prussia could be dangerous to England only if allied to Russia.

> The right line for Prussia to follow is that of reconciliation and close alliance with Austria. . . . Together [they] are a check on both Russian and French ambition. . . . Anything we can do to bring about the result—though it can be but little—will be very willingly done, as far as I am concerned.[1]

Consequently the aggressiveness of Prussia and the authoritarian system within that country, repeatedly pointed out by the British ministers in Germany,[2] made little difference to Stanley. At the same time the warnings from Lyons about the shaky position of Napoleon III, though recognized by the foreign secretary, did not unduly worry him. 'The real danger to Europe appears however to be in the difficulties of the Emperor Napoleon at home. . . . I think that Europe, and England in particular, are more interested in maintaining the Emperor, than in almost anything else.'[3]

But Stanley felt the way to preserve peace and British interests was not by helping the stumbling Napoleon III, but by doing nothing to prevent the expansion of Prussia in Germany. Yet if Britain had actively co-operated with Bismarck, a co-operation Stanley would have opposed on the general grounds of non-involvement, France might have paid almost any price in the East for Russian support in the West. So the foreign secretary could safely remain quiet and look to a strong Prussia to neutralize both Russia and France. He hoped that the passage of time would enable the French to reconcile themselves to the expansion of Prussia and their own consequently diminished importance in Europe.

British prestige continued to decline because it seemed that her interest in Europe had been reduced to a concern only for Belgium and Constantinople. The Government, recognizing

---

[1] Stanley to Loftus, private, 8 Jan. 1868, Stan. Pap., Prussia.

[2] Howard to Stanley, Munich, confidential, 2 Apr. 1867, PRO FO 9/181, no. 77; same to same, Munich, 31 Dec. 1867, ibid. 183, no. 272; Crowe to Stanley, Leipzig, 15 Apr. 1868, PRO FO 68/148, no. 1. 'The govt. of Northern Germany is daily tending to become as much of a personal govt. as that of France' (Morier to Stanley, Darmstadt, private, 10 Mar. 1868, Stan. Pap., Germany—Bavaria). 'Bismarck . . . reigns supreme. . . . The Prussian ministers are reduced to cyphers' (Loftus to Stanley, 19 Oct. 1867, RA J 39/24).

[3] Lyons to Stanley, Paris, confidential, Lyons Pap. RC 2.

the public mood, approved of the diminution of its own interests on the Continent.[1] Forceful intervention, except on behalf of Belgium or Constantinople, could hardly be contemplated. What weight and influence Britain commanded in Europe was limited to her two special interests, and all Europe recognized the importance England attached to them. Napoleon III, grasping for straws to revive his position in Europe and France, now threatened one of these special interests.

[1] In April the annually passed Mutiny Bill was amended. Deleted from it was the traditional phrase concerning the necessity of preserving the balance of power in Europe (Gordon Craig, 'Great Britain and the Belgian Railways Dispute of 1869', *American Historical Review*, l [July, 1945], 741).

VI

BELGIUM

Clarendon and Crete

THE Franco-Austrian and Russo-Prussian *rapprochements* in the winter of 1867–8 had little if any effect on British policy at Constantinople or along the Rhine. Stanley's refusal to join France and Russia in putting pressure on the Sultan undoubtedly saved Crete for Turkey and possibly prevented the disintegration of the Ottoman empire. Now that France and Russia were on more formal terms, the urgency of the Cretan question declined, though the rebellion continued. Beust's attempt to align England with France and Austria in an anti-Russian policy in the East failed, as Stanley politely declined any joint action.[1] The foreign secretary's wish to preserve the 'sick man' was still the basis for British policy in the East, and it meant keeping Russia out of the Balkans.[2]

In the spring of 1868, talk of a Franco-Prussian war[3] only strengthened Stanley's uncommitted position. An appeal to intercede with Prussia was refused by the foreign secretary.

[The French government] thought it right . . . to say that any movement of an annexationist character affecting south Germany could not fail to create in France an impression to which the French government could hardly remain indifferent.

Mons. de Moustier hoped therefore, that in the event of any necessity for such a step arising, Her Majesty's government would

[1] Bloomfield to Stanley, private, Vienna, 19 Nov. 1867, PRO FO 356/40. In December Stanley did, however, propose to France that the two countries might suggest to the Sultan local self-government for Crete (Lyons to Stanley, confidential, Paris, 12 Dec. 1867, PRO FO 27/1671, no. 161).

[2] Stanley instructed the British representatives at Bucharest and Belgrade in a pro-Turkish sense and asked the Prussian Government to support the British advice. The English ministers were directed that 'if the facts which might come to their knowledge should warrant their doing so, to warn the governments of those Principalities of the danger they would incur by furthering any scheme for the disturbance of the neighboring Turkish provinces' (Loftus to Stanley, Berlin, 22 Feb. 1868, PRO FO 64/639, no. 121).

[3] Colonel Claremont, the British military attaché, was confirmed 'in the fear that there will be a war this year between France and Prussia' (Claremont to Lyons, confidential, Paris, 7 Apr. 1868, PRO FO 27/1704, no. 25).

tender their advice to that of Prussia in such a sense as to avert the possibility of danger.[1]

Stanley declined to do this, 'as it is in fact advising Bismarck to give way, and implying that the French demands are intrinsically reasonable—a matter very open to doubt'.[2] Stanley openly admitted to La Tour that it was inevitable that all Germany would be united. While he did not hide his satisfaction at such an occurrence, he felt that Bismarck would not compromise his past achievements by pushing matters too quickly.[3] In September Lyons reported from Paris that 'the war panic does not seem to diminish'.[4] Two months later Stanley made a speech at King's Lynn which presented events in Europe in a way which both justified England's refusal to intervene, and pointed up the futility of war. The foreign secretary argued the fruitlessness of struggling against German unity; it was a natural and inevitable event and France had no need to fear it. In the East the danger to Turkish integrity was ascribed to internal causes—governmental bankruptcy and provincial rebellion.[5] Stanley told La Tour that the days were over when England would fight to uphold Ottoman integrity, only 'the possession of Constantinople itself' would bring Britain into the field.[6]

In December the Conservative Government fell when the Liberals obtained a majority in the Commons. Stanley justified the Government's action to his father:

It is possible that at almost any moment trouble may break out in Roumania, involving the whole eastern question: in another part of the world, Seward . . . is raising difficulties. . . . As a provisional

---

[1] Stanley to Lyons, confidential, 14 Apr. 1868, PRO FO 27/1697, no. 239.

[2] Stanley to Bloomfield, private, 14 Apr. 1868, PRO FO 356/33.

[3] La Tour to Moustier, London, 5 July 1868, *Orig.* xvi. 395. Moustier pointed to 'gloomy reports from Germany' which referred to Germany's being united at once (Lyons to Stanley, confidential, Paris, 31 July 1868, PRO FO 27/1707, no. 485). Stanley undoubtedly shared Russell's sentiments, and of course the queen's, that German unification would not justify France's making a war (Russell to Clarendon, 20 Sept. 1868, Maxwell, ii. 349).

[4] Lyons to Stanley, private, 17 Sept. 1868, Stan. Pap. X 6.

[5] La Tour to Moustier, telegram, London, 14 Nov. 1868, *Orig.* xxii. 237–9. Moustier was much upset by Stanley's speech (ibid.).

[6] La Tour to Moustier, confidential, London, 22 Nov. 1868, *Orig.* xxii. 279–80. There is little doubt but that Stanley reflected the opinion of Parliament. 'The debate of Friday last shewed great indifference on the Cretan question. . . . The general wish appeared to be to continue to keep us as much out of the quarrel as possible' (Stanley to Lyons, private, 28 Apr. 1868, Stan. Pap., France).

minister, I could hardly convert the country to a decided course of action in the east . . . and . . . such action . . . may arise at any moment—and thus England will be paralyzed at what may be a very critical juncture.[1]

It was generally expected by Englishmen and foreigners alike that the post of foreign secretary in the new Government would be filled by Lord Clarendon. The only objection to Clarendon was a serious one privately expressed by Victoria. The queen felt he was 'impertinent' and also that he did not favour German unity.[2] Grey told Gladstone of the queen's feelings:

As regards Lord Clarendon it seems enough to say, that the two years and a half he has spent in Opposition, have completely changed the opinion your Majesty entertained in 1866 of his fitness for the Foreign Office.—His language during that time has been very indiscreet, and has created an impression abroad and especially in Germany, as to his present views and feelings, which it is most desirable, in the present state of the Continent, should not be entertained of the English Foreign Secretary.[3]

But there was no satisfactory alternative and Victoria dropped her objections. Clarendon became foreign secretary. He was the only really important British statesman at the time who was more French than German in his sympathies.

Just at the moment when Britain was changing governments the Cretan embers again flared into fire. Greek aid to Crete was

[1] Stanley to Derby, private, 30 Nov. 1868, Derby Pap. 107.

[2] Lord Halifax's journal, 26 Nov. 1868, Maxwell, ii. 353. On the latter score Clarendon probably told Napoleon that England would support a proposal to guarantee the *status quo* in Germany (Metternich to Beust, Paris, 28 Oct. 1868, D. W. Houston, *The Negotiations for a Triple Alliance between France, Austria, and Italy 1869–70* [University of Pennsylvania Dissertation, 1959], p. 57). Bismarck instructed Bernstorff to refute Clarendon's confidential suggestion of a European guarantee of the Treaty of Prague (Bismarck to Bernstorff, Berlin, telegram, 7 Dec. 1868, *GW* vi A, no. 1221; same to same, Berlin, 8 Dec. 1868, ibid., no. 1222). In January of 1869 La Valette told Lyons that peace could be preserved if some 'third power' would suggest 'the neutralization of the states south of the Main' (Lyons to Clarendon, private, Paris, 26 Jan. 1869, Lyons Pap. RC 2).

[3] Grey to Victoria, 1 Dec. 1868, RA C 32/142, Mosse, pp. 295–6. 'I propose to say to Ld. Halifax that Y.M. wd. not find Clarendon personably agreeable and that his feelings & opinions about Ger. & Pr. have been almost offensively expressed [therefore] . . . we can't have him when we shd preserve a good understanding with Germany. . . . His hostile opinions to Ger. are well known' (Grey to Victoria,? Nov. 1868, ibid., no. 129).

making a Graeco-Turkish war a real possibility at the end of 1869.[1] Stanley wrote to the English minister at Athens.

Since matter is urgent I give you instructions tho I would rather leave question to my successor. Warn Greek Govt. of serious danger & certainty that they can expect no support from the other powers . . . in a contest with Turkey, wantonly provoked on the part of Greece.[2]

Stanley was certain that England would not and could not fight for Turkey as she had done fifteen years before.

However the English people may dislike the advance of Russian power in the East, they will hardly embark in a second Crimean war. There is a general feeling that we have not been repaid for the sacrifices of 1854–5 by the result, as exhibited in the present state of the Turkish Empire. . . . I feel nearly sure that if the question were to become one of fighting . . . neither the present cabinet, nor any that may follow would be able to induce the country to repeat the armed interference of 15 years ago. . . . We have a good and safe pilot in Lord Clarendon, and we must hope for the best.[3]

Clarendon followed Stanley's lead and warned the Greek Government that England would not restrain the Porte.[4] He differed from his predecessor, however, in the emphasis he placed upon acting with France and Russia in the East,[5] but his initiative for three-power co-operation was blunted when Bismarck proposed a six-power conference.[6] Both La Valette, who had replaced Moustier as foreign minister, and Gorchakov favoured a conference. Only Clarendon seemed to fear the consequences of a meeting that might reopen the whole Eastern question.[7] When Italy and Austria agreed and Turkey did not object to such a meeting, Clarendon gave way.[8] He qualified

[1] Lyons to Stanley, Compiègne, 8 Dec. 1868, PRO FO 27/1712, no. 1027; La Tour to Moustier, 9 Dec. 1868, *Orig.* xxii. 341–2.
[2] Stanley to Erskine, 7 Dec. 1868, PRO FO 146/1344, no. 87.
[3] Stanley to Buchanan, private, 16 Dec. 1868, Stan. Pap., Russia.
[4] Clarendon to Erskine, telegram, 16 Dec. 1868, PRO FO 146/1344; Hammond to Lyons, telegram, 18 Dec. 1868, PRO FO 146/1344, no. 25.
[5] La Tour to Moustier, 18 Dec. 1868, *Orig.* xxii. 386. Clarendon's desire to concert with Russia was to prevent her from acting independently (Clarendon to Lyons, private, 19 Dec. 1868, Clar. Pap. C 148).
[6] Lyons to Clarendon, telegram, 20 Dec. 1868, PRO FO 27/1712, no. 1061.
[7] Lyons to Clarendon, confidential, 20 Dec. 1868, PRO FO 27/1712, no. 1062; same to same, 21 Dec. 1868, PRO FO 27/1713, no. 1069.
[8] Ibid. Lyons favoured a conference if only to stay well with France (Lyons to Clarendon, private, 21 Dec. 1868, Lyons Pap. RC 2). Gladstone felt England should not object too strongly since a conference was certain (Gladstone to Clarendon, 21 Dec. 1868, Glad. Pap. 44133, 149).

England's adhesion to the conference, however, with the stipulation that the integrity of the Ottoman empire must be respected.[1]

The conference met in Paris in January 1869. Greece was compelled to stop interfering in Crete and fomenting insurrection against Turkey. A secondary fact of hardly less significance was the closeness of France and England in bringing the Cretan affair to a close. The British ambassador in Paris wrote: 'The conference has had this good effect that it has produced an intimacy between La Valette and me which is agreeable and very useful.'[2]

Earlier in the Cretan affair, Stanley's justification for inaction was that France was obviously playing Russia's game of discomfiting the Turks, and Stanley would have no part of it. When France cooled towards her Russian connexion, she explained to London that she had co-operated with Russia only with a view to controlling her. Stanley still kept his distance, however, because he felt Russia would not push matters as far as war.[3] Consequently French and then later Austrian attempts to obtain British aid in the East by picturing Russia as an iniquitous pirate failed; the foreign secretary was insufficiently impressed by the Russian spectre. Clarendon's alacrity to associate with France was not because his estimate of Russian intentions was different but because, unlike Stanley, he had a predisposition towards the French and was willing to exhibit it.

Belgium

Ironically Clarendon's sympathies were frustrated by Napoleon's move towards Belgium. Before the Belgian railroads dis-

---

[1] Clarendon to Lyons, 23 Dec. 1868, PRO FO 27/1699, no. 50; same to same, 30 Dec. 1868, ibid., no. 78.

[2] Lyons to Clarendon, Paris, private, 22 Jan. 1869, Lyons Pap. RC 2.

[3] 'I partly believe what he [Brunnow] says, that Russia does not wish to precipitate an eastern crisis. (She has reasons—finances disordered, southern railways not made, Poland not wholly quieted, and the peasantry hardly settled down under the new system. This he did not say, but I do.)'. (Stanley to Cowley, private, 18 Sept. 1866, PRO FO 579/182; Stanley to Derby, private, 19 Sept. 1866, Derby Pap. 161/2; La Tour to Moustier, London, 5 Nov. 1866, *Orig.* xiii. 57; Stanley to Denbigh, private, 30 May 1867, Stan. Pap., Miscellaneous; Stuart to Stanley, secret, St. Petersburg, 15 Jan. 1868, PRO FO 146/1329, no. 13; Apponyi to Beust, London, 25 Sept. 1867, HHSA, England, no. 60.)

pute Bismarck had played up French designs in the hope of winning a measure of English support. The French Government now gave substance to the rumours of French plots to obtain Belgium. The British attitude towards this small country was one of the crucial factors, if not the most important, in determining British policy towards France and Prussia before the war of 1870. Professor Pribram has discerned what he refers to as the two great principles or aims of British foreign policy. One has been the maintenance of balance among the great powers; the other the preservation of Belgian independence—'for it was from here that the greatest danger could threaten the island kingdom whose strongest defence was the sea'.[1] Sir. J. Headlam-Morley expressed a similar point of view:

As an island, we depend for our security on our fleet and on the naval control of the surrounding seas. . . . It is an essential principle of our policy to insure that on the opposite shores there shall never arise a nation which by superiority of wealth and numbers could beat us in ship building, and which at the same time has command of the sea coast. Apart from the Channel ports, the most important position is the delta formed by the estuaries of the great rivers, the Scheldt, the Meuse and the Rhine. This delta would provide an impregnable base in which resources which come from the continent behind it, could be provided with all the equipment of a great naval arsenal. It is for this reason that so large a part of English history is occupied with this district.[2]

Throughout much of the eighteenth and nineteenth centuries the dominant power on the Continent was also the power posing the greatest threat to the security of the Low Countries. Pitt refused to 'see with indifference that France shall make herself, either directly or indirectly, sovereign of the Low Countries'.[3] Castlereagh and Canning both agreed that 'the importance of preventing the Low Countries, the Military Barrier of Europe, from being lost, by being melted down into the general Mass of French Power . . . might enable the British Govt to act more promptly upon this, than perhaps upon any other Case of an internal Character that can be

---

[1] A. F. Pribram, *England and the International Policy of the European Great Powers 1871–1914* (Oxford, 1931), pp. 1–4.
[2] Sir J. Headlam-Morley, *Studies in Diplomatic History* (London, 1930), pp. 157–8.
[3] Grenville to Chauvelin, 31 Dec. 1792, Temperley and Penson, p. 7.

stated'.[1] Palmerston, who was instrumental in creating an independent Belgium, left little doubt but that he was willing to fight to defend his creation. 'One thing is certain—the French must go out of Belgium, or we have a general war, and war in a given number of days.'[2] As late as 1865 he wrote the following to Russell: 'As to France, we know how restless and aggressive she is, and how ready to break loose for Belgium, for the Rhine, for everything she would be likely to get without too great an exertion.'[3] England's long historical interest in the Low Countries, which was a natural manifestation of geographical proximity, was reinforced in the nineteenth century by nightmares of a French move towards Belgium, epitomizing the fear of general French expansion.

In 1863 Palmerston had said:

Antwerp is quite as much in his [Napoleon's] thoughts as Brussels and his real Object and that which lies at the Bottom of his Heart, as well as that of every Frenchman, is the humbling of England, the traditional Rival of France, and the main Obstacle to French Supremacy in Europe and all over the World. The Emperor would wish to bring us upon our Marrow bones in the most friendly manner if we would let him do so.[4]

To this historical residue of geography, commerce, and French expansion, must be added the guarantee of 1839, the dynastic tie, and the position of Belgium as a pawn in Franco-Prussian relations in the 1860's. Clarendon seems to have been particularly conscious of the English obligation to defend Belgian integrity, or to put it more precisely of the European recognition that Britain had a special interest in doing so.[5] On the eve of the Austro-Prussian war, he wrote to Cowley that 'our

[1] The state paper of 5 May 1820, Temperley and Penson p. 62.

[2] Palmerston to Granville, private, 17 Aug. 1831, ibid., p. 92. In 1876 Gladstone, speaking on the Belgian guarantee, attempted to minimize its obligation. 'I have often heard Lord Palmerston give his opinion of guarantees . . . that while a guarantee gave a right of interference, it did not constitute of itself an obligation to interfere' (W. E. Lingelbach, 'Belgian Neutrality: its Origin and Interpretation', *American Historical Review*, xxxix [October, 1933], 66–67).

[3] Palmerston to Russell, 13 Sept. 1865, W. H. Dawson, *Richard Cobden and foreign policy* (London, 1926), p. 280.

[4] Palmerston to Russell, 7 Apr. 1863, PRO FO 30/22, no. 14. Professor Mosse kindly supplied this quotation and generously advised me concerning British feeling about Belgium.

[5] 'The preservation of Belgium is supposed in Germany to be mainly an English interest' (Napier to Clarendon, Berlin, 5 Jan. 1866, RA I 43/1).

great care must be for Belgium & our resources of all kinds must
be husbanded for fulfilling our treaty engagements respecting
that country'.[1] Further, in the same paragraph, Clarendon,
perhaps unconsciously, reveals the reason for his concern. 'He
[Napoleon] will probably admit our position & not try to
embarrass us by meddling with Belgium.'[1] The word used is
not hurt or threaten, but 'embarrass'. Clarendon seemed most
aware that everyone recognized Belgium as a British charge, and
that consequently England would lose face if she upset general
expectation by not defending its independence. The argument
that Clarendon recognized the British obligation contracted
in 1839, by supporting the distinction Derby and Stanley were
making between the guarantees of 1839 and 1867, does not stand
up. In this light his private letter to Hammond is significant:

> The so called guarantee given in the Luxg Treaty is as you said in
> your note the other day no guarantee at all because it is collective
> and no power engages to enforce it individually, but I cannot say
> that the guarantee of 39 has much more validity or binding force—
> the words . . . wd not make it obligatory upon any single power to
> interfere, & the same obstacles to collective action wd probably
> arise as those wh. are now thought to render the Luxg guarantee
> a nullity.[2]

England would be 'embarrassed' then not because it was
'obligatory' that she 'interfere', but because it was expected
that she would, an expectation which in Clarendon's mind would
be difficult if not impossible to satisfy.

Europe assumed that Belgium was for Britain a vital interest
because England seemed to take it for granted. 'Be sure that I
never allow any opportunity to escape of reminding the
Emperor that Belgium is the sanctum sanctorum.'[3] No one
assumed this more than Leopold II, and one cannot but feel
that he took undue advantage of it. The alarm of Leopold in

---

[1] Clarendon to Cowley, private, 11 Apr. 1866, PRO FO 519/180.

[2] Clarendon to Hammond, private, 17 June 1867, PRO FO 391/4. When the
foreign secretary told the queen that 'Belgium we were bound to defend', he was
referring only in part to the guarantee of 1839 (Victoria memorandum, 6 May
1866, *QVL*, 2nd ser., i. 325–6).

[3] Cowley to Clarendon, Paris, private, 13 Apr. 1866, PRO FO 519/232. 'I took
the opportunity, as I did also yesterday with Drouyn to hint that I know of no
question which wd really produce a rupture between the two countries except an
attempt to annex Belgium' (Cowley to Clarendon, private, 11 May 1866, PRO FO
519/232).

July 1866 was translated into a letter from Clarendon to Cowley
to obtain French assurances concerning Belgium.[1] From 1866
to 1871 Belgium so often told England that her integrity was in
danger that London became preoccupied with attempting to
establish the validity of the threat.[2] At the same time the
rumours as they accumulated became all too familiar and bred
perhaps a certain contempt. 'It cd hardly be anything relating
to Belgium, because offers, as far as Prussia make them, have
been made over & over again.'[3]

During Napoleon's quest for compensation after the Austro-
Prussian war, Stanley attempted to distract the emperor from
Belgium by referring to the 'formal engagement' Britain had
to defend it.[4] Like Clarendon, Stanley asked for and got French
assurances concerning her Channel neighbour.[5] Ironically, at
the same time that the Benedetti draft treaty was proposed
Stanley confessed that he 'believed firmly . . . that there is no
present danger of Belgium being annexed to France'.[6] Perhaps
the wish was father to the thought. The prime minister agreed
with his son's estimate. 'I should think the case of Belgium
serious, if it were not for the more than antagonism which sub-
sists between France and Prussia.'[7] Disraeli was much less
certain,[8] but the foreign secretary remained firm in his conviction.[9]

Victoria's concern for Belgian independence was based on
considerations of prestige and family feeling, both the throne of
cousin Leopold and England's prestige in upholding it being
involved. The queen felt her small neighbour was in danger,

[1] Clarendon to Cowley, private, 5 July 1866, PRO FO 519/180.
[2] The threat seemed genuine in July and August of 1866. The Foreign Office
was sure that Belgium was being used to buy Napoleon's acquiescence to Prussian
expansion. 'He [Goltz] again urged the Emperor to take possession of Belgium'
(Cowley to Clarendon, confidential, Paris, 6 July 1866, PRO FO 27/9620, no. 902).
[3] Cowley to Stanley, private, Paris, 20 July 1866, PRO FO 519/233.
[4] La Tour to Drouyn, 29 July 1866, Orig. xi. 293–4.
[5] Stanley to Cowley, telegram, 10 Aug. 1866, PRO FO 27/1608, no. 129;
Cowley to Stanley, telegram, Paris, 14 Aug. 1866, PRO FO 27/1621, no. 161.
[6] Stanley to Cowley, private, 30 Aug. 1866, PRO FO 519/182; ibid., Stan. Pap.,
France.
[7] Derby to Stanley, private, 23 Sept. 1866, Stan. Pap., Derby.
[8] Disraeli to Stanley, 30 Dec. 1866, Buckle, iv. 469.
[9] 'At present I can hardly believe in a deliberate proposal to annex Belgium'
(Stanley to Disraeli, confidential, 31 Dec. 1866, Stan. Pap., Disraeli). Stanley was
concerned, however, as he asked Fane to make an 'enquiry' (Fane to Stanley,
private, Paris, 4 Jan. 1867, Stan. Pap. X 6).

but wanted it 'understood, beyond the possibility of mistake, that England will never stand quietly by, or remain a passive spectator of any attempt against the integrity or independence of Belgium'.[1] Victoria stood ready to fight;[2] not so her foreign secretary who seemed to minimize Belgium's importance for England. If Clarendon cast doubt upon Britain's obligation to fight, Stanley questioned her interest in doing so. 'Whether we should fight in that quarrel [if France tried to take Belgium] I don't know; but I am sure no other power would.'[3]

During the Luxemburg affair, Bismarck attempted to exploit British anxiety over Belgium in order to secure British support in the event of a Franco-Prussian war. Stanley replied that Luxemburg was distinct from Belgium and only concerning the latter country had there been 'promises solemnly & repeatedly given'.[4] The foreign secretary's implication that Britain would fight if Belgium were harmed had a hollow ring. On the same day, 3 April, he instructed Cowley to obtain further French assurances about Belgium.[5] Stanley's strategy seemed to be to make Napoleon declare his honest intentions so many times that he would be too embarrassed to go back on his promises.[6] This was one reason why he was able to remain so

---

[1] Grey to Stanley, 9 Jan. 1867, *QVL*, 2nd ser., i. 386–7.

[2] Grey told Bernstorff that the queen would 'actively intervene if the independence of Belgium were menaced' (Bernstorff to William I, 3 Apr. 1867, *APP* viii. 575). Apponyi believed that to England, Belgium was a question of honour and interest and one upon which the British Government might fight (Apponyi to Beust, London, 16 Mar. 1869, HHSA, England). Bernstorff and his subordinate, Katte, had strong doubts whether Britain would fight to save Belgium from France (Bernstorff to Bismarck, secret, 18 Feb. 1867, *APP* viii. 403–7; Katte to Bismarck, confidential, London, 20 Sept. 1868, *APP* x. 187–91).

[3] Stanley to Fane, private, 6 Feb. 1867, Stan. Pap., France. Bismarck seemed indisposed to do so, as he privately informed Bernstorff (Bismarck to Bernstorff, 14 Jan. 1867, Oncken, ii. 185). Nor did there seem to be any Russian inclination to fight. Budberg told Moustier to take Belgium, that it was an affair between France and England (Moustier to Talleyrand, 18 Feb. 1867, *Orig.* xiv. 320–1). General Grey felt that Stanley 'seemed to imply . . . doubt as to whether it would be expedient to fight for it [Belgium]' (Grey to Victoria, 18 Apr. 1867, RA I 71/101).

[4] Stanley to Cowley, 3 Apr. 1867, PRO FO 27/1652, no. 83. Stanley informed Bernstorff, though not for publication, that if France violently annexed Belgium, the British public would ask for war on account of the guarantee of 1839 and not because of material interests (Bernstorff to Bismarck, telegram, 8 Apr. 1867, *APP* viii. 624–5). [5] Ibid., no. 84.

[6] The foreign secretary wrote to Cowley that his 'having extracted a fresh declaration about Belgium is a good thing done' (Stanley to Cowley, private, 6 Apr. 1867, PRO FO 356/33).

unmoved by Bismarckian hints about a Franco-Prussian understanding[1] on Belgium.

In April 1867 a Franco-Prussian war over Luxemburg seemed probable. As Victoria became more excitable about Belgium, Stanley characteristically became more cautious, and even intimated to Grey the inexpediency of fighting for it. This, of course, increased Victoria's concern, especially as it was learned that Napoleon had asked Leopold to enter a customs union with France.[2] The queen, who never had much confidence in Stanley, appealed to his father, and her words are significant. If Belgium were overrun, she said, England would be 'placed in a most painful & Humiliating position'.[3] The country would be humiliated rather than threatened, and the reason why she would be more humiliated than, say, Austria or Russia or Prussia if they permitted such a violation was undoubtedly because it was so widely recognized and assumed that Belgium was Britain's particular responsibility. The queen's letter continued:

E[ngland] must show the World that she is not prepared to abdicate her position as a great Power . . . & that . . . she is determined to fulfill her obligations, & (even single handed if need be) to defend the Independence of Belgium with the whole strength of the British Empire.[4]

Forsaking Belgium would be tantamount to Britain's abdication as a great power, because it was recognized as one of the two vital interests on the Continent that entitled her to that status. Victoria concluded that she would not 'be a party to the national disgrace that E[ngland] would incur'[5] if she stood by while France seized Belgium.

Disraeli attempted to reassure the queen by telling her that Stanley 'would . . . act, if necessary'.[6] The foreign secretary, as he wrote to Disraeli, was not so sure.

I am ready to go so far as may be necessary in support of Belgium,

---

[1] Stanley to Cowley, private, 8 Apr. 1867, PRO FO 356/33; Loftus to Stanley, confidential, Berlin, 13 Apr. 1867, PRO FO 64/619, no. 205; ibid., *APP* viii. 650–2.

[2] Cowley to Stanley, private, Paris, 18 Apr. 1867, PRO FO 519/233. In June Leopold excitedly wrote to England about such a union. Stanley felt that the king 'has got into the habit of thinking that we are bound to help him out of all his troubles' (Stanley note, 9 June 1867, Stan. Pap., Belgium).

[3] Victoria to Derby, 19 Apr. 1867, *QVL*, 2nd ser., i. 419–20.

[4] Ibid.   [5] Ibid.

[6] Disraeli to Stanley, 22 Apr. 1867, Buckle, iv. 470–1.

short of giving an absolute pledge to fight for its independence. Suppose we gave such a pledge, that France and Prussia came to an understanding. Russia and Austria standing aloof, where should we be. But I say nothing in an opposite sense, lest we should lose our influence.[1]

'Influence' is the key word. England could not afford to abandon Belgium even if she would.

Victoria and Grey continued their campaign to swing the reluctant Stanley round to their views. The court used Derby, Disraeli, and Malmesbury in the hope that they might influence the foreign secretary to take a more courageous stand on Belgian integrity. Malmesbury, who remembered Napoleon's departure for St. Helena and was very conscious of what had been once a real threat to England, emphasized Britain's strategic interests.

I consider the independence of the *Dutch* coast as bona fide *Dutch* & that of *Antwerp* of the most vital importance to us, in fact indispensable to our future safety; & I know that this was the decided opinion of both the Duke [of Wellington] & Palmerston who urged it upon me over & over again as an axiom when I took the F.O. in 1852.[2]

Malmesbury was almost alone in emphasizing Belgium's strategic importance in the 1860's.[3] If his view was more widely held, it was assumed and not put forward. In any case, Stanley was not impressed.

The Belgian government, backed by our Queen, desires to turn the European guarantee which now exists into what will be de facto an exclusive British protectorate. Results—the loss of all the military

---

[1] Stanley to Disraeli, private, 23 Apr. 1867, Stan. Pap., Disraeli. In 1874 Stanley, now Lord Derby, spoke much more definitely to the German ambassador. 'I said that the maintenance of the territorial integrity and independence of Belgium was a principle to which successive Administrations in this Country had again and again pledged themselves. . . . The national honour was . . . bound up with the observance of these promises. . . . I had no doubt . . . [if Belgium were violated] what our duty would be' (Temperley and Penson, pp. 350–1).

[2] Malmesbury to Stanley, private, 23 Apr. 1867, Stan. Pap. X 6, cabinet. Disraeli did the same in August 1870 (Hansard, *Parliamentary Debates* [3rd series] cciii. 1289–92).

[3] One exception was General Grey and possibly the queen, also. 'Were the French in possession of Antwerp—or were that port open to her for offensive purposes, in the event of war between France and England, we shd be in a very different position as regards the danger of invasion, from that in which we now are, when there is no port higher than Cherbourg from wh a French invading force can issue' (Grey to Clarendon, Windsor, 5 Apr. 1869, RA Q 3/104).

advantage which our insular position gives us, and the creation of a second Hanover.[1]

Great Britain's interest in Belgium was a compound of many elements: a diplomatic tradition going back at least to the time of Louis XIV, the guarantee of 1839, family ties, commercial interests, strategic considerations, an obsessive fear of French expansion, Belgian reliance upon her, and, finally, Belgium's geographical position which offered England, even in a period of retrenchment, the apparent means to take naval and military action to implement her interest and fulfil her obligation.[2]

In 1864, England's honour had been tarnished and her prestige lowered as a result of the attack on Denmark. To rectify the policy of 'meddle and muddle' and to satisfy English opinion that had become overwhelmingly averse to continental entanglements, both political parties veered away from the policy of Palmerston and Russell. Europe interpreted British abstention from the Continent as a sign of weakness, and a cautious policy instead of raising England's worth in the eyes of others lowered it. But to have cast aside at this moment what Europe had long been led to believe was a vital interest would have resulted in an ignominy far worse than that courted in 1864. Most of whatever prestige Britain had retained was tied up with Belgium, and constant concern and anxiety about Belgium was in large part an English reaction to what was expected of her, and what she expected of herself. In the decade before the war of 1870 the strategic and commercial importance of Belgium,[3] however valid, was accepted by England as an act of faith. The Belgian railroads affair challenged England's vision of herself and her importance in Europe.

[1] Stanley to Disraeli, private, 1 Oct. 1868, Stan. Pap., Disraeli. Stanley seemed more aware of England's commercial interest in Belgium (Apponyi to Beust, 30 Apr. 1867, *HHSA*, England, VIII/75 no. 33c, Temperley and Penson, p. 310).

[2] When the Franco-Prussian war began, Gladstone wrote to Cardwell that 'what I should like is to study the means of sending 20,000 men to Antwerp' (Gladstone to Cardwell, 16 July 1870, Morley, i. 339).

[3] Approximately one-third of all Belgium's trade was with France (Lumley to Clarendon, Brussels, 12 Dec. 1868, PRO FO 10/287, no. 5, commercial). Bernstorff believed that England's interest in Belgium was commercial and strategic, particularly the latter, as he felt that Britain would interpret a French fortress at Antwerp as a 'pistol pointed at the heart of England'. Nevertheless the Prussian ambassador doubted whether England would go to war to defend Belgium and was almost certain that she would not if France took Belgium with Belgium's consent (Bernstorff to Bismarck, secret, 18 Feb. 1867, *APP* viii. 403–7).

A Commercial Dispute

In January 1868 a French railway, the Compagnie de l'Est, obtained from a privately owned company in Luxemburg, the Compagnie Guillaume-Luxembourg, the right to operate the latter's lines for a period of forty-five years.[1] It gave the French concern, which was financially backed by the French Government, control of a railroad which ran from Basle to the city of Luxemburg and then into Belgium to the outskirts of Liège.

Early in 1868 two Belgian railroads, which had received charters from the Belgian Government, the Grand Luxembourg company and the Liégeois–Limbourgeois company, were heavily in debt.[2] In October 1868 both Belgian lines opened negotiations for cession to the Compagnie de l'Est. The month before, Leopold, anxious about prospects of a customs union with France and the appointment of La Guéronnière as minister to Brussels,[3] wrote to Victoria. She showed the letter to Stanley, who was annoyed at what he considered to be the unreasonable anxiety of the king and his Government.

What I have always told the Belgian government on the question of a commercial union is, that if it should be proposed to them they have the clearest right to refuse, and that then if any attempt should be made to use pressure to induce them to reconsider their decision, it will be time for them to appeal to us.

What they want is, that we should interfere to prevent any overture of the kind being made, so as to save them from incurring the responsibility of a refusal.

I do not think the request reasonable.[4]

The Liège–Limburg line, which was not contiguous with the track of the French company, applied for control of a state-owned line to effect a junction between the two. The Belgian Government refused this application, and yet the Liège–

---

[1] Stanley was not disposed to interfere in what he considered to be a convention of a commercial nature (Stanley to Lyons, confidential, 20 June 1868, PRO FO 27/1697, no. 31).

[2] The early phases of these negotiations are outlined in two letters: Lumley to Clarendon, Brussels, 12 Mar. 1869, PRO FO 146/1383, no. 100; Clarendon to Lyons, confidential, 16 Mar. 1869, PRO FO 146/1383, no. 274. One should also consult: Paul Hymans, Frère-Orban (Brussels, 1905); Emile Banning, *Les Origines et les phases de la neutralité belge* (Brussels, 1927); R. Grenu, *La Question belge dans la politique européenne de 1866 à 1870* (Paris, 1931).

[3] The new French ambassador was an outspoken advocate of French absorption of Belgium.   [4] Stanley to Disraeli, private, 25 Sept. 1868, Stan. Pap., Disraeli.

Limburg company on 22 December petitioned the Government for approval to cede the working of its line to the Compagnie de l'Est. Shortly after this, the Belgian railroad submitted to its shareholders a contract made with the French railway. On 10 February 1869, the Belgian Government informed the Liège–Limburg company that consent to this contract was denied.[1]

The Grand Luxembourg line was contiguous with the French railroad. In April 1868, according to Fenton who was a director of the Grand Luxembourg, overtures made to the Belgian Government to purchase the line were ignored. On 1 November Tesch, another of the railway's directors, informed Frère-Orban, the Belgian first minister, that his company hoped to find a purchaser in the Compagnie de l'Est. The Government, which had previously considered purchasing the line, appointed a committee to determine with the officers of the company a price at which the Government might buy. But on 5 December the Grand Luxembourg line informed Jamar, the Belgian minister of public works, that unless the Government were prepared to settle immediately a convention would be signed on 7 December with the Compagnie de l'Est. Jamar at once replied that the Government would never ratify this convention. On 8 December a contract, subject to the approval of the two companies, was signed between the two railways. Three days later Jamar, in answer to a question in the Belgian lower house, stated that no cession was possible without government authorization and this authorization would never be given.[2]

[1] According to Belgian law no concession connected with routes or means of communication could be granted without government approval. This law, in force since 1829, prohibited the transference of concessions from one party to another without previous governmental permission. A law of 1864 stated that the Liège–Limburg line may cede its line with governmental approval. In the charter of the Grand Luxembourg company of 1846, it was stated that cession or fusion of the line required governmental consent (Lumley to Clarendon, Brussels, 12 Mar. 1869, PRO FO 146/1383, no. 100). A brief but excellent discussion of the railroad crisis is contained in G. A. Craig, 'Great Britain and the Belgian Railways Dispute of 1869', American Historical Review, l (no. 4, 1945), 738–61. D.H. Thomas has used the Lumley papers in his short but interesting 'English Investors and the Franco-Belgian Railway Crisis of 1869', The Historian, xxvi (no. 2, 1964), 228–243.

[2] Lumley to Clarendon, 12 Dec. 1868, PRO FO 146/1345, no. 1, commercial. The Grand Luxembourg company claimed that a clause barring cession or fusion was not in their contract with the government (Clarendon to Lyons, confidential, 16 Mar. 1869, PRO FO 146/1383, no. 274).

The Belgian Government warned the Compagnie de l'Est that the contracts signed with the Belgian companies would never be ratified by Brussels. Daviste, president of the French line, assured Beyens, the Belgian minister in Paris, that the convention signed on 8 December would in consequence be dropped as it had not yet been submitted to the administrative board of the French company. It was not, however, dropped and the Compagnie de l'Est ratified the convention on 30 January 1869.

It is difficult to conceive how the French Compagnie de l'Est could have acted in defiance of Brussels without the financial and political support of its own government.[1] The French Government stood to gain if the contemplated arrangement took effect. If the French company managed to obtain the two Belgian lines, these, together with the already acquired Luxemburg railroad, would give France a railway network extending from Switzerland through Luxemburg to Brussels in one direction, and from Luxemburg through Liège into Holland in the other. Such a network would have been invaluable in a war with Prussia, and also a step leading to the annexation of Belgium. There were more immediate economic advantages to be derived, too. Districts in north-east France and the area around Liège and Charleroi in Belgium were competitors in iron production. If a French railway served both it is unlikely that the French iron-masters would have suffered.[2]

Clarendon, who had replaced Stanley, was obviously annoyed when on 16 January Dujardin, the Belgian minister, officially communicated the railroad imbroglio and alluded to the 'numerous' British shareholders in the Grand Luxemburg company who intended to petition for the intervention of the British Government. Clarendon criticized the lack of initiative taken by Brussels in preventing the proposed arrangements and advised the Belgian government to 'stop . . . the sale, not by a veto, but by a purchase of the railway'.[3] Frère-Orban replied

[1] Professor Craig emphasizes the roles played by La Guéronnière and Rouher in this (Craig, pp. 745–6).

[2] Clarendon to Lyons, confidential, 16 Mar. 1869, PRO FO 146/1383, no. 274; Lumley to Clarendon, confidential, 21 Mar. 1869, ibid., no. 120; same to same, confidential, 26 Mar. 1869, ibid., 1384, no. 129.

[3] Clarendon to Lumley, 16 Jan. 1869, PRO FO 146/1378, no. 6. Two days before this the foreign secretary had been warned by the queen that the French

that his Government was attempting to do just that, but that caution was necessary or every railroad company in the country would use the threat of selling out to a foreign concern to force the Belgian Government to purchase its line.[1]

In January the French Government had not yet shown its hand and the affair still appeared to be primarily a commercial matter. On 30 January Lumley, the British ambassador to Belgium, requested a month's leave of absence. Clarendon seemed more annoyed by the business than alarmed and Gladstone felt that any serious consequences could be avoided:

A war between France & Germany would be sad, but the compulsory or fraudulent extinction by annexation of the free state of Belgium would be worse. I cannot however believe that this can be effected by force & I hope we may assume that the public opinion of Belgium will remain true to itself.[2]

The queen was most anxious of all,[3] and in retrospect the most realistic, for what had been begun as a commercial arrangement would now become much more serious.

Government 'might seek to obtain a footing in Belgium' by means of a railway purchase (Grey to Clarendon, private, Osborne, 14 Jan. 1869, RA Q 2/103).
[1] Lumley to Clarendon, confidential, Brussels, 23 Jan. 1869, PRO FO 10/292, no. 22.
[2] Gladstone to Clarendon, 30 Jan. 1869, Glad. Pap. ccccli, letter-book 1866–9.
[3] Grey to Clarendon, Osborne, 14 Jan. 1869, Lord Newton, *Lord Lyons* (London, 1913), pp. 211–12.

VII

THE BELGIAN RAILWAYS

DESPITE the previously stated objections of the Belgian government, the Grand Luxembourg and the Compagnie de l'Est continued to negotiate. A final contract between the two companies was signed on 30 January. The defiant conduct of the Grand Luxembourg line was hardly disguised by the fact that the contract reserved the right of government approval.[1] The grandiose designs of the French railroad became evident. A contract was made with the other Belgian line, the Liège–Limburg, and still another which gave the Compagnie de l'Est half control of the Rotterdam railway station. On 6 February the Belgian Cabinet submitted to the legislature a new railroad bill, the purpose of which was to prohibit the leasing and cession of railways without government sanction, a right which Brussels had claimed they already possessed.[2] The bill became law on 25 February. The Government was still ready to take over the Grand Luxembourg, although not on such favourable terms as offered by the Compagnie de l'Est.[3]

The haste with which the Belgian law was passed reflected the fact that the French Government was considering a financial guarantee to support the Compagnie de l'Est in its attempted expansion.[4] La Valette, who had replaced Moustier, spoke to Beyens, the Belgian ambassador at Paris. The foreign minister expressed dismay at the 'offensive' jealousy and distrust of France on the part of Belgium, which he added was

[1] Lumley to Clarendon, confidential, Brussels, 5 Feb. 1869, PRO FO 146/1379, no. 40.

[2] Lumley to Clarendon, Brussels, 7 Feb. 1869, PRO FO 146/1379, no. 41; same to same, confidential, 10 Feb. 1869, ibid., no. 47.

[3] Clarendon to Lyons, confidential, 16 Mar. 1869, PRO FO 146/1383, no. 274; Lumley to Clarendon, confidential, Brussels, 12 Feb. 1869, PRO FO 146/1379, no. 52.

[4] First official French concern occurred in reaction to Jamar's speech in the Belgian Legislature on 13 December (La Guéronnière to Moustier, telegram, 13 Dec. 1868, *Orig.* xxii. 355).

unwarranted.[1] He told Lyons that he felt that Bismarck had instigated the whole question and that Belgium 'had been guilty of a very *mauvais procédé* towards Fr'.[2] La Valette went further by declaring 'it to be quite impossible that any friendship could hereafter exist between the Fr Govt & the present Belgian Ministry'.[3] Clarendon was as suspicious of France as the Belgian government:

I am getting rather anxious about the Belgian railway business which is an audacious attempt on the part of the French govt to incorporate Belgium. It is absurd for La V[alette] to say or rather complain that the objections raised by Belgium shew mistrust of France—what would the French govt and public say if the Ligne du Nord was bought at a ruinously high price by the Chatham and Dover Comp[anie]s and that English officials were to be in charge of the line up to the walls of Paris? . . . The Queen is very uneasy about the designs of France on Belgium.[4]

The French press following the Government's lead had complained with great vituperativeness, advocating the annexation of Belgium because that small country was in league with Prussia.[5] Clarendon instructed Lyons to state confidentially to La Valette that Belgium was not acting at Prussia's behest and 'if the relations between France and Prussia were on a better footing, the course that the Belgium government has taken . . . would [not] have produced the slightest impression at Paris'.[6] Privately the foreign secretary was disgusted with the Belgian Government:

The Belgian govt has been 1st neglectful—then stingy and lastly clumsy, but they *are in the right* and public opinion, out of France, will assuredly be on their side.

The extraordinary and uncalled for violence of the French papers is not understood here, and Delane who has just been here says that

[1] Lyons to Clarendon, very confidential, 12 Feb. 1869, PRO FO 27/1748, no. 175; La Valette to La Guéronnière, telegram, 12 Feb. 1869, *Orig.* xxiii. 237–8.
[2] Lyons to Clarendon, 16 Feb. 1869, Newton, pp. 213–14.   [3] Ibid.
[4] Clarendon to Lyons, private, 16 Feb. 1869, Clar. MSS. C 148.
[5] Lyons to Clarendon, 16 Feb. 1869, PRO FO 27/1748, no. 189.
[6] Clarendon to Lyons, confidential, 18 Feb. 1869, PRO FO 27/1739, no. 195. Clarendon spoke to La Tour in the same sense, acquitting Belgium of any connexion with Prussia over the railroads (La Tour to La Valette, confidential, 18 Feb. 1869, *Orig.* xxiii. 278–9). Clarendon was assured on this point by Loftus (Loftus to Clarendon, confidential, Berlin, 20 Feb. 1869, PRO FO 64/660, no. 100). La Tour to La Valette, London, confidential, 18 Feb. 1869, *Orig.* xxiii, 278–80.

alarm is spreading, for it is of course thought that we can't shirk our treaty obligations to stand by Belgium.[1]

Gladstone, who referred to a French annexation of Belgium as 'a terrible spectre', believed it was necessary 'to have France . . . with strong neighbours' to guard 'against this demon of ambition & aggression which seems still to linger within her'.[2] French quickness to take offence at Belgium's passing a new railroad law was a corollary of Franco-Prussian tension.[3] Frustration, rebuff, and embarrassment since 1863 had made Napoleon and his ministers so susceptible to insult that any check to French plans was seen as a piece of Bismarckian intrigue. Such was French feeling in 1867 when the Roman question arose again due to Mentana. Such was the feeling in 1869 during the Belgian railways controversy. So would it be on 3 July 1870.

On 19 February 1869 Napoleon wrote to Marshal Niel of the possibility of a French war on Belgium. Since the letter contains no reference to England, Professor Craig has interpreted it as an indication 'of the complete disregard in which England was held at this time'.[4] Craig's own translation of the letter indicates another possible interpretation.

The Belgian Government is demonstrating its illwill toward France, and public opinion is convinced, rightly or wrongly, that Belgium would not be so arrogant were not Prussia behind her. In these circumstances to be conciliatory and to retreat in the face of a proceeding which injures us would be to surrender, before the face of Europe, all our legitimate influence. Must war arise out of this conflict? I do not know. But it is necessary to act as if it will arise.[5]

Napoleon did not want a war with Belgium, but he did desire for present economic[6] and possible future political reasons the

---

[1] Clarendon to Lyons, private, 18 Feb. 1869, Clar. Pap. C 148.

[2] Gladstone to Clarendon, 18 Feb. 1869, Glad. MSS. ccccli, letter-book 1866-9; Gladstone to Clarendon, private, 28 Feb. 1869, Clar. Pap. C 497.

[3] In 1854 and 1856 the Belgian Government refused its permission to arrangements concluded by a French railway, the Compagnie du Nord (Lumley to Clarendon, 20 Feb. 1869, PRO FO 10/293, no. 61).

[4] Craig, p. 747. Professor Craig's source for the letter is E. Ollivier, L'Empire libéral (Paris, 1895), xi. 375. Apparently Drouyn was concerned about English feelings, for he warned Napoleon of the British reaction to any annexation of Belgium (Drouyn to Napoleon, 5 Apr. 1869, Orig. xxiv. 137-9).

[5] Craig, p. 747.

[6] Lumley to Clarendon, Brussels, 20 Feb. 1869, PRO FO 146/1380, no. 62; same to same, confidential, 23 Feb. 1869, ibid., no. 69.

acceptance of the railway contracts by the Belgian Government. He hoped by threatening war to obtain Belgian acquiescence to the expansion of the Compagnie de l'Est. This was one reason why, in his own words, 'it is necessary to act as if it [war] will arise'.[1] The emperor's 'disregard' of England was therefore relative to the fact that British intervention was probable only in war which he himself wished to avoid.

Clarendon was well aware that French anger was not due to the passage of a railway law but to what Paris felt was a public insult. This only increased the foreign secretary's irritation at Belgian maladroitness:

The Belgian government [he wrote] was negligent of what was passing under their noses—then stingy in not buying the Luxembourg railway & at last hasty, because frightened, & they passed a bill in a manner that might have offended people less prone to take offence than the French.[2]

Clarendon was not, however, unaware of Parisian motives.

The French on the other hand wanted to get in the fine end of the wedge & as they cd not annex Belgium they hoped to incorporate the country by means of railway tariffs & officials, but they have been checked & therefore are angry far beyond what they have any just excuse to be. They at last have come down in their pretensions & propose a mixed commission of inquiry as to how the two railways can best serve the interests of the two countries.[3]

Since 1866 rumours of French designs on Belgium had been as numerous as French protestations of innocence concerning them. The passage of the new railroad bill by the Belgian legislature was received as a public accusation in official circles in Paris; feelings of guilt were transformed into proclamations of injury and then into demands for compensation.

The French Government was led to believe that the railway contracts would take effect by the reports they received from their minister in Brussels. La Guéronnière wished the Compagnie de l'Est to proceed at full speed, not only because

[1] Napoleon mentioned the 'possibility of a war against Belgium' to Metternich, perhaps for the effect it would have (La Valette to La Tour, 28 Feb. 1869, *Orig.* xxiii. 282–3).

[2] Clarendon to Bloomfield, private, 23 Feb. 1869, PRO FO 356/33.

[3] Ibid.; Lumley to Clarendon, Brussels, 21 Feb. 1869, PRO FO 146/1380, no. 65. According to Lumley the idea of a mixed commission was La Guéronnière's (Lumley to Clarendon, Brussels, 2 Mar. 1869, PRO FO 10/293, no. 83).

the Grand Luxembourg was bankrupt but also because, as he claimed, there was no clause in the Belgian line's charter necessitating government approval of cession.[1] He did not pay much attention to Jamar's declaration to the legislature that the contracts would never receive government consent. 'It seems to me', he wrote to Paris, 'it depends a little on us whether the conflict is reduced to simple proportions, or whether we give to it a more important character.'[2] La Guéron-nière contended further that some of Jamar's colleagues in the Cabinet disagreed with his statement and that there were strong economic interests in Belgium which supported the railroad contracts, and much more. 'I estimate that in the economic and political conditions in which Belgium finds herself, there is today an excellent opportunity for France to master the passions and mistrust which repel her [France], by taking for allies the interests which call her.'[3] When on 30 January the final railroad contracts were signed, La Guéronnière hoped 'that the inevitable resistance of the government would find a decisive counterweight in the powerful league of interests.'[4]

The French Government maintained its air of injured innocence over the passing of the railway law. La Valette instructed La Guéronnière to inform Brussels that no one contested Belgium's right to pass such a law but that the manner in which it was passed was abrupt and unfriendly.[5] The ambassador had anticipated his orders by telling Frère-Orban that France had been challenged and she must not appear to have been wounded.[6]

By 23 February the Belgian Government seemed more disposed to recognize the wounded feelings of France. Frère-Orban still refused to give way on the cession of the Grand Luxembourg,

[1] La Guéronnière to Moustier, Brussels, 17 Dec. 1868, *Orig.* xxii. 376–80.

[2] Ibid. The French ambassador pointed out that the directors of the Belgian railway wished to sell despite the opposition of the Belgian Government (La Guéronnière to La Valette, Brussels, telegram, 30 Dec. 1868, *Orig.* xxii. 99).

[3] La Guéronnière to La Valette, Brussels, 3 Jan. 1869, *Orig.* xxiii. 112–14.

[4] La Guéronnière to La Valette, Brussels, 31 Jan. 1869, ibid., pp. 202–3.

[5] La Valette to La Guéronnière, 17 Feb. 1869, *Orig.* xxiii. 267–71.

[6] La Guéronnière to La Valette, Brussels, 16 Feb. 1869, ibid., pp. 253–71. Metternich, who was on close terms with Napoleon, assumed that he judged it useful for the French Government to remain in the background in the railroad negotiations, as their successful culmination would have given France an overwhelming influence in Belgium (Metternich to Beust, confidential, Paris, 19 Feb. 1869, ibid., pp. 410–11).

but proposed to negotiate a service convention which would give to the French railroad some of the advantages it would have gained had the contract for cession been accepted.[1] On the following day Van der Stichelen, the Belgian foreign minister, expanded on Frère-Orban's suggestion. He agreed to a mixed commission of three French and three Belgian delegates to negotiate the means of transport which would benefit the industry and commerce of both countries.[2] Clarendon, who favoured the mixed commission, advised Belgium to be moderate and La Valette felt that his advice contributed to the more conciliatory spirit in Brussels.[3]

However, the Belgian Government still refused to examine the contract between the two railroad companies, which according to La Valette was the purpose of the mixed commission.[4] Failing agreement, rumours of war again circulated in Paris and Brussels.[5] Lyons observed that 'the most disquieting sign for the future is the extraordinary irritability of the French with regard to Prussia'.[6] Clarendon was concerned lest Belgium aggravate that 'irritability'.

Her Majesty's Government [Clarendon wrote] cannot too earnestly recommend the government of Belgium to abstain from taking any step or holding any language indicating apprehension on its part of a military movement against Belgium on the part of France. . . . Her Majesty's Government considers it of the utmost importance that Belgium should show no distrust of French intentions whatever she may feel.[7]

The foreign secretary wrote privately to Lyons that he had 'not hesitated to advise the B[elgian] govt. to meet the wishes of the Fr. govt. as far as possible . . . [and to] make this known to M. de La V[alette]'.[8]

[1] La Guéronnière to La Valette, Brussels, telegram, 23 Feb. 1869, ibid., p. 294.
[2] La Guéronnière to La Valette, Brussels, telegram, 24 Feb. 1869, ibid., p. 298; same to same, 24 Feb. 1869, ibid., pp. 299–306.
[3] Clarendon to Lyons, confidential, 24 Feb. 1869, PRO FO 146/1380, no. 214; Lumley to Clarendon, confidential, Brussels, 27 Feb. 1869, PRO FO 10/293, no. 76.
[4] Lyons to Clarendon, confidential, Paris, 4 Mar. 1869, PRO FO 27/1749, no. 248.
[5] Lyons to Clarendon, very confidential, Paris, 2 Mar. 1869, PRO FO 27/1749, no. 236; Clarendon to Lyons, telegram, 2 Mar. 1869, PRO FO 146/1383, no. 260.
[6] Lyons to Clarendon, ibid.
[7] Clarendon to Lumley, telegram, 2 Mar. 1869, PRO FO 146/1383, no. 260.
[8] Clarendon to Lyons, private, 2 Mar. 1869, Clar. Pap. C 148.

It would appear that Gladstone suspected that Clarendon was ready to write off Belgium:

I am sure that if it [Belgium] was absorbed by France the thing would produce a most painful impression here. I don't mean to say that the misunderstanding would be of a hostile character, but there would no longer exist the confidence which is now felt in the Empr.[1]

It would be a misfortune if France could, on account of your tone, suppose either that you sympathised with or understood her proposals in the matter, or that the independence of Belgium was anything else than an object of the first interest to the mind of the British people.[2]

Yet the prime minister himself was no more willing to intimate the use of force to defend Belgium than was his foreign secretary.[3] Clarendon wished to avoid the mistake of Palmerston and Russell in 1864, and Lyons at Paris was conscious of his feelings.

I am glad to see that our papers have not as yet taken up the matter violently. I am terribly afraid of their making the mess they did in the Danish question—leading the small powers to think that public opinion in England wd do wonders for it, and then leaving it to declare itself betrayed because the people of England would not go to war for it.[4]

In Paris it was 'doubted whether, if Prussia connived at spoliation [of Belgium], England would be willing, or indeed able, to make any effectual resistance to it'.[5] It was doubted in London also and Clarendon continued in his efforts to prevent the Government in Brussels from expecting too much. He wrote to Lumley:

You must do all in your power (tho not as being instructed to that effect) to abate any such reliance [of Belgium on England]. . . . In the present state of public opinion here I apprehend that the govt would not be allowed to go single handed into a defence of treaty obligations while other guarantors stood aloof. Nor have we the

---

[1] Ibid. Clarendon's moderation reflected Lyons's opinion that the British people 'were too full of the Irish Church Bill to think of foreign politics' (Lyons to Bloomfield, Paris, private, 30 June 1869, Lyons Pap. RC 2).
[2] Gladstone to Clarendon, 3 Mar. 1869, Glad. MSS. ccccli, letter-book 1866–9.
[3] Ibid. 'Mr. Gladstone seemed averse to any language that would bind us to act . . . to defend the independence of Belgium' (Grey to Victoria, 2 Mar. 1869, RA Q 2/59).
[4] Lyons to Clarendon, private, Paris, 4 Mar. 1869, Lyons Pap. RC 2.
[5] Lyons to Clarendon, very confidential, Paris, 4 Mar. 1869, PRO FO 27/1749, no. 249.

means even if we had the will to go to war with France and as that
must be as well known to the Belgian govt as to ourselves it should
make them chary of relying upon our aid.[1]

On 6 March Clarendon learned from Lumley that the French
minister at Brussels would be recalled unless Belgium accepted
France's ideas for the mixed commission.[2] In his dispatches to
Lyons and Lumley, the foreign secretary considered the views
of the Cabinet and followed the advice of Gladstone.[3]

It is hard to perceive how the action of the Belgian government
can be viewed as a deliberate affront to the French government.
[There may be] ground for a claim for damages.

But to magnify a mere commercial claim, however originating,
into a cause of offence between government and government, is
surely to invest it with a degree of importance which is hardly compatible with its character.

The question then really turns upon the verification of any loss
which the French company may allege that it has sustained, and that
question it seems to Her Majesty's Government might well be solved
without importing into the discussion of it the extraneous question
of national dignity.[4]

Lyons was to speak to La Valette on the subject and request
information on 'the exact nature of the affront'.[5] If La Valette
was still opposed to modifying his country's demands, Lyons
was to suggest 'the good offices of some third state', as stipulated
by the mediatorial clause of the Paris Treaty of 1856.[6] Lumley
at Brussels was instructed to tell Frère-Orban that England
'cannot too strongly recommend the employment of all means
consistent with national honour and independence to calm
the feelings which are entertained by the Imperial Govt'.[7]
The relative ineffectiveness of unofficial British mediation was
due to Clarendon's desire to avoid involvement even on behalf

---

[1] Clarendon to Lumley, private, 6 Mar. 1869, Clar. Pap. C 475.

[2] Lumley to Clarendon, Brussels, telegram, 6 Mar. 1869, PRO FO 10/293.

[3] The prime minister referred 'to a solution by means of "good offices"', and
stressed the 'pecuniary' rather than the 'political question' (Gladstone to Hammond, 6 Mar. 1869, Glad. MSS. ccccli, letter-book 1866-9).

[4] Clarendon to Lyons, confidential, 6 Mar. 1869, PRO FO 27/1740, no. 240.

[5] Ibid.

[6] Ibid., no. 241. Lyons did not make this suggestion, as he detected a more
conciliatory attitude on the part of La Valette (Lyons to Clarendon, very confidential, Paris, 8 Mar. 1869, PRO FO 27/1750, no. 268).

[7] Clarendon to Lumley, confidential, 6 Mar. 1869, PRO FO 146/1382, no. 249.

of Belgium.[1] His criticism of Belgian maladroitness and of French vanity led both sides to assume that England recognized the righteousness of their causes. Yet the Cabinet and the foreign secretary would not publicly state their real convictions, for to do so might have led to an English war with France. Clarendon, who had continually assured France that Prussia was not at all implicated in the affair, now seemed to imply to La Tour that she was not unwilling to interfere. He told him that 'it was to be feared that Prussia would draw . . . encouragement to intervene'.[2] While this view was taking effect in Paris, Clarendon was startled by a telegram from Brussels. Lumley wired that 'the King is confident that Your Lordship will let him know whether and when you think he should commence military preparations'.[3] The foreign secretary wired back that any war preparations were premature.[4] The prime minister was of the same feeling.

> Genl Grey is himself inclined to be valiant on the subject of fighting even alone for Belgium but I do not see how it is safe to go beyond making it known that the day when this nation seriously suspects France of meaning ill to Belgian independence will be the last day of friendship with that country.[5]

By the second week in March both France and Belgium were

[1] Part of the difficulty was Lumley's unconcealed suspicion of French intentions, which must have caused some Belgian intransigence toward France (Lumley to Clarendon, most confidential, 13 Mar. 1869, PRO FO 10/293, no. 101).

[2] La Tour to La Valette, confidential, London, 7 Mar. 1869, *Orig.* xxiii. 352–4. Clarendon wrote privately to Bloomfield that Belgium would bring 'grists to the Prussian mill' (Clarendon to Bloomfield, private, 23 Mar. 1869, PRO FO 356/33). Bismarck was willing to assist England in order to preserve Belgium but only if Britain would make an alliance with Prussia against France, an alliance the scope of which would not be restricted to Belgium. Bismarck maintained that England had more interest in preserving and protecting north Germany than Belgium, but that in present circumstances Berlin could not depend on London. This letter was never sent to Bernstorff (Bismarck to Bernstorff, Berlin 16 Mar. 1869, *GW* vi B, no. 1344). Bismarck did tell Bernstorff that Prussia's policy was presently one of wait and see and that initiative must come from the English side rather than the Prussian (Bismarck to Bernstorff, confidential, Berlin, 21 Mar. 1869, ibid., no. 1351). Bismarck probably hoped that Britain would become embroiled with France so that he could then have his alliance with England on his own terms.

[3] Lumley to Clarendon, telegram, 9 Mar. 1869, PRO FO 10/293.

[4] Clarendon to Lumley, telegram, 9 Mar. 1869, PRO FO 10/291. Three days later Clarendon impressed upon Lumley that it was of the 'utmost importance that Belgium should show no distrust of French intentions whatever she may feel' (Clarendon to Lumley, telegram, 12 Mar. 1869, PRO FO 10/291, no. 38).

[5] Gladstone to Clarendon, private, 9 Mar. 1869, Clar. Pap. C 497; ibid., Glad. MSS. ccccli, letter-book 1866–9.

wavering in the direction of concession and compromise. Brussels agreed to a mixed commission to consider everything except the already signed railroad contracts, which was what the French were most anxious to discuss.[1] La Valette was running back and forth to Napoleon, who appears to have been influenced by English feelings.[2] Clarendon was not convinced, however, that Napoleon meant no harm to Belgium. He told Lyons that if Prussia in accordance with the treaty of 1839 aided Belgium and asked England 'to do the same, I believe that the call would be responded to because the Engl[ish] people would think that they couldn't hold aloof without dishonour'.[3]

On 14 March 1869 La Valette telegraphed to La Guéronnière that the French Government could not compromise on an examination of the railway contracts which Belgium still hesitated to accept categorically.[4] The next day, before Frère-Orban saw La Guéronnière, Lumley informed the Belgian minister as instructed that Britain advised the Belgian Government to accept France's position on the subjects to be discussed by the mixed commission, since she was not herself bound to ratify the contracts.[5] La Valette, informed of Clarendon's advice by La Tour, felt strengthened in his efforts to compel Brussels to give way.[6] On the sixteenth, the Belgian Government finally accepted

[1] La Tour to Siméon, Paris, 12 Mar. 1869, *Orig.* xxiv. 10–15. The queen had written privately to the King of Belgium advising him to accept the commission (Grey to King of Belgium, Windsor, 7 Mar. 1869, RA Q 2/171).

[2] Lyons to Clarendon, private, 11 Mar. 1869, Clar. Pap. RC 2. 'The fear [on the part of Napoleon and La Valette] of being ill with us acts as a restraint the more from being left a little vague. If we pull the string tight, it will snap' (ibid.).

[3] Clarendon to Lyons, private, 13 Mar. 1869, Clar. Pap. C 148. This in part contradicts the foreign secretary's words to Lumley on 6 March, where he claimed that the Government 'would not be allowed' to defend 'single-handed' the treaty of 1839 if the 'other guarantors stood aloof' (Clarendon to Lumley, private, 6 Mar. 1869, Clar. Pap. C 475). It is difficult to estimate exactly what Clarendon really did believe. His words to Lyons were obviously to frustrate French aggression toward Belgium, while his words to Lumley were meant to moderate Brussels so as not to provoke France. The probability is that Clarendon's personal concern to avoid fighting for Belgium was being influenced by court pressure and the possibility of an ally in Prussia, although he did not trust Bismarck in the slightest degree.

[4] La Valette to La Guéronnière, Paris, telegram, 14 Mar. 1869, *Orig.* xxiv. 25; La Guéronnière to La Valette, Brussels, telegram, 14 Mar. 1869, ibid., p. 25.

[5] Lumley to Clarendon, most confidential, 15 Mar. 1869, PRO FO 10/294, no. 107; ibid. 146/1383, no. 107.

[6] La Valette to La Guéronnière, Paris, telegram, 15 Mar. 1869, *Orig.* xxiv. 32; La Guéronnière to La Valette, Brussels, telegram, 15 Mar. 1869, ibid., pp. 32–33.

the French proposal.¹ La Guéronnière attributed this to British advice, and Frère-Orban justified his consent by reference to the same counsels.² The desire of Victoria and Grey to warn France off Belgium, and Clarendon's own growing conviction 'that the Empr. has evil designs upon Belgium and that the railway is a mere pretext',³ resulted in a dispatch to Lyons. The foreign secretary pointed out⁴ that a French attack on Belgium would probably result in a European war and 'Her Majesty's Government would lament the interruption of those cordial relations with France'.⁵ The use to be made of the dispatch was left to Lyons's judgement.

The mode of dealing with that dispatch may be delicate and difficult and we therefore leave the decision on that point to your discretion. You can either read it, or tell the substance of it at once to M. de La Valette, or you may keep it for a short time and until some crisis arrives when it could best be turned to account.⁶

The ambassador delayed communicating the dispatch in order to suggest an alteration which he thought would make it more effective.⁷ Clarendon agreed, after learning of the Franco-Belgian agreement of the day before, that the time had not yet come to deliver it;⁸ he was also inclined to hold it back because it might be useful if things actually came to war.

If the Empr. chooses to quarrel with Belgium and we are to be dragged in we must be able to shew that nothing on our part has been neglected to avert the calamity of the war that might ensue and in which we might by the force of circ[umstanc]es be compelled to take part.⁹

---

¹ La Guéronnière to La Valette, Brussels, telegram, 16 Mar. 1869, ibid., pp. 42–43.

² La Guéronnière to La Valette, Brussels, confidential, 16 Mar. 1869, ibid., pp. 44–46; Lumley to Clarendon, Brussels, most confidential, telegram, 16 Mar. 1869, PRO FO 10/294. Frère-Orban did stipulate in his acceptance that questions to be discussed by the commission should be settled before it met (Lumley to Clarendon, secret, 16 Mar. 1869, PRO FO 146/1383, no. 109).

³ Clarendon to Lyons, private, 13 Mar. 1869, Clar. MSS. C 148.

⁴ Gladstone helped write the dispatch (Gladstone to Clarendon, 13 Mar. 1869, Glad. MSS. ccccli, letter-book 1866–9).

⁵ Clarendon to Lyons, 16 Mar. 1869, PRO FO 27/1740, no. 286.

⁶ Clarendon to Lyons, private, 16 Mar. 1869, Clar. Pap. C 148. Notice the foreign secretary's use of the word 'we' to indicate Cabinet responsibility.

⁷ Lyons to Clarendon, Paris, 17 Mar. 1869, PRO FO 27/1750, no. 297.

⁸ Clarendon to Lyons, 18 Mar. 1869, PRO FO 27/1740, no. 287.

⁹ Clarendon to Lyons, private, House of Lords, 18 Mar. 1869, Clar. Pap. C 148.

It was to prevent war feeling arising that Clarendon had muzzled *The Times* and the *Daily Telegraph*.[1] He also instructed Lyons to 'keep telling M. de L. [a Valette] how anxious we all are, notwithstanding the outward appearance of an improved state of things'.[2]

On the first day of April Frère-Orban arrived at Paris to arrange preliminaries for the mixed commission. La Valette at once spoke to him of concluding arrangements between the Grand Luxembourg and the Compagnie de l'Est.[3] On 3 April the Belgian first minister saw Napoleon, who seemed to be ignorant of the details of the railway dispute.[4] Rouher, even more than La Valette, pressed for the amalgamation of the two railroads when he talked with Frère-Orban.[5] On the sixth the Belgian statesman had a satisfactory and agreeable conference with La Valette, Rouher, and Gressier, the minister of public works.[6] It appeared that agreement would be reached without the necessity for a mixed commission. A week later, however, Frère-Orban's suggestions were meeting with a cool reception in Paris.[7] Since the first week in March La Valette had been conscious of Britain's displeasure with France. He assured Lyons that even if Frère-Orban returned to Brussels without an arrangement, the French Government would content itself with nothing 'more serious' than economic reprisals.[8] Lyons replied that the 'mere' breaking off of the negotiations would produce 'in England . . . pain and alarm'.[9] Despite these words Franco-Belgian discussions reached an impasse with no sign of resolution.[10]

---

[1] Clarendon to Lyons, private, 20 Mar. 1869, Clar. Pap. C 148. According to the Belgian minister in London, the British press was more Belgian than the Cabinet, and pushed that body into recognizing one of the traditional interests of England (Van Praet to Frère-Orban, 5 Apr. 1869, P. Hymans, *Frère-Orban* [Brussels, 1905], ii. 245).

[2] Same to same, private, 22 Mar. 1869, ibid.

[3] Lyons to Clarendon, confidential, Paris, 2 Apr. 1869, PRO FO 27/1751, no. 345; Lumley to Clarendon, confidential, Brussels, 4 Apr. 1869, PRO FO 146/1385, no. 143.

[4] Lyons to Clarendon, Paris, 6 Apr. 1869, PRO FO 27/1751, no. 360.   [5] Ibid.

[6] Lyons to Clarendon, confidential, Paris, 8 Apr. 1869, PRO FO 27/1752, no. 378; Lumley to Clarendon, confidential, Brussels, 9 Apr. 1869, PRO FO 146/1385, no. 148.

[7] Lyons to Clarendon, confidential, Paris, 13 Apr. 1869, PRO FO 27/1752, no. 404.   [8] Ibid.   [9] Ibid.

[10] Lyons to Clarendon, Paris, telegram, 17 Apr. 1869, PRO FO 27/1753, no. 430; same to same, telegram, 18 Apr. 1869, ibid., no. 432.

The queen took this occasion to point out to Clarendon that 'if it were generally understood that we could not any longer be relied upon, except for moral support, E[ngland] would soon lose her position in Europe'.[1] The foreign secretary justified his reticence and caution:

> The object of the Belgian & Portuguese Govts. is to hold out as a menace to their real or supposed enemies that the whole material force of E[ngland] is at their disposal; the object of Lord Clarendon is to preserve an entire freedom of action for your Majesty's Govt.

It would seem more honourable & dignified on the part of E[ngland] not to menace if she is not sure of being able to strike, & not to promise more than she may be able to perform; though at the same time neither saying nor doing anything to warrant the supposition that on a real necessity arising, E[ngland] would shrink from any obligation that she might be rightfully called upon to perform.

In every quarrel there are at least 2 principals, & that we are bound to consider not only the deterring effect which menace would have on one of them, but also the stimulating effect it would be at least as likely to produce on the other.[2]

The queen, while generally in agreement with Clarendon's letter, stuck to her guns. She alluded to 'a disposition on the Continent to believe that E[ngland] is not to be moved, either by interest, or the obligation of Treaties, into giving more than moral support in any complications that may arise'. Victoria concluded that England should avoid the use of threats but never the 'obligation of Treaties, wherever her honour or her interest may call upon her to do so'.[3] Gladstone supported the foreign secretary:

> I think your letter will do good [he wrote to Clarendon]—The Queen is essentially fair: her prejudices are I think never original, always imbibed: & her good sense & equity enable her to overcome them. It did not occur to me until after I had written to you yesterday,

---

[1] Victoria to Clarendon, 15 Apr. 1869, *QVL*, 2nd ser., i. 589.
[2] Clarendon to Victoria, 16 Apr. 1869, ibid., pp. 589–91. In this dispatch Clarendon repeated the advice of Gladstone, in part almost word for word. The prime minister wrote to the foreign secretary: 'I need not say I quite agree with you about this fancy which the Queen has taken about the salutary effect to be produced by British threats in anticipation. . . . I think H.M. should consider . . . that you are bound to consider not only the deterring effect which it is assumed your menaces would have on one, but the stimulating effect it would be at least as likely to produce on the other' (Gladstone to Clarendon, 16 Apr. 1869, Clar. Pap. C 497).
[3] Victoria to Clarendon, 17 Apr. 1869, *QVL*, 2nd ser., i. 591–2.

but I ought perhaps to have explained what I felt namely a perfect willingness to be trotted out in your rear in support of your doctrine that menace is a bad basis for a system of international communication upon the arrival of difficulty.[1]

When the queen appealed to Gladstone, the prime minister replied at great length. He asserted that England would never turn her back on Europe, but that her power 'should be thriftily used' lest there be an 'exhaustion of her means, or a collapse in the day of performance'. England should interpret her own obligations and 'come what may, it is better for her to promise too little than too much. She [England] should seek to develop & mature the action of a common, or public, or European opinion, as the best standing bulwark against wrong, but should beware of seeming to lay down the law of that opinion by her own authority.'[2] The prime minister's view of foreign policy as something directed by domestic economy was further complicated by the need to rest such a policy upon a moral basis.

On 12 March Bismarck told Loftus that as Prussia had no special interest in Belgium she would not defend it alone. He could not understand, however, why England had not invited Prussian co-operation on this question, for it was 'of vital importance to her prestige and her interests'. Bismarck observed that if France took Belgium, Prussia would find her own compensation somewhere else. When Loftus referred to this as 'bandit politics', Bismarck made no reply. The Prussian minister concluded by saying that British abstention forced him 'into almost a state of vassalage to Russia, and the only way . . . [he] can recompense Russia is by supporting her interests in the East'.[3]

Clarendon was not impressed.

The leading object of B[ismarck] is to detach us from Fr[ance].

---

[1] Gladstone to Clarendon, 17 Apr. 1869, Glad. MSS. ccccli, letter-book 1866–9.

[2] Gladstone to Grey, 17 Apr. 1869, Morley, ii. 317–18. Prince Napoleon told Lumley that 'the old public law has disappeared and has not yet been replaced by any new law of nations' (Lumley to Clarendon, Brussels, most confidential, 18 Apr. 1869, PRO FO 10/295, no. 164).

[3] Loftus to Clarendon, Berlin, most confidential, 17 Apr. 1869, PRO FO 64/662, no. 198. Bismarck maintained that he never told Loftus 'positively' that Prussia would defend Belgium if England did, but that if France took Belgium Prussia might fight or take South Germany (Bismarck to Bernstorff, Berlin, very confidential, 7 Apr. 1869, *GW* vi B, no. 1363; same to same, Berlin, confidential, 15 Apr. 1869, ibid., no. 1368).

We might tomorrow, if we pleased, enter into a coalition with Pr[ussia] against Fr[ance] for the protection of Belgian independence . . . but we will do nothing of the kind so long as there is hope that Fr[ance] will act with common honesty.

Bernstorff, who never speaks without instructions, has said on more than one occasion to Gladstone & to me that though Pr[ussia] would not undertake to defend Bel[gium] single-handed, as that country concerned E[ngland] more nearly than Pr[ussia], yet that we had but to say the word, & we should soon come to terms. I treated this . . . as a ruse to detach us from Fr[ance], which is B[ismarck]'s main object.[1]

By 20 April a rupture of the Franco-Belgian negotiations appeared imminent. Lumley excitedly telegraphed asking whether London thought the 'time had arrived' for Belgium 'to make an appeal to [the] guaranteeing powers'.[2] Clarendon expressed his concern to La Tour and instructed Lyons to do the same with La Valette. 'Her Majesty's government looked forward with . . . regret . . . to the risk of an interruption of those cordial and friendly relations between England and France'.[3] The foreign secretary was purposely and wisely vague as to how serious an 'interruption' he anticipated. La Tour reported home Clarendon's feeling that 'Berlin sees without regret France engaged in a way which would fatally compromise her friendly relations with England'.[4] The foreign secretary intimated to the French ambassador that Russia, Austria, and Prussia shared English concern for Belgian neutrality and independence.[5]

---

[1] Clarendon to Lyons, 19 Apr. 1869, Newton, pp. 217–18. Bismarck had intimated such an alliance in his talks with Loftus (Bismarck to Bernstorff, Berlin, confidential, 20 Apr. 1869, *GW* vi B, no. 1371).

[2] Lumley to Clarendon, Brussels, telegram, 20 Apr. 1869, PRO FO 10/295. Clarendon was furious with Lumley, who was a troublemaker and seemed also to be something of an ass. 'We are not pleased with your recent comm[unication] & fear that you increase rather than endeavour to allay the alarm of the King & His govt. . . . As I do not wish to put this and some more in a public dispatch I write privately to beg you to be *very discreet* as the moment is a critical one' (Clarendon to Lumley, private, 21 Apr. 1869, Clar. Pap. C 475). In fairness to Lumley it should be noted that in 1866 Clarendon referred to him as 'a very able, intelligent man' (Clarendon to Victoria, 14 June 1866, RA B 22/75).

[3] Clarendon to Lyons, 22 Apr. 1869, PRO FO 27/1740, no. 248; ibid. 146/1368, no. 428. Before Lyons communicated this, La Valette told the British minister that England need not fear a 'military' or 'diplomatic quarrel' (Lyons to Clarendon, Paris, confidential, 22 Apr. 1869, PRO FO 1753, no. 450).

[4] La Tour to La Valette, London, confidential, 22 Apr. 1869, *Orig.* xxiv. 185–7.

[5] La Tour to La Valette, London, confidential, 24 Apr. 1869, ibid., pp. 201–2.

Despite Rouher's attempts to make Frère-Orban back down it was France in the end who gave way.[1] A protocol was signed on 27 April cancelling the railroad contracts but affirming that Belgium would offer 'equivalent advantages' to those which would have accrued had the contracts been confirmed,[2] a proposal which Belgium had offered almost from the beginning of the affair. It was mutually agreed that a commission would settle the details. As it seemed that the dispute had ended, Lyons added a postscript: 'The great points now are for the Belgians not to sing songs of triumph & for us & everybody to avoid all appearance of having exercised any pressure. The Emperor cannot safely take a snub from any foreign nation, & he feels this very strongly.'[3]

In June the slow progress of three French and three Belgian commissioners in Paris caused concern in London. The chastened Lumley 'urged . . . in the strongest manner the necessity for settling the railway question with the utmost expedition'.[4] Clarendon advised Beaulieu, the Belgian ambassador, to go to Brussels 'in order to expedite matters if possible, as the gravity of the position and the danger of delay don't seem to be fully appreciated'.[5] Further British pressure on Belgium became unnecessary when agreement was reached on 9 July and service conventions were concluded between the Belgian and French railroads.

Why did France give way? The uncertainty and inconsistency of Napoleon, elections to the legislative body in May, negotiations for a triple alliance with Austria-Hungary and Italy, Prussian designs on south Germany—all tended to moderate French ardour. It was, however, the attitude of Great Britain that was decisive, if any single factor was, in restraining the French.

[1] Rouher refused to attend the final conferences with Frère-Orban, Gressier, and La Valette (Lumley to Clarendon, 30 Apr. 1869, PRO FO 146/1387, no. 181).

[2] Lyons to Clarendon, Paris, confidential, 27 Apr. 1869, PRO FO 27/1754, no. 477; Lumley to Clarendon, Brussels, most confidential, 30 Apr. 1869, PRO FO 10/295, no. 181.

[3] Lyons to Clarendon, Paris, 28 Apr. 1869, Newton, pp. 219–20.

[4] Lumley to Clarendon, Brussels, confidential, 13 June 1869, PRO FO 10/296, no. 244; Lyons to Clarendon, confidential, 14 June 1869, PRO FO 27/1756, no. 630.

[5] Clarendon to Lumley, private, 23 June 1869, Clar. Pap. C 475.

Bismarck's contention that Clarendon's unauthorized assumption of Prussian support prevented Napoleon from annexing Belgium[1] is completely unsubstantiated. Clarendon in fact intimated to La Tour that Prussia would possibly take advantage of a French imbroglio in Belgium, but he never alluded to an Anglo-Prussian alliance. Paris, if she feared anything, feared a Prussian move into south Germany, to which she could hardly have objected if she had herself just obtained Belgium. British concern for Belgian integrity was more effective in Paris because it was understated and did not threaten war. In Lyons's words, to have pulled the string too tightly would have caused it to snap. An English threat of war might have created one since the emperor could not have backed down before such intimidation. Clarendon avoided such language because he realized this.

The emperor's wish to be on good terms with England was another reflection of Franco-Prussian tension. It was obvious to the Austrian ambassador that British public sentiment considered Belgium to be a question of honour, and even an ardent abstentionist would fight to prevent its absorption.[2] Whether or not the French Government thought England would go to war was a lesser consideration than the loss of British friendship, which would be a catalyst for Bismarck's version of German unification. The French Government was aware that the absorption of Belgium would bring with it British hatred. This in itself was enough to deter the emperor in the light of Prussian animosity and the lack of an alliance with either Austria or Italy.

Clarendon repeatedly told the French that Prussia was not involved in the Belgian affair in order to soothe ruffled gallic feathers.[3] He knew that any hint of an Anglo-Prussian agreement would excite the French whom he was attempting to pacify, and he did not bite at the Prussian bait for an alliance because he did not trust Bismarck nor did he wish to become involved. Once the crisis was over Bismarck himself was not

[1] Craig, pp. 755–60. As a matter of fact on 12 April 1869 Loftus read to Bismarck a letter from Clarendon which asked the Prussian Government not to provoke or excite France (Bismarck to Bernstorff, Berlin, confidential, 15 Apr. 1869, GW vi B, no. 1368). Bismarck was irritated that he could not make use of the Belgian situation in order to draw England closer to Prussia.

[2] Apponyi to Beust, London, 16 Mar. 1869, England, HHSA.

[3] Bernstorff to Bismarck, telegram, 17 Feb. 1869, APP x. 563.

unduly anxious for an alliance with England,[1] since he was more conscious of the obligations it would entail than any benefits it would confer.

Finally it seems that the emperor, if he contemplated the annexation of Belgium, only did so for a flickering moment. Consequently the French withdrew, not from a war of annexation but from demanding the consummation of the already signed railway agreements. La Valette repeatedly told Lyons, before the middle of April, that France would take only economic measures in the event of a rupture with Belgium. This was made clear well before Clarendon had intimated anything about possible Prussian action. British displeasure, coupled of course with strong Belgian resistance, caused the emperor to drop his plans for putting the railroad agreements into operation. It was also British pressure at Brussels which in large part restrained the Belgians from provoking the French into a war which Napoleon had the good sense to realize was unjustifiable and dangerous.

The Belgian railroads dispute provided an occasion for British interference on the Continent, however reluctantly advantage was taken of it. Clarendon, who was almost as cautious as Stanley, was much less pro-German than his predecessor and much more sympathetic to the difficult position of Napoleon. This sympathy was initially frustrated by the Belgian imbroglio, which also emphasized the military inadequacy of England, especially when contrasted with the growing armaments on the continent. Clarendon, alive to his country's military impotence, recognized the large part armaments played in creating tension between France and Prussia. The interests of England and Europe prompted the foreign secretary to lend his efforts to achieving Franco-Prussian disarmament.

---

[1] Bernstorff to Bismarck, 31 July 1869, Karl Ringhoffer, *Bernstorff Papers: The Life of Count Albrecht von Bernstorff* (New York, 1908), ii. 267–70. Bismarck also felt that British ministers could not undertake a definite commitment because they were not sure what England's policy would be in a given situation. Would England's obsequious desire for peace prevail over 'excited patriotism' and concern for Belgium? (Bismarck to Bernstorff, Berlin, confidential, 29 June 1869, *GW* vi B, no. 1416). Apparently Bismarck did not think so. An article in *The Times* on 21 Aug. 1866 commented that if France attacked Belgium and took part of that country, England would probably not act because of her military unpreparedness (*APP* viii. 302, note).

VIII

DISARMAMENT

The Army

THE Belgian railways crisis was especially discomforting for England because her honour might have compelled the Government to undertake military action. Such intervention was repugnant in itself, the more so since the country was so ill-prepared to conduct it successfully. While the continental powers had increased the size and efficiency of their forces Britain in the sixties had done neither, but rather reduced the strength of her army for the sake of economy. British security was based upon her navy,[1] and Prussia was not yet regarded as the great threat to the continental balance of power which with the one exception of the preservation of Belgium could justify English military intervention in Europe.

During the Danish crisis of 1864, and just before the Austro–Prussia conflict of 1866, the Duke of Cambridge complained of the inadequate strength of the British military.[2] Russell saw no reason to oppose the contemplated reductions in the army[3] and was supported by Parliament, particularly in view of the surplus which Gladstone brought in for the year 1866–7.[4] The dominant British opinion in 1866 was summed up by General Peel: 'Any proposal for an augmentation of the army would be most unpopular, and I am sure we could not carry it in the House of Commons unless there is a prospect of war, which God forbid.'[5]

Disraeli was almost as vocal on economy as Gladstone. He hoped 'that no department of the state shall exceed the amount

---

[1] Taylor has pointed out that in 1870 England spent almost four million pounds more on her army than on her navy (A. J. P. Taylor, *The Struggle for Mastery in Europe* (Oxford, 1954), p. xxvii).

[2] Duke of Cambridge to Lord de Grey, 2 Feb. 1864, 10 Jan. 1866, W. Verner, *The Military Life of George, Duke of Cambridge* (London, 1905), i. 287, 292.

[3] Russell to Duke of Cambridge, 26 Jan. 1866, ibid., p. 294.

[4] The duke remained unconvinced (Duke of Cambridge to Hartington, 6 May 1866, ibid., p. 295).

[5] General Peel to Derby, 11 July 1866, Derby Pap. 161/11.

of the estimates of 1866–7, with a hope that they may not reach them: otherwise we shall get into a scrape.'[1] Both Stanley and Disraeli urged Peel to avoid any increase in the army estimates for 1867–8.[2] Consequently, in spite of the Austro-Prussian war, there was no proposed augmentation of the army over what it had been in 1866–7.[3] The lack of any real reserve was generally recognized even by those who were opposed to any increase in the size of the army.

In 1868 it was decided to cut down the numbers of the military for 1869–70 by 8,000 men, reducing the total force to 130,000, and the money allocated to it by £1,000,000.[4] However, it was considered advisable to increase the size of the force stationed in England. In May of 1869, Colonel Walker, the British military attaché at Berlin, after four years observing the Prussian army offered an analysis of its English counterpart. He commented on the lack of cohesion and a single 'central authority' in the British forces:

That we should ever again play the part of earlier days in great Continental wars is impossible, the magnitude of the disciplined and expansive forces of other nations, whose armies are supplied by conscription . . . precluded us from a participation in the numerical contest for supremacy.

Walker, however, was not ready to join the peace-at-any-price group:

On that day when the Continent becomes convinced that we are incapable of holding the balance, the influence of England on European questions will cease. . . . As far as regards brotherly offers of peaceful advice, I have long since learnt that to advise, you must be strong, or your advice may be taken but will not be respected.

He felt that with a small mobile army and a sufficient reserve, intervention was possible in a continental war. 'England . . . may hold the balance and dictate the terms of peace to an exhausted Europe.'[5] General Grey was of the same mind.

---

[1] Disraeli to Pakington, confidential, 23 Oct. 1866, Disraeli Pap., Box 59.

[2] Stanley to Disraeli, confidential, 15 Dec. 1866, Stan. Pap., Disraeli.

[3] There was actually a proposed increase of seventy-two men for 1867–8. The total number of men in England was about 90,000 of which less than half were in the infantry.

[4] S. Walpole, *The History of Twenty-five Years* (London, 1904), ii. 415.

[5] Walker to Loftus, confidential, Berlin, 7 May 1869, PRO FO 64/663, no. 37.

'What we require as an *Army*—is a comparatively small, well organized body of men, ready to move in any part of the world.'[1]
Victoria too expressed her anxiety about the state of the army:

The queen is happy to find from Mr. Gladstone's letter . . . that the Cabinet have already entertained the question of national defences & she fully considers that no public action shall be taken, so as to create alarm.
There are 88,000 regular troops in the United Kingdom.
Mr. Cardwell's opinion is that 20,000 of these cld be made available for Foreign Service in 3 weeks with great exertion.
The Queen cannot conceal her disappointment & uneasiness at reading this statement. . . . The Queen trusts that this subject will receive Mr. Cardwell's serious attention & that no time will be lost in placing the army in a state of preparation for any calls that may be made upon it.[2]

The difficulty was that in order to increase the army a vote of the Parliament was necessary, and even if granted it was feared that such a step would create a financial panic. Cardwell, who became secretary of state for war in 1868, was acutely aware of his burden. He told Gladstone that he was 'not prepared to be responsible for sending an expedition abroad, unless the army is fitted for that object by measures taken to increase its force'.[3]
The prime minister replied immediately:

I feel, however, rather uneasy at what seems to have been extreme susceptibility, on our side of the case of some members of the Cabinet. I hope it will be balanced by considering the effect of any forward step by appeal to Parliament, in compromising the . . . neutrality of our position, and in distracting . . . the mind of the public & of Parliament.
It is only a fear outlook which . . . [wishes to send] a force to Antwerp.
Should the day arrive [to send such a force] we shall then be on the very edge of war, with scarcely a hope of not passing onwards into the abyss.[4]

The publication of the Bismarck–Benedetti draft treaty and the combined pressure of Victoria and Cardwell caused Gladstone to give way. He informed Disraeli of the Government's

[1] Grey to Cardwell, private, 24 Dec. 1869, PRO FO 30/48, 1/1.
[2] Victoria memorandum, Osborne, 18 July 1870, PRO FO 30/48, 1/2.
[3] Cardwell to Gladstone, 24 July 1870, ibid. 2/7.
[4] Gladstone to Cardwell, private, 24 July 1870, ibid.

intention. 'It may be convenient for you to know before the
House meets today that we shall lay upon the table . . . a vote
empowering govt to add 20,000 men to the army, and a vote
of credit in aid of the naval & military services for two millions.'[1]

A few in parliament objected to the extra twenty thousand,
but they were outnumbered by those who criticized the weaken-
ing of the army by the previous reductions. Both the increase
and the vote of credit were passed. In December of 1870 the
Cabinet decided upon no further augmentation of forces for
1871–2, other than the already approved 20,000.[2] This created
a regular army in the United Kingdom of 107,000 men, which
together with the non-regular units it was hoped would be
sufficient for defensive purposes. But the military complacency
of England had been exposed by the outbreak of the Franco-
Prussian war before Cardwell's reforms had taken effect.

The Navy

Opinion in England in the 1860's, though not weighed down
by the earlier fears of invasion, interpreted warfare in a naval
sense and in terms of defence and security. It was generally
assumed that the British navy was invincible. There were some,
however, even in England, who refused to make such an assumption. One student has said of this period that 'in prestige even
when not in sheer power—the Royal Navy . . . overshadowed
all its rivals'. He adds, however, that 'Britain's naval policy in
the sixties becomes harder to defend: she lagged behind'.[3]

The naval estimates for 1866–7 contained a reduction of
1,300 men from the previous year. The Duke of Somerset, in
a curious analysis, felt that the English fleet was superior to the

---

[1] Gladstone to Disraeli, 1 Aug. 1870, Glad. Pap., ccccliv, letter-book 1870–1.
[2] Cardwell to Victoria, 1 Dec. 1870, PRO FO 30/48, 1/2.
[3] M. Lewis, 'Armed Forces and the Art of War: Navies', vol. x of *The New Cambridge Modern History*, ed. by J. P. T. Bury (Cambridge, 1960), pp. 274, 279.
Apponyi believed the passivity of England was due to the Irish situation and the
poor state of the British navy (Apponyi to Mensdorff, 8 Apr. 1866, England,
HHSA, no. 53). Bartlett maintained that 'in ships of the line, whether of sail or
steam, Britain maintained and even increased her lead over France down to the
Crimean War' (C. J. Bartlett, *Great Britain and Sea Power 1815–1853* [Oxford, 1963],
p. 302). This was, of course, prior to the introduction of ironclads. An article in
The Times on 4 Sept. 1866 questioned the strength of the fleet whilst pointing to
the great amount of money spent on naval experimentation (*APP* viii. 302, note).

French, but that 'the Americans have more to cope with us than the French have'.[1] Disraeli seemed more concerned with naval expenditure than naval strength.[2] He scorned 'the obstinacy with wh. the Admi[ralt]y has declined building iron ships, & the vast sums wh. they have vainly expended in cobbling up old wooden vessels'.[3] Malmesbury was genuinely anxious. 'I have been for a long time anxious about the state of our *navy* wh. from unavoidable circumstances does not bear nearly the same relative position as regards other navies wh. it formerly did, & wh. it should do.' His anxiety was not motivated by fear of invasion but by concern for England's food supply. 'We cannot grow or supply half the food we want for our increased population.'[4]

Stanley, needless to say, was at one with Derby and Disraeli on the necessity for economy. 'In case of an Admiralty row on the estimates, it may be worth your knowing that our naval attaché at Washington . . . assures me that our seagoing iron-clad fleet is far superior at the present moment to that of the U.S.'[5] The foreign secretary did feel some doubt about England's harbour defences, and so forwarded a letter to his father which contained a proposal to meet attack or invasion: 'The commission would have the advantage of examining a plan of attack on this country drawn up with great care, & after much enquiry & research, by a French officer about 10 years since.'[6] Lord Derby replied 'that the question raised . . . in the enclosed letter is one which should not be decided without reference to the cabinet'.[7]

At the end of 1867 and the beginning of 1868 the Cabinet,

---

[1] Duke of Somerset to Russell, private, 17 June 1866, PRO FO 30/22, 16.

[2] Derby felt the same way (Derby to Disraeli, private, 16 Sept. 1866, Derby Pap. L–B 191/2).

[3] Disraeli to Derby, confidential, 20 Aug. 1866, Derby Pap. 146/2; ibid., Disraeli Pap., box 59 (XIII).

[4] Malmesbury to Derby, 13 Sept. 1866, Derby Pap. 105. This was probably an exaggeration. 'Until the international trade in foodstuffs developed after 1873, Great Britain was reasonably self-sufficient, although not wholly so, in meat and wheat. She could have stood a siege, not of course without danger and inconvenience' (W. H. B. Court, *A Concise Economic History of Britain* [Cambridge, 1954], p. 161).

[5] Stanley to Disraeli, private, 19 Dec. 1866, Disraeli Pap., box 111.

[6] Sir H. Verney to Stanley, 16 Apr. 1869, Stan. Pap. X 6, miscellaneous.

[7] Derby to Stanley, 24 Apr. 1867, ibid. Apparently invasion was a contingency not seriously considered, as nothing came as a result of the question.

admiralty, and the court engaged in a serious and very private analysis of the British navy. Grave concern was indicated in a long memorandum drawn up by Mr. Corry and presented to the Cabinet and Victoria.[1] Corry mentioned the lack of a naval reserve and a reduction of active seamen by one thousand over the past ten years. More seriously he pointed out that at Cherbourg and Toulon France had fifteen ironclads, with an additional one in the Pacific, and that she was building seven more. England's inferiority in the Mediterranean and the Channel was clear, as she had but ten ironclads there and was building only eight. There were in addition two British ironclads in the West Indies and one each off China and in the Pacific. All told France had afloat thirty-five ironclads and was building eleven. England had thirty-one and was building eight.[2] Even allowing for a certain amount of exaggeration England was at best the equal of France in ironclads, and compared to France and Russia combined no match at all. Considering the world-wide naval needs of Britain, French superiority in Europe was evident, at least to Corry. He argued that before armour-clads were introduced, the British navy was almost double that of France. 'The opinion wh. is [now] becoming prevalent & finds expression in H. of Commons [is] that it is sufficient if our navy is = to Fr's.'[3]

The admiralty, which of course had a vested interest in increased naval estimates, supported Corry's case. An admiralty memorandum stated:

To arrive at a bare equality in ironclad ships, with France alone, it will be necessary to build 2 first class ironclads and 5 second class.

France has 46 of all classes . . . England has 39, of which 3 are absent on foreign stations.

If France was to collect her ironclads in her Atlantic Ports she

---

[1] Corry memorandum, confidential, 2 Dec. 1867, Stan. Pap., memorandum (2), 1867. Corry was first lord of the admiralty and, according to the article in *The Dictionary of National Biography*, 'his knowledge of naval affairs was unquestioned'.

[2] According to Corry's figures Russia had twenty-five armour-clads and was building four. For a contrary view of the naval strength of Britain and France see J. P. Baxter, *The Introduction of the Ironclad Warship* (Cambridge, 1933). Marder maintains that in the nineteenth century the British fleet was larger than the French (A. J. Marder, *Anatomy of British sea power* [New York 1940]).

[3] Corry memorandum, ibid. Bernstorff reported that the English and French fleets were about equal and that British superiority in the Channel was offset by French preponderance in the Mediterranean (Bernstorff to Bismarck, 16 Apr. 1867, *APP* viii. 676–7).

would command the Channel—The mere assembling of such a fleet in troubled times, without actual war, would by its effect on trade and credit, be in itself a disgrace and a disaster. The naval members of the Board therefore urge upon Her Majesty's Government the necessity of a large and efficient force of ironclads being provided and constantly maintained.[1]

Sir Thomas Biddulph, the keeper of her majesty's privy purse, shared some of the admiralty's anxiety, but for financial reasons and the desire to await further experimentation was disinclined to any crash building programme. Grey, Victoria's private secretary, also opposed a naval race with France.

Disraeli expressed irritation and disbelief at the admiralty's figures and arguments:

The state of our finances will not permit any increase in our expenditure. . . . The requisitions of the Admiralty are unwise & unnecessary.

Last year, there was the same pressure on the ground of the great increase of the American navy. We successfully resisted the appeal & it now turns out that the Americans have no navy, & not an ironclad except for coast defence.

Now it is the old bugbear of the French navy.

The Admiralty wants a large increase of our iron-clad fleet, but it offers no plan how this increase is to be effected except by the vulgar expedient of a large increase of the navy estimates.

As for the Adm[iralt]y view of the present condition of the French navy, I believe it is marked by the usual exaggeration & false colouring, wh. always accompanies these estimates.[2]

Derby seemed much more concerned with the admiralty's report.

I must confess that for the last few years the comparison of the relative strength of the British navy with that of the two other navies of the world [presumably the French and Russian] has not been altogether of a satisfactory character. . . . We do not possess the preponderance of power, which used to be considered as essential for our safety. But on the other hand, there has been a continual

---

[1] Memorandum of naval members of the board for consideration of the first lord of the admiralty and the Cabinet, 16/17 Dec. 1867, Derby Pap. 58/1.
[2] Disraeli to Derby, confidential, 28 Jan. 1868, Derby Pap. 146/4; same to same, ibid., Morley, iv. 578-9.

increase of expenditure upon our naval estimates, which is very difficult to justify or to explain.[1]

But for all this he agreed with Disraeli that the admiralty should be informed 'that a further increase in the naval estimates cannot be sanctioned'.[2]

Disraeli prevailed with the Cabinet and the estimates were not increased. However it is significant that the Cabinet ordered immediately the building of three additional ironclads, a decision which apparently Disraeli did not oppose.[3] Gladstone's effort to reduce the naval estimates failed, but once prime minister he was able to impose the reduction he failed to obtain when in opposition. In 1869 the prime minister announced that the naval estimates for 1870-1 proposed to diminish the number of men in the navy by 1,800, leaving a force of 61,000. He seemed prepared to legislate to permanent impotence the military and naval force of England.[4]

Fortunately for the successive governments between 1866 and 1870, British opinion either assumed the predominance of the royal navy, which was questionable, or was not concerned about lagging behind.[5] But deficiencies in the military and naval forces weakened the effectiveness of British diplomacy. Even if Britain had absolutely no intention of intervening militarily on the Continent, her influence fell because such intervention would have been difficult if not impossible to execute successfully. This is in part what Clarendon meant when he referred to 'our horribly defenceless position'. A Franco-

---

[1] Derby to Disraeli, confidential, 30 Jan. 1868, Derby Pap. L–B 195/1; ibid., Disraeli Pap., box 111.   [2] Ibid.

[3] 'He [Disraeli] . . . has induced the cabinet, this day, unanimously to adopt his views; that the naval estimates have been re-constructed; & without any material increase of expenditure, your Majesty will now have a real & we hope, rapidly increasing naval reserve. The cabinet determined today to lay down immediately three more ironclads' (Disraeli to Victoria, 15 Feb. 1868, RA E 52/26).

[4] The increase in British ironclads from thirteen in 1866 to twenty-three in 1870 was due more to the Conservatives than the Liberals.

[5] The admiralty was constantly concerned with the naval challenge presented by France or a Franco-Russian combination. There were few, at this time, who saw any Prussian or German threat. One who did was Cowley (Cowley to Stanley, private, Paris, 23 Apr. 1867, PRO FO 519/233). In May 1869 Clarendon's eagerness to send a British warship to participate in a naval gala at Wilhelmshaven had an interesting explanation. 'I can't quite say it but the *real* reason of our readiness . . . was the desire of the Admiralty to get plans of Jahde [Wilhelmshaven] and to know what was really doing and preparing' (Clarendon to Lyons, private, 24 May 1869, Clar. Pap. C 148).

Russian combination in the East might have been dire for England, and for this and other reasons Clarendon and Stanley attempted to separate Paris and St. Petersburg. Stanley's refusal to consider military measures in the East was as much a naval and military assessment of the possible as an awareness of the change in attitude towards the Turk on the part of British opinion. In the West, though England could not match the army of France or Prussia, there was at least the possibility that, because of Antwerp and Belgium's geographical position, she had the means to take some naval and military action.

In the middle and late 1860's a French invasion of England was extremely remote, but the possibility of French hegemony in the Channel was not. The attitude of successive British governments toward Prussia and France was at least coloured by the fact that Prussia had no navy to speak of whereas France had. France could pose the greatest threat to English trade, and it is usually argued that Britain's policy of peace in this period was for the sake of her trade and industry. David Thompson has said:

Her policy was peaceful because war . . . interfered with trade and damaged her industrial production. One of the most persuasive arguments brought forward by Cobden and Bright in favour of free trade was that it would eliminate some of the main causes of war and bind nations together by bonds of mutual interest.[1]

Though England's policy was the preservation of peace, her ability to engage in war and effectuate her diplomacy were frustrated by her relative military weakness. Britain's position on disarmament therefore was not entirely based on the general grounds of the prevention of war. If continental disarmament would reduce tension it would also raise England's influence in Europe by narrowing the disparity between her forces and those of the continental powers. Clarendon's efforts to bring about Franco-Prussian disarmament were therefore not entirely altruistic.

Efforts to obtain Continental Disarmament

In April of 1866 Clarendon brought friendly pressure to bear on Austria and Prussia in order to persuade them to

---

[1] D. Thompson, 'The United Kingdom and Its Worldwide Interest', vol. x of *The New Cambridge Modern History*, ed. by J. P. T. Bury (Cambridge, 1960), p. 349.

reduce their forces to a peace establishment.[1] Bismarck avoided the foreign secretary's *démarche*, but in the following year complained of French armaments.[2] Loftus's comments on Bismarck's complaint are interesting:

> The experience I [Loftus] have had . . . convinces me that if the question of armaments should be made the subject of diplomatic remonstrances between the Parties at issue or should be brought under discussion in the conference [on Luxemburg] the result will only be to precipitate war. . . . The question of armaments . . . [should] not be made the question of diplomatic discussion.[3]

In June of 1867 Cowley wrote that he was 'quite convinced' that Paris would not hear of 'an appeal for a general disarmament'.[4] In 1868 Prussia was extending her military system in north Germany, whilst at the same time France was adopting a new programme. In this situation Lyons felt disarmament appeals would meet with little favour in either Paris or Berlin.[5] Stanley agreed, even though Bismarck announced some paper reductions in Prussian military strength.[6] An attempt by Gorchakov in July of 1868 to outlaw the use of 'explosive projectiles' provoked a sceptical reaction in both London and Berlin.

At the close of 1868 Stanley, in his speech at King's Lynn, referred to 'the monster armaments' of the powers as a source of danger.[7] Clarendon in a conversation with La Tour expressed his feeling that neither France nor Prussia would disarm so long as the tension existing between them remained.[8] Clarendon was greatly in favour of disarmament but hesitated himself to intrude in the affairs of Prussia or France—but Austria or Russia might do so. To Buchanan in Vienna he wrote:

> The maintenance of peace shd be the paramount purpose of every European govt, not withstanding their monster armaments that are a disgrace to our age & civilization, & none shd be ashamed

[1] Clarendon to Bloomfield, telegram, 17 Apr. 1866, PRO FO 146/1246, no. 117; Clarendon to Loftus, 24 Apr. 1866, ibid. 64/588, no. 67.

[2] Loftus to Stanley, confidential, Berlin, 27 Apr. 1867, ibid. 620, no. 243.

[3] Cowley to Clarendon, Paris, 12 June 1867, Maxwell, ii. 336–7.

[4] Lyons to Stanley, Paris, 24 Apr. 1868, PRO FO 27/1704, no. 405.

[5] Loftus to Stanley, confidential, Berlin, 25 Apr. 1868, *APP* ix. 908–9.

[6] Loftus to Stanley, Berlin, 11 July 1868, PRO FO 146/1339, no. 311; Stanley to Buchanan, 25 July 1868, ibid., no. 72.

[7] La Tour to Moustier, telegram, 14 Nov. 1868, *Orig.* xxii. 238–9.

[8] Same to same, confidential, 15 Nov. 1868, ibid., pp. 241–3.

of avowing that purpose & adopting its policy to the end in view.
. . . Speak in this sense to Beust.[1]

In the early autumn of 1869 Clarendon also asked Gorchakov
to propose a reduction of armaments. The Russian minister
was sympathetic but replied that France ought to take the
initiative.[2] The foreign secretary in a talk with Napoleon again
alluded to 'the monster armaments . . . & the constant danger
of war they created'. The emperor replied that the responsibility for them was Prussia's.[3] Nor did Berlin seem amenable
to disarmament. 'I [Clarendon] quite agree with you [Loftus]
that the King [of Prussia] is *inabordable* about military reductions
but I hope that the taxpayers bring him to understand their
difficulties.'[4] It would seem that the foreign secretary was
generalizing on the basis of his English experience.

In January 1870 Daru, the new foreign minister in the
Ollivier government, approached Clarendon on disarmament.[5]
But before that the foreign secretary had received a pessimistic
communication from Loftus:

It is not the actual army—but the Prussian system which is a
standing menace to her neighbours. A state counting 30 millions—
with a peace army of 300,000 and the means of raising that army to
900,000 in 6 weeks—is a very formidable power—and altho you
may reduce its peace contingent 100,000 men you still have the
possibility of her placing 900,000 men under arms in 6 weeks. Turn
the question how you like the Prussian military system is a standing
menace to her neighbours, and is the chief cause of the large armaments in Europe, and so long as that system is continued there is not
a chance of her neighbours disarming.[6]

---

[1] Clarendon to Bloomfield, private, 16 Feb. 1869, PRO FO 356/33.
[2] Clarendon to Buchanan, confidential, Wiesbaden, 3 Sept. 1869, PRO FO
146/1394, no. 122.
[3] Clarendon to Gladstone, private, Paris, 18 Sept. 1869, Glad. Pap. xlix. 19–25.
[4] Clarendon to Loftus, private, 20 Oct. 1869, Clar. Pap. C 474.
[5] It appears to this writer that though the French were sincere in wishing to
disarm, they wished Bismarck to bear the responsibility for any failure to do so. See
Taylor, p. 199. In his private report to Clarendon, Lyons reported that Daru 'did
not wish simply to put Ct. Bismarck in the wrong' but that 'he [Daru] thought
[that] Ct. Bismarck would be more likely to be influenced by a desp[atch] which
might be laid before Parliament & thus become public in Germany & in the rest
of Europe, than by a confidential communication' (Lyons to Clarendon, very confidential, Paris, 1 Feb. 1870, RA J 83/117).
[6] Loftus to Clarendon, private, Berlin, 1 Jan. 1870, Clar. Pap. C 478. The
French army numbered in all about 430,000 and had a reserve of about 200,000
(Claremont to Lyons, Paris, 25 Jan. 1870, PRO FO 27/1798, no. 4).

Daru nevertheless suggested that England should take the initiative in proposing Franco-Prussian disarmament.[1] Clarendon informed the queen that he intended to comply with this request even though he felt that failure was certain, as the King of Prussia idolized his army and would 'not listen to any proposal for its reduction or ... change'.[2] It was due to Prussian sensitivity about disarming and the wish to avoid a public snub that Clarendon decided to broach the subject at Berlin in a private and confidential manner.[3] Ollivier told Lyons that reduction was necessary to conciliate the peasant population of France, but that a 'public rebuff from Prussia would be fatal'. Consequently a secret approach by Clarendon was best.[4]

At the end of January the foreign secretary composed a draft letter to Loftus, evidently pleased that 'the French govt had addressed themselves to [England] ... for assistance & support'.[5] He asked Gladstone's consent to his proposed action, and as might be expected the prime minister was more than pleased: 'The object of Y.L. on disarmament is noble [he replied], & I do not see how the terms of the draft can be improved. I presume you will let the Q[ueen] know what you are abt. & possibly circ[umstance]s might arrive in wh. she cd. help?'[6]

Clarendon's letter to Loftus instructed the ambassador to ask Bismarck in the foreign secretary's name to suggest disarmament to the King of Prussia, and to inform the German minister that he, Clarendon, was sure that France would agree to a military reduction.[7] Bismarck officially hesitated to broach the subject with his king, and complained that Prussia's only security against France was her army.[8] Gladstone was

---

[1] Daru to La Valette, Paris, 24 Jan. 1870, *QVL*, 2nd ser., ii. 5.

[2] Clarendon to Victoria, 26 Jan. 1870, *QVL*, 2nd ser., ii. 5.

[3] La Valette to Daru, London, 27 Jan. 1870, *Orig.* xxvi. 230–4.

[4] Lyons to Clarendon, Paris, 30 Jan. 1870, Newton, pp. 248–50.

[5] Clarendon to Gladstone, 31 Jan. 1870, Glad. Pap. xlix. 143–5.

[6] Gladstone to Clarendon, 31 Jan. 1870, Glad. Pap. cccliii, letter-book 1869–70. Clarendon heeding Gladstone's advice sent the private draft to Victoria for her information (Clarendon to Victoria, 1 Feb. 1870, *QVL*, 2nd ser., ii. 8).

[7] Clarendon to Loftus, 2 Feb. 1870, Newton, pp. 250–3; La Valette to Daru, London, 3 Feb. 1870, *Orig.* xxvi. 261–3; Bismarck to Bernstorff, Berlin, 9 Feb. 1870, *GW* vi B, no. 1495.

[8] Loftus to Clarendon, Berlin, 5 Feb. 1870, Newton, pp. 254–6; Clarendon to Victoria, 9 Feb. 1870, *QVL*, 2nd ser., ii. 8; La Valette to Daru, London, 9 Feb. 1870, *Orig.* xxvi. 280–2. Lyons believed that Bismarck's fear of showing Clarendon's letter to his king was sincere and not a 'diplomatic pretext' (Lyons to Clarendon,

dissatisfied with the answer and suggested that the queen 'could venture in her gentle way upon a separate & independent attempt.'[1] Daru's reaction to Bismarck's refusal, as he told Lyons, was nevertheless 'to reduce the annual French contingent from 100,000 men to 90,000',[2] a decision that pleased both Clarendon and Gladstone.[3] The latter wrote to Clarendon: 'I hope, with Daru, that you will not desist fr. yr. efforts, whatever be the best mode of prosecuting the good design. I thought Bismarck's case, on Loftus' l[ette]r, a very bad one.'[4] The foreign secretary had no intention of desisting.[5]

Bismarck's negative reply through Bernstorff reaffirmed his earlier answer to Loftus.[6] Gladstone was extremely disappointed and expressed a certain vindictiveness towards the Prussian minister, suggesting that 'he [Bismarck] ought at any rate to be made to feel his responsibility which I daresay you will contrive'.[7] Bismarck, in his turn, stressed the necessity for 'guarantees' if Prussia were to disarm. One such guarantee might have been an Anglo-Prussian alliance. The queen's advice to Clarendon to write directly to the crown prince or princess of Prussia was not acted upon.[8]

In the second week in March, Clarendon made another attempt in Berlin:[9]

private, Paris, 15 Feb. 1870, Lyons Pap., RC2.) Lyons was partly wrong. Bismarck did consult the king, but did not want this known because he did not wish to give the disarmament proposal an official character which would enable France to throw the blame of its failure upon Prussian intransigence. Bismarck suspected France of insincerity and requested guarantees if Prussia weakened herself by disarming. He did not think that Clarendon was consciously making himself a tool of France, but that he was 'a cool friend' of Prussia imbued with 'Utopian' ideas (Bismarck to Bernstorff, Berlin, 9 Feb. 1870, *GW* vi B, no. 1495; same to same, very confidential and secret, 9 Feb. 1870, ibid., no. 1496).

[1] Gladstone to Clarendon, 7 Feb. 1870, Glad. Pap. ccccliii, letter-book 1869–70.
[2] Lyons to Clarendon, Paris, 11 Feb. 1870, Newton, pp. 256–9.
[3] Clarendon to Victoria, 12 Feb. 1870, *QVL*, 2nd ser., ii. 8–9.
[4] Gladstone to Clarendon, 12 Feb. 1870, Glad. Pap. ccccliii, letter-book 1869–70; same to same, ibid., Morley, ii. 322.
[5] La Valette to Daru, London, 16 Feb. 1870, *Orig.* xxvi. 312–13.
[6] Clarendon to Gladstone, 18 Feb. 1870, Glad. Pap. xlix. 151; Clarendon to Lyons, 19 Feb. 1870, Newton, pp. 261–5; Bismarck to Bernstorff, 9 Feb. 1870, *GW* vi B, no. 1495; ibid., no. 1496.
[7] Gladstone to Clarendon, 18 Feb. 1870, Glad. Pap. ccccliii, letter-book 1869–70; same to same, 23 Feb. 1870, ibid.; same to same, private, 18 Feb. 1870, Clar. Pap. C 498. General Grey was very sympathetic to Bismarck's reply.
[8] Clarendon to Loftus, private, 2 Mar. 1870, PRO FO 361/1.
[9] He did not expect it would succeed (Clarendon to Lyons, 12 Mar. 1870, Newton, p. 266).

The question to my mind appears quite simple [he wrote to Loftus]. The military forces of the great Continental Powers have a certain proportion to each other; in order to maintain that proportion, very heavy burdens are imposed upon each country, but if by common agreement, each reduces its army by a certain no. of men, the same proportions will be maintained, while the burdens . . . will be alleviated.

A minute discussion of guarantees would be endless & dangerous.

I have reason to know that the reduction in the Fr. army would have been carried further if the Govt. could have hoped that the example would be followed by Pr.[1]

Loftus read his chief's letter to Bismarck, who would not be moved beyond remarking 'that without some guarantee . . . disarmament would be difficult'.[2] The foreign secretary now gave up. 'I send you a copy of Loftus' letter, & you will, I am sure, agree with me that more harm than good would be done by further pressing the question of disarmament.'[3] Clarendon evidently sensed Bismarck's irritation when the latter alluded to naval disarmament. The last words were Gladstone's:

If inclined to touch the point you [Clarendon] might with perfect justice say that while our naval responsibilities for overseas defence have no parallel or analogue in the world, we have taken not far short of 2 million off our estimates, & have not announced that the work of reduction is at an end; which whether satisfactory or not is enough to show that you do not preach wholly without practicing.[4]

The failure to bring about continental disarmament weakened the justification, for the sake of economy, of British retrenchment. It also frustrated a demand for greater reductions which Gladstone, at least, would have been happy to see. The failure had little effect on England's relations with either Prussia or France, since it was recognized from the beginning that an

---

[1] Clarendon to Loftus, 9 Mar. 1870, ibid., pp. 266–70. Clarendon's dispatch was almost a word-for-word version of Daru's view of the question as reported by Lyons (Lyons to Clarendon, private and confidential, Paris, 22 Feb. 1870, RA J 83/127).

[2] Loftus to Clarendon, Berlin, 12 Mar. 1870, ibid., pp. 270–3; Bismarck to Bernstorff, very confidential, Berlin, 25 Mar. 1870, *GW* vi B, no. 1541.

[3] Clarendon to Lyons, 23 Mar. 1870, ibid., pp. 276–7.

[4] Gladstone to Clarendon, 9 Apr. 1870, Glad. Pap. ccccliii, letter-book 1869–70; ibid., Morley, ii. 322. Bismarck expressed his views in a letter of 25 March to Bernstorff, which the Prussian minister gave to Clarendon. This letter contained Bismarck's reference to naval disarmament (Bismarck to Bernstorff, very confidential, Berlin, 25 Mar. 1870, *GW* vi B, no. 1541).

attempt to induce disarmament in the face of Franco-Prussian tension and sensitivity was like whispering in the wind.

The Eastern Question

At the end of 1869 Clarendon's natural pro-French feelings were reinforced by a quarrel between Egypt and the Ottoman Empire over Egypt's autonomous position under the Sultan. The need for French co-operation was recognized by both Gladstone and Clarendon.

The affair between the Sultan and the Khedive is getting serious. . . . The Khedive [has] . . . been ordering ironclads . . . [and] a number of rifles . . . & I must admit that this to a certain extent justifies the Porte in believing that he aims at independence.[1]

Lyons's fear that if a war took place 'France wd take the Khedive's side'[2] only made it more necessary that London should act with Paris. The prime minister wrote to Clarendon of the advisability of 'acting in union with France on this point which . . . might be . . . such a sore one'.[3] Clarendon agreed.

I rejoice that as yet we have been able to keep in perfect harmony with France respecting the Turco-Egyptian difficulty & pray assure La Tour that we mean to act with France, tho neither the French or English govt can be blind to the fact that the Khedive has gone outrageously beyond his tether & that the Porte is justified in considering that he aims at independence and that this ought not to be allowed.[4]

Towards the end of October, Clarendon thought the conflict had become 'very serious', and was rather out of humour with Paris. 'If the French govt had done in Egypt 1/2 what I have done at C[onstantino]ple to produce an arrangement it would all have been settled long ago.'[5] The foreign secretary believed that without French support the Khedive 'would not have dared to act as he has done towards his sovereign'.[6] Gladstone desired a settlement upon which England '& the French appear

---

[1] Clarendon to Lyons, private, 5 Aug. 1869, Clar. Pap. C 149.
[2] Lyons to Clarendon, private, Paris, 20 Aug. 1869, Lyons Pap. RC 2.
[3] Gladstone to Clarendon, 24 Aug. 1869, Glad. Pap. ccccliii, letter-book 1869.
[4] Clarendon to Lyons, private, Wiesbaden, 31 Aug. 1869, Clar. Pap. C 149.
[5] Clarendon to West, private, 20 Oct. 1869, ibid.
[6] Same to same, private, 30 Oct. 1869, ibid.

to be agreed'.[1] The foreign secretary followed the advice of the prime minister and urged upon Constantinople the acceptance of the *status quo*,[2] rather than the taking of any coercive measures against Egypt. When it appeared that the Porte would not listen to reason, Gladstone told Clarendon that 'having done your best . . . I am now chiefly anxious that we should stand clear of responsibility in the business'.[3]

Napoleon appeared to Lyons not to have been 'up in the Porte–Khedive question'.[4] Yet at the beginning of December, with no solution in sight, the prime minister expressed concern about a 'breach between England & France in this affair', than which 'nothing could be so bad'.[5] A few days later the dispute was resolved and the British Government heaved a sigh of relief. 'We have got out of the Khedive affair just in time, for the Emperor and the ministers had got very angry with the Porte, and could not have been kept within bounds much longer'.[6]

The prime minister, however, was still not assured. 'I shall be glad therefore if we can limit ourselves to watching against foul play & keep France from it if she has evil propensities of which I do not feel sure.'[7]

England's co-operation with the emperor in the eastern question in the 1860's was judged by London to be a necessity: sometimes, as in the Ottoman–Egyptian quarrel, a necessary evil. In part English mistrust of France in the East was a residue of French threats to Belgium and along the Rhine; in part it was due to the fact that Napoleon was playing a double game at Constantinople because English support was uncertain and limited in nature. In any event, co-operation with France, whether based upon sympathy or motivated by the desire to control her designs, stood between England and diplomatic isolation in the East. Clarendon was much less willing than Stanley to run this risk, and even Stanley recognized the danger. Consequently the British Government had no option but to

---

[1] Gladstone to Clarendon, 4 Nov. 1869, Glad. Pap. ccclii, letter-book 1869.
[2] Ibid., Clarendon to Elliot, 5 Nov. 1869, PRO FO 146/1397, no. 364.
[3] Gladstone to Clarendon, 17 Nov. 1869, Glad. Pap. ccli, letter-book 1869.
[4] Lyons to Clarendon, private, Paris, 26 Nov. 1869, Lyons Pap. RC 2.
[5] Gladstone to Clarendon, 2 Dec. 1869, ibid., Clar. Pap. C 498.
[6] Lyons to Clarendon, private, Paris, 9 Dec. 1869, Lyons Pap. RC 2.
[7] Gladstone to Clarendon, 8 Jan. 1870, Glad. Pap. ccccliii, letter-book 1869–70.

work with the emperor, and it was only a question of the degree to which the Government was prepared to co-operate with her Channel neighbour.

This fact, French willingness to disarm, and Clarendon's own natural sympathies indicated much closer Anglo-French relations. Daru's disposition to foster such relations and Clarendon's mistrust and dislike of Bismarck only reinforced the possibility of a *rapprochement*. 'Holding the balance even' seemed more likely under Clarendon than Stanley, but neither Berlin nor Paris mistook sympathy for active support. It was the unanimous feeling of all continental statesmen that if Belgium were left alone, a Franco-Prussian conflict would elicit immediate English neutrality. Clarendon himself justified this feeling.[1]

[1] In September of 1869 the foreign secretary told Gorchakov that in the event of a Franco-Prussian war he 'could see nothing to interfere with the strictest neutrality of England' (Clarendon to Buchanan, confidential, Wiesbaden, 3 Sept. 1869, PRO FO 146/1394, no. 122).

IX

THE BALANCE OF POWER AND THE HOHENZOLLERNS[1]

THE significance of the Hohenzollern candidature[2] for the throne of Spain lies in the fact that it was the culminating incident in a series of events. In other circumstances it would have been of less importance. Against the background of Prussian expansion and French failure to offset it, it was explosive and therefore kept secret. The connexion of the candidature with the relationship between the North German Confederation and south Germany complicated and exacerbated the already tense Franco-Prussian situation.

In March 1869 Clarendon noted that 'the aversion of the south to incorporate itself with the north seems to be on the increase which I am glad of as the contrary would be provocation of France'.[3] A few days later the foreign secretary wrote to Lyons about Spain: 'If France was engaged in war the Empr wd find a wonderful unanimity among Spaniards to take part with his enemies and there has been evidence already that Bismarck has his eye on Spain as an auxiliary.'[4] It is difficult to say what the foreign secretary meant by 'evidence', probably no more than the frequent newspaper articles referring to Leopold and the other possible candidates for the Spanish throne. In January of 1869 the foreign secretary was approached by the Spanish ambassador to France.

The reason that Olozaga sent his secr. to report to me [Clarendon]

---

[1] One should consult R. H. Lord, *The Origins of the War of 1870* (Cambridge, 1924); G. Bonnin, *Bismarck and the Hohenzollern Candidature for the Spanish Throne* (London, 1957); L. D. Steefel, *Bismarck, the Hohenzollern Candidacy, and the Origins of the Franco-German War of 1870* (Cambridge, 1962).

[2] In September 1868 a revolution in Spain resulted in the queen's flight to France. A Spanish provisional government sought a replacement, and Leopold of Hohenzollern-Sigmaringen was one of the many possibilities mentioned.

[3] Clarendon to Bloomfield, private, 23 Mar. 1869, PRO FO 356/33.

[4] Clarendon to Lyons, private, 27 Mar. 1869, Clar. Pap. C 148. According to Professor Steefel this was a common and erroneous opinion (Steefel, pp. 11–13).

his interview with the Empr. was that both the Empr. and he had agreed that Don Fernando of Portugal would be the right man for the place and that I was the only person who could sound him on the subject without France or Spain being thereby in any way committed.

I said I should not object to desire Murray confidentially to make enquiry of Don F. himself . . . but it would be for my own information and not for that of the gov't.[1]

La Tour commented upon English indifference to events in Spain and Clarendon's choice of Ferdinand of Portugal for the throne.[2]

There is some evidence to support the contention that Bismarck's interest in the Spanish throne was due to a possible alliance between France, Austria, and Italy. Steefel believes that 'Bismarck did not create the Hohenzollern candidacy as a countermine to explode the projected triple alliance, but the fear of such an alliance was a major factor, perhaps the major factor, in his decision to urge the acceptance of the Spanish offer'.[3] Loftus interpreted the anti-Austrian press warfare in Berlin as an expression of Bismarck's annoyance over the threat of a triple alliance.[4] In one dispatch he wrote:

The reported alliance between Austria, Italy and France . . . has occupied of late the attention of the Berlin press. Although in well informed circles no great credence is given to this reported alliance the civilities lately exchanged between the Emperor of Austria and King Victor Emmanuel, . . . has given an apparent consistency to the report in question.[5]

The Prussians were no more unaware of the triple alliance than the French were of the Hohenzollern candidacy. Benedetti informed La Valette of the latter possibility in March 1869.[6] The foreign minister telegraphed his objection to the candidature,

---

[1] Clarendon to Lyons, private, 2 Jan. 1869, Clar. Pap. C 148.

[2] La Tour to La Valette, confidential, London, 1 Feb. 1869, *Orig.* xxiii. 206–7.

[3] Steefel, p. 239. In 1868 and 1869 Bismarck mentioned his concern about such a coalition to Bernstorff on several occasions.

[4] Loftus to Clarendon, Berlin, 27 Mar. 1869, PRO FO 64/661, no 157.

[5] Same to same, ibid., no. 156. 'I am *secretly* told that an enquiry was made from here [Berlin] at Florence as to the truth of the reported triple alliance. . . . Menebrea, I am told, gave an evasive answer' (Loftus to Clarendon, private, Berlin, 10 Apr. 1869, Clar. Pap. C 478).

[6] V. Benedetti, *Ma mission en Prusse* (Paris, 1871), pp. 302–6; Steefel, pp. 36–37 : Benedetti to La Valette, Berlin, 27 Mar. 1869, *Orig.* xxiv. 104–5.

delegated the responsibility for deciding the extent to which his objection should be made known, and requested further information.[1] When Benedetti, in Bismarck's absence at Varzin, questioned von Thile, the secretary of state assured him there was nothing in the rumours.[2] Unaware of any French anxieties over the candidature, Clarendon was more concerned about German unification:

> Now if Ct. Bismarck does not wish for war . . . it would be worth while for him . . . to make it evident that the unification must be delayed for some years.
>
> I hope Ct. Bismarck to whom I beg you [Loftus] to make this suggestion will not think I am taking too great a liberty *purely in the interest of peace.*[3]

Loftus thought it would be best not to make such a communication, as any expression of advice or opinion with respect to German affairs would be distasteful to Bismarck.[4] The foreign secretary's fears on this count were partially allayed by a pacific speech by La Valette in the legislature,[5] and word from Loftus that Bismarck would not 'disturb the existing status quo' in Germany.[6]

Throughout 1869 the British ambassador in Berlin was certain that Bismarck did not desire war and consequently suggested that England could best preach words of peace in Paris.

> If England hopes to succeed in maintaining the peace of Europe, it will not be effected by sedatives or palliatives to either party, but by firmly stating that Her neutrality must not be counted upon, and that if any power should willfully break the peace, that power will find England across her path.
>
> Be assured that Bismarck will do nothing which can give umbrage to France. . . . Till now Bismarck has placed full confidence in the wish of the Emperor to preserve peace . . . but if Bismarck should . . . suspect the sincerity or the power of the Emperor, he may then alter his course.
>
> I believe . . . that the Emperor Napoleon would not embark in a war against Germany, were he to fear that England would be

---

[1] La Valette to Benedetti, Paris, teleg., 30 Mar. 1869, ibid., p. 116.
[2] Benedetti to La Valette, 31 Mar. 1869, ibid., pp. 118–20.
[3] Clarendon to Loftus, private, 31 Mar. 1869, Clar. Pap. C 474.
[4] Loftus to Clarendon, private, Berlin, 3 Apr. 1869, ibid., C 478.
[5] *Orig.*, xxiv. 159.
[6] Loftus to Clarendon, confidential, Berlin, 10 Apr. 1869, PRO FO 64/662, no. 187.

opposed to him. It is therefore at Paris that friendly but firm language may work on the vacillating mind of the Emperor.

If anything could precipitate that unification [of Germany] it would be war. Southern Germany at this moment is receding from— not approaching to Northern Germany, and the aversion of the South for Prussian rule and gov't is becoming daily stronger.[1]

Nevertheless, following his earlier instructions Loftus made known to Bismarck Clarendon's feelings about hasty or precipitous German unification.[2] Bismarck claimed indifference and even aversion to a union of his confederation and south Germany. Loftus felt that 'the governments' and 'public opinion' of south Germany were 'at the present moment far less favourably disposed to an union with the Northern Confederation than . . . [they were] in the summer of 1867'. He was alive to the possibility 'that the indifference [of Bismarck] . . . may be but a strategem intended to conceal other designs'.[3] Clarendon was pleased with the independent tendencies of south Germany, as he wrote to Bloomfield:

As the complete unification of Germany is the great bugbear in France and the event most likely to lead to war I observe with pleasure that the south is becoming daily less disposed to be Prussianized and that the north seems unready for the disturbing elements that the south would introduce.[4]

In May of 1869 Benedetti discussed the Hohenzollern rumours with Bismarck. The latter stressed their improbability, and this led the French ambassador to assume the absence of any formal offer of the throne to Leopold.[5] If the words of the Portuguese ambassador to France are to be trusted, Rouher was much more concerned with the candidature than the emperor. At the end of July 1870 the Duke of Saldanha told Murray, the British minister to Portugal, of conversations he had had with Napoleon and Rouher in May 1869.

---

[1] Loftus to Clarendon, private, Berlin, 10 Apr. 1869, Clar. Pap. C 478.

[2] Clarendon had asked Loftus 'whether it would be prudent to suggest to Ct. Bismarck . . . any postponement of the unification of Germany [since it would] . . . calm French susceptibilities and fear, and . . . any guarantee of the maintenance of the Treaty of Prague' (Clarendon to Victoria, 7 Apr. 1869, RA Q 3/108).

[3] Loftus to Clarendon, most confidential, Berlin, 17 Apr. 1869, PRO FO 64/662, no. 198.

[4] Clarendon to Bloomfield, private, 27 Apr. 1869, PRO FO 356/33.

[5] Benedetti to Rouher, confidential, Berlin, 11 May 1869, *Orig.* xxiv. 285-9.

I [Murray] have just returned from an interview with the Duke of Saldanha and . . . he mentioned a circumstance . . . when he was at Paris in May, '69'. . . . He spoke to the Emperor, to whom in mentioning the subject the Duke said he feared that on some grounds this . . . would not be agreeable to H.M. 'My dear Duke,' was the reply, 'I have before told you that so long as the Spaniards do not proclaim Montpensier [youngest son of Louis Phillippe] or a republic, I do not care who they take—in no other case shall we meddle with their selection.' It is to be presumed that H.M. mentioned the conversation to Rouher for next day Rouher sent to arrange a meeting with the Duke and . . . exclaimed apparently in great excitement 'M. le duc, what have you been doing with the Emperor with respect to the candidature of the Spanish throne? You must have taken H.M. at a moment when he was off-guard. . . . We [i.e., the government] well know that any attempt at placing a Prussian on that throne would occasion such a storm in France that we could not control it—that project cannot and must not be entertained.'[1]

In the meantime, Salazar sounded out the Hohenzollerns in September of 1869 and the door to further negotiations was left open.

Napoleon's announced liberal intentions in the summer of 1869 raised as many problems as solutions. Lyons was very anxious for the emperor's position.

I grieve to say that the Emperor seems to lose ground. . . . What is serious is that this doubt is strong among the generals. They would stick to him if they felt sure of him, because a reduction of the army is one of the leading doctrines of his opponents.[2]

The death of Marshal Niel in August was interpreted as a further 'embarrassment to the Empr.'.[3] Lyons hoped that 'foreign governments may perhaps do something towards

---

[1] Murray to Granville, 29 July 1870, PRO FO 30/29, no. 84. According to Benedetti, during his stay in Paris between 26 April and 5 May the emperor spoke decidedly against the Hohenzollern candidature (Benedetti, pp. 306–7). Murray's report is supported by a letter of Layard, the British minister at Madrid. 'I am assured that Leopold's candidature was fully discussed in the Bonaparte family, that sometime ago the Princess Mathilde recommended a person to speak to the Emp[eror] and Emp[eror] did not express any great objection to it but referred person in question to Rouher who did say it would be ill viewed in France' (Layard to Granville, private, Madrid, 28 July 1870, RA I 64/4).

[2] Lyons to Clarendon, private, Paris, 27 July 1869, Lyons Pap. RC 2. See also same to same, very confidential, Paris, 27 Aug. 1869, PRO FO 27/1760, no. 904.

[3] Clarendon to Lyons, private, Wiesbaden, 17 Aug. 1869, Clar. Pap. C 149.

supporting the Emperor, by treating international questions in such a way as to raise ... his reputation for sagacity and influence'.[1] The adverse change in the balance of power, which in large part had caused Napoleon's loss of influence in France, seemed to have been at least temporarily stabilized. The emperor was well aware, as Clarendon told him, that 'if Fr. was aggressive, it would do more in a month to cement Germany together than Bismarck would achieve in 5 yrs.'[2] Loftus remained 'confident' that Bismarck did not desire to hasten unification, and that the entry of the South into the North German Confederation was 'reserved for a distant future'.[3] The foreign secretary, publicly and privately, expressed his belief that the peace would be preserved.[4] 'Bismarck has shown so much tact and wisdom in the relations between France and Prussia that I cannot doubt his desire now to prevent a misunderstanding.'[5] Rumours of Baden's entry into the North German Confederation were played down by Clarendon.[6]

Until his death in 1870 Clarendon was building an image as an honest peacemaker. He evidently liked the role of self-appointed go-between for Paris and Berlin, particularly as the avoidance of war was his Government's main aim. His silence on the Hohenzollern question between October 1869 and March 1870 was due to the information he had received, which pointed to the Duke of Genoa as the future king of Spain.[7] He was unaware, as can be seen in his instruction to the English minister at Madrid, of any foreign intrigue in Spain:

Happily there is no longer a question as in former times of attempts on the part of foreign powers to turn to their own advantage the variations of Spanish politics. There is no desire on the part of any of them to disturb the balance of power in Europe by seeking to acquire dynastic influence in Spain.

---

[1] Ibid.

[2] Clarendon to Gladstone, Paris, 18 Sept. 1869, QVL, 2nd ser., i. 624–6.

[3] Loftus to Clarendon, Berlin, 25 Sept. 1869, PRO FO 64/666, no. 444.

[4] Contades to La Tour, London, 29 Sept. 1869, Orig. xxv. 272.

[5] Clarendon to Loftus, private, 29 Sept. 1869, Clar. Pap. C 474.

[6] Clarendon to Gladstone, 4 Oct. 1869, Glad. Pap. xlix. 48–49; Contades to La Tour, confidential, London, 5 Oct. 1869, Orig. xxv. 299–300. 'It is not here thought that Bismarck would risk a war with France for the mere accession of Baden' (Howard to Clarendon, most confidential, Munich, 8 Oct. 1869, PRO FO 244/234, no. 150).

[7] Ffrench to Clarendon, confidential, Madrid, 29 Oct. 1869, PRO FO 146/1397, no. 176; West to Clarendon, confidential, Paris, ibid. 27/1762, no. 104.

I have, therefore, no occasion to instruct you to watch in an anxious spirit the policy of other powers at Madrid.[1]

Foreign interference in Spain would 'disturb the balance of power', a balance which since 1866 had been greatly altered. Extreme French sensitiveness was a result of this fact.

In January 1870 Loftus assured Clarendon that Bismarck had no intention of doing 'anything venturesome about Baden'.[2] The King of Bavaria in a speech before the opening of the legislature said that he would 'only agree' to a German union 'as shall not threaten the independence of Bavaria'.[3] The only unsettling information was a report from Loftus that Bismarck was preparing the way for the King of Prussia to become emperor of North Germany.[4] The foreign secretary expressed the opinion that this would be a dangerous step.[5]

He was quite unaware that in the middle of February a dangerous step had already been taken. Salazar arrived in Germany with letters from Prim to the King of Prussia, Bismarck, and Leopold.[6] Leopold and Karl Anton, his father, in conversations with Salazar, informed the Spanish deputy that any decision must come from William. Bismarck strongly urged acceptance of the offer and told Leopold that if he refused 'a Bavarian prince might be elected'.[7] He also urged William to use his influence to secure acceptance.

There is some indication, though it should not perhaps be too much stressed, that at the end of 1869 and the beginning of 1870 Bismarck was becoming uneasy. Among his other

---

[1] Clarendon to Layard, 8 Nov. 1869, PRO FO 72/1206, no. 2.

[2] Loftus to Clarendon, private, Berlin, 22 Jan. 1870, Clar. Pap. 478.

[3] Howard to Clarendon, Munich, 17 Jan. 1870, PRO FO 9/200, no. 7.

[4] Loftus to Clarendon, most confidential, Berlin, 8 Jan. 1870, PRO FO 64/684, no. 17; same to same, private, Berlin, 22 Jan. 1870, Clar. Pap. C 478. On this see Otto Pflanze, *Bismarck and the Development of Germany* (Princeton, 1963), pp. 417–18.

[5] La Valette to Daru, London, 28 Jan. 1870, *Orig.* xxvi. 233. In February 1870 Bismarck casually told Loftus that if 'serious disturbances took place in Bavaria Prussians would immediately march in' (Loftus to Clarendon, confidential, Berlin, telegram, 15 Feb. 1870, PRO FO 64/685, no. 79). Clarendon was greatly concerned with this report (Clarendon to Lyons, teleg. secret, 15 Feb. 1870, PRO FO 27/1389, no. 111). Gladstone was also anxious (Gladstone to Clarendon, 16 Feb. 1870, Glad. Pap. ccccliii, letter-book 1869–70).

[6] Negotiations with the other possible candidates for the Spanish throne were generally known. Arrangements with a Hohenzollern were kept secret because of French feelings (Lord, p. 19).

[7] Leopold to Karl Anton, 1 Mar. 1870, Steefel, p. 55.

difficulties, events in southern Germany were not to his liking.[1] Even if he assumed German unification to be inevitable, the questions when and how had not been definitely answered.[2] The already mentioned indications of anti-Prussian sentiment south of the Main continued in 1870. Bismarck's desire for a Hohenzollern king of Spain in 1870 reflected this situation. He could not be sure that France would make war to prevent the candidature, only that she would object to it. In either case Napoleon would push south Germany closer to Prussia. This had occurred in 1866 and 1867 when the emperor demanded compensation and then Luxemburg. As long as France remained quiet the particularist tendencies of south Germany might grow.[3]

In Bavaria the anti-Prussian clericalist party had gained strength, and the military treaty signed with Prussia in 1866 was questioned in the legislature. On 10 February Bismarck inserted in the *Norddeutsche Allgemeine Zeitung* an article maintaining that the south German states did not have the right to determine when a *casus foederis* has arisen.[4] Varnbüler, of Württemberg, disagreed and claimed 'that in case of a treaty between nations each interpreted the stipulations in the way it considered itself justified in doing'.[5] He argued that Württemberg had the right 'to determine as to whether any special combination of events involved a *casus foederis* or not'.[6] Freydorf, the foreign minister of Baden, agreed with Varnbüler that each signatory to the treaty had the right of free decision.[7] Hohenlohe of Bavaria, who was being pressed to resign by the anti-Prussian faction, would only say that he had received no word from Prussia on this question.[8] Even Leopold of Hohenzollern noted

---

[1] See Steefel, pp. 233–8; E. Eyck, *Bismarck and the German Empire* (London, 1950), pp. 162–3.

[2] According to Busch, Bismarck in February 1870 told him that 'the question of German unity is making good progress; but it requires time—one year perhaps, or five, or indeed possibly even ten years' (Moritz Busch, *Bismarck: Some Secret Pages of His History* [London, 1898], i. 4).

[3] Pflanze presents a similar view (Pflanze, pp. 448–9).

[4] The King of Prussia in his speech at the opening of the federal parliament claimed that the treaties were reciprocally binding (Loftus to Clarendon, confidential, Berlin, 19 Feb. 1870, PRO FO 64/685, no. 87).

[5] Gordon to Clarendon, Stuttgart, 14 Feb. 1870, PRO FO 244/242.

[6] Same to same, confidential, Stuttgart, 16 Feb. 1870, ibid., no. 16.

[7] Gordon to Clarendon, Stuttgart, 18 Feb. 1870, ibid., no. 18.

[8] Howard to Clarendon, Munich, 18 Feb. 1870, PRO FO 146/1436, no. 43.

that 'South German conditions seem to be seriously preoccupy-
ing the [Prussian] government at the moment'.[1]

Bismarck's disinclination to use force or overt pressure on
the south German states was due only in part to consideration
for France or the fear of provoking her. He did not wish to
strengthen the particularist elements south of the Main by
frightening when he hoped to entice, or by demanding what
he hoped to be offered. While he did not flagrantly wish to
excite France on the question of German unity, this consideration was subordinate to the completion of unification on his own
or Hohenzollern terms. Consequently, when the issue of
Baden's entry into the North German Confederation arose in
March 1870, Bismarck poured cold water on the idea[2] for the
sake of his allies in Bavaria and Württemberg.[3]

On 12 March the Crown Princess of Prussia wrote to
Victoria, her mother:

> General Prim has sent a Spaniard here with several autograph
> letters from himself to Leopold Hohenzollern, urging him most
> earnestly to accept the Crown of Spain, saying he would be elected
> by 2/3 of the Cortes. They do not wish the French to know it, but
> the K., Prince Hohenzollern, Leopold and Fritz wish to know
> your opinion in private; as it is so great a secret, there is no way of
> communicating with Lord Clarendon on the subject, except your
> speaking to him confidentially.
>
> Neither the K. nor Prince Hohenzollern, nor Antoinette [Princess
> Leopold] and Leopold, nor Fritz are in favour of the idea, thinking
> it painful and unpleasant to accept a position which has legitimate
> claimants. . . . Will you please let me have an answer which I can
> show the persons mentioned?[4]

The queen communicated the letter to her foreign secretary

His successor, Count Bray, believed that Bavaria had the right 'to examine the
validity of the "casus foederis", before taking a decision' (Howard to Clarendon,
confidential, Munich, 26 Mar. 1870, PRO FO 9/201, no. 72).

[1] Leopold to Karl Anton, 1 Mar. 1870, Steefel, p. 55.

[2] Howard to Clarendon, confidential, Munich, 3 Mar. 1870, PRO FO 146/1437,
no. 50; Gordon to Clarendon, Stuttgart, 4 Mar. 1870, ibid., no. 23.

[3] In Bavaria there was an especially strong faction opposed to joining the north
on almost any basis (Howard to Clarendon, ibid.). Renouvin feels that Bismarck's
motivation was to give French opinion time to accustom itself to German union
(Renouvin, pp. 377–82).

[4] Crown Princess of Prussia to Victoria, Berlin, 12 Mar. 1870, QVL, 2nd ser., ii.
10. Fritz had asked his wife to write this letter to the queen (ibid., Letters of Queen
Victoria: from the archives of Brandenburg—Prussia [New Haven, 1938], p. 71).

whose reply was enigmatic, considering his efforts to retard German unification so as not to provoke France.

It would not be expedient for your Majesty to give any advice upon a matter in which no British interest is concerned and which can only be decided according to the feeling and the interests of the family.

Lord Clarendon has little doubt that the proposed arrangement would produce an unfavourable impression in France.[1]

Clarendon, perhaps, saw no reason to give an opinion on an improbable eventuality, and the queen gave no opinion in her reply to her son-in-law:

About the letters from General Prim to the Prince of Hohenzollern I have spoken quite confidentially to Lord Clarendon and we Both agree that I can express no opinion—either in favour or against, as it is a matter on which only the Prince and his son must come to a decision on which I would not care to exercise the least influence.[2]

At the same time as the above correspondence, and on Bismarck's initiative, a dinner was held in Berlin in order to discuss the question. Present were the king, crown prince, Bismarck, Karl Anton, Leopold, von Roon, von Moltke, Delbruck, Schleinitz, and von Thile.[3] Opinion was much in favour of the acceptance of the offer of the Spanish throne, but Leopold declined to do so except at the king's wish, and this the king refused to give.[4] Throughout the rest of March and April little progress was made, though Bismarck had established closer contacts with Prim in Spain, and Karl Anton seemed to be wavering towards acceptance.

In France all attention was focused on constitutional reform, which resulted in the resignation of some of the emperor's ministers, including Daru.[5] Napoleon's use of plebiscites was viewed with disfavour by the British prime minister.

If the Emperor is really striking for the right to refer when he

---

[1] Clarendon to Victoria, Windsor Castle, 14 Mar. 1870, *QVL*, 2nd ser., ii. 10–11. Undoubtedly the nature of the communication tied the foreign secretary's hands as to the possibility of taking action on the contents of the letter.

[2] Victoria to Frederick William, Windsor Castle, 16 Mar. 1870, Bonnin, p. 84.

[3] Lord, pp. 20–21; Steefel, pp. 61–65.　　　　[4] Ibid.

[5] Lyons believed that Daru's party, 'the left centre, wd not go with him, and felt that in that case he should have a weak position in the cabinet' (Lyons to Clarendon, private, 14 Apr. 1870, Lyons Pap. RC 2).

pleases to the people for an aye or no upon a proposition which he is to frame, that in my opinion reduces constitutional gov't to an absolute mockery, just as it would reduce to a shadow the power of a legislative assembly.[1]

In France, too, the feeling was growing that a really successful plebiscite would lead the emperor to 'personal gov't'.[2] The nomination of Gramont as Daru's successor caused regret both at London and Berlin. 'Gramont will be a very bad for. min. and one can only say that he is preferable to the detested rogue La Guerroniere who was the other candidate.'[3] Bloomfield, who knew him at Vienna, seemed even more anxious: 'Gramont is favourable to the English alliance but he is violently anti-Prussian and Russian, and he certainly would not be sorry to stir up a feeling against the N. German confed. and stand out against any Prussian advance s[outh] of the Main.'[4] In April and May, though there was more than a little evidence for German union, the anti-Prussian tendencies of south Germany continued.

At the beginning of April there was talk of establishing a south German confederation, which according to Gordon, the British minister in Stuttgart, was being inspired by Hohenlohe[5] because it would mean Bavarian hegemony. In Gordon's estimation a south German confederation was unlikely as all but five members of the Baden legislature would vote for annexation to the north; in Württemberg 33 out of 92 would do so; in Bavaria a little less than half; and in Hesse the overwhelming majority were inclined to the North German Confederation.[6] Morier seemed more impressed with the anti-Prussian tendencies of the south than Gordon. He pointed out that in Baden the Government wanted union with the north but was opposed by an active ultramontane element. In

[1] Gladstone to Clarendon, 14 Apr. 1870, Glad. Pap., ccccliii, letter-book 1869–70. Clarendon also disliked the idea of plebiscites (Clarendon to Lyons, 12 May 1870, Newton, p. 287).
[2] Lyons to Clarendon, 21 Apr. 1870, Newton, p. 283.
[3] Clarendon to Bloomfield, private, 8 May 1870, PRO FO 361/1. Clarendon felt he was 'an empty headed unreliable coxcombe quite unfit for the post' (Clarendon to Lyons, private, 11 May 1870, Clar. Pap. C 474); Clarendon to Bloomfield, private, 18 May 1870, PRO FO 356/33.
[4] Bloomfield to Clarendon, private, Vienna, 12 May 1870, PRO FO 356/40.
[5] Gordon to Clarendon, Stuttgart, 13 Apr. 1870, PRO FO 146/1441, no. 45.
[6] Ibid.

Württemberg there was an energetic and vocal party for independence and in Bavaria the patriotic and ultramontane group 'is embarrassed with the victory it has won and knows not to what use to put it'.[1] He felt, however, that the 'outlines of a unified national state are daily becoming more discernible'.[2] Five days later he wrote that 'the anti-Prussian stream is running higher at the present moment in South Germany than I have ever known it since 1866'.[3] Morier was certain that the reason for this was the strong demand for military reduction which it was believed Prussia would prevent.[4]

Rumours concerning unification increased in May.[5] 'The project for unifying Germany and making the K [of Prussia] Emperor . . . is suspended not dropped.'[6] Clarendon was worried because, as Lyons reported, 'a war unmistakably provoked by Pr., would be hailed by many [in France] as a welcome diversion from internal difficulties'.[7] The foreign secretary seemed more concerned than Napoleon, who told Beyens that he was 'perfectly tranquil with regard to Prussia'.[8]

It was generally agreed that if Prussia crossed the Main river there would be war,[9] and indications of Bavarian resistance to such a step pleased Clarendon.[10] The foreign secretary cautioned the Spanish about electing Montpensier because it might make France 'uncomfortable'.[11] In May his attempts to prevent the provocation of France met resistance in Berlin and Madrid as the Hohenzollern candidature took new life.

The King of Prussia was both surprised and annoyed that

---

[1] Morier to Clarendon, Darmstadt, 20 Apr. 1870, PRO FO 30/238, no. 4.
[2] Ibid.
[3] Morier to Clarendon, private and confidential, Carlsbad, 25 Apr. 1870, Clar. Pap. C 498.   [4] Ibid.
[5] Howard to Clarendon, most confidential, Munich, 12 May 1870, PRO FO 146/1444, no. 108.
[6] Clarendon to Victoria, 3 May 1870, QVL, 2nd ser., ii. 19; Clarendon to Loftus, private, 4 May 1870, Clar. Pap. C 474.
[7] Lyons to Clarendon, Paris, 6 May 1870, Newton, pp. 285–6.
[8] Lumley to Clarendon, private, Brussels, 8 May 1870, Clar. Pap. C 495.
[9] Clarendon to Loftus, private, 18 May 1870, PRO FO 361/1. When Bismarck mentioned the possibility of a closer connexion with south Germany to Benedetti, the French ambassador made no comment (Bismarck to Bernstorff, Berlin, 29 Mar. 1870, GW vi B, no. 1544).
[10] Clarendon to Howard, private, 18 May 1870, PRO FO 361/1.
[11] Clarendon to Layard, private, 20 May 1870, C. J. Bartlett, 'Clarendon, the Foreign Office and the Hohenzollern Candidature, 1868–70', English Historical Review, lxxv (1960), 279.

the candidature was alive again.[1] Bismarck convinced Karl Anton, who in turn persuaded Leopold, that it was not necessary for the King of Prussia to command the latter to accept the crown. By the beginning of June the decision had been taken to accept, and Prim eagerly began to prepare for Leopold's election. In June, final arrangements still pending, Prim spoke to the Cortes of the difficulty of finding an acceptable sovereign, and in doing so mentioned the names of Ferdinand of Portugal, Amadeus of Savoy, the Duke of Genoa, and a fourth candidate whose name he would not mention.[2] The secret candidate had all the necessary qualifications, but according to Prim the Government had nothing definite to report.

It was no secret that the fourth candidate was Leopold of Hohenzollern, but so many names had been put forth as possibilities for the throne of Spain that one more stirred no undue excitement. Lyons referred to the 'g[rea]t diplomatic calm all over the world',[3] despite the fact that Layard reported from Spain that he had 'been assured that a Hohenzollern . . . [was] Prim's fourth candidate'.[4] The British minister further commented that he had been informed by a reliable source that Napoleon would be compelled by opinion in France to oppose such a candidature.[5] Clarendon, who had been so concerned lest German unification should provoke France to war, would have been at least as concerned about a confirmed Hohenzollern candidature. But he died on the morning of 27 June and never saw Layard's letter.

Clarendon's death, the interim until his successor entered office, and Granville's own lack of forcefulness, which Gladstone did not offset, prevented the British Government from having the influence it might have had on the Hohenzollern candidacy and the events leading to war. However limited it might have been, Clarendon's weight on the Continent was greater than that of any other British statesman. Gladstone remarked that he 'was the only living British statesman whose name carried any influence in the councils of Europe'.[6] His prestige did not

---

[1] Steefel, p. 82; *Bismarck's Pen; the Life of Heinrich Abeken*, trans. C. E. Barrett-Lennard and M. W. Hoper (London, 1911), pp. 243–4, 247.   [2] Steefel, pp. 93–94.
[3] Lyons to Adolphus, private, 24 Apr. 1870, Lyons Pap. RC 2.
[4] Layard to Clarendon, private, Madrid, 25 June 1870, PRO FO 361/1.
[5] Ibid.
[6] Morley, i. 254–5. Granville agreed with this estimate (E. G. P. Fitzmaurice, *Life of the Second Earl of Granville* [London, 1905], ii. 26).

derive from policy, for it was little different from Stanley's or Granville's, but from personality and diplomatic experience. Unlike Stanley or Granville he was conscious of his importance in Europe and was willing, short of involvement, to exercise it. Stanley was unsure of himself and Granville's sense of propriety was overwhelming. Clarendon's intervention in the question of German unification was superfluous. Bismarck did not need to be told what he already knew and what France made little attempt to hide. Lyons summed up the problem:

> Prussia holds that it is not conquest or aggression to annex any German state. France considers that the annexation of any of the states south of the Main wd be as much conquest or aggression on the part of Prussia, as it wd be, on the part of France to annex them herself.
>
> Prussia will never declare that she will not complete the unity of Germany.
>
> France will never declare that she will not interfere to prevent this.[1]

Nevertheless the foreign secretary hoped, as the King of Prussia told him, that unification 'would not take place in his [the king's] lifetime, possibly not in that of his son'.[2] If unity took long enough, France might grow accustomed to the prospect.

The existence of a strong and compact power in central Europe as an offset to France and Russia was pleasing to British opinion. It was felt that a united Germany would preserve the balance of power on the Continent and at the same time help to guarantee the peace. It is surprising in the light of Bismarck's actions in 1864 and 1866 that Prussia was viewed as a peaceful power by most Englishmen. The parochial *Times* led and upheld this view. Prussia was considered as 'the natural friend of all who wish . . . peace'.[3] Clarendon at least had the commonsense to see what was before his eyes, but among Englishmen he was almost alone in this.[4] 'One asks

---

[1] Lyons to Clarendon, private, Paris, 11 Mar. 1870, Lyons Pap. RC 2.

[2] Clarendon to Lyons, 12 Mar. 1870, Newton, p. 266. Stanley also hoped that if German unification were gradual, time would temper French objections to it and war would not result (Katte to Bismarck, London, 6 Aug. 1868, *APP* x. 138–9).

[3] D. N. Raymond, *British Policy and Opinion during the Franco-Prussian War* (New York, 1921), p. 27.

[4] The Duke of Cambridge shared Clarendon's feeling. Loftus wrote that 'so long as England and France remain united—we are predominant—and England will have an ally . . . whose interests are the same as our own' (Loftus to Clarendon, secret and confidential, Berlin, 10 July 1869, Clar. Pap. C 478).

oneself however what possible interest Russia can have in favouring Prussian ambition, in forfeiting the French alliance and endangering the peace of Europe.'[1]

Napoleon was much upset by the anti-French tone of the English press and told Lyons so.[2] Though English feeling was pro-Prussian it was only partially opposed to the emperor, despite the fact that he was French. He was regarded as an apostle of free trade and as a bulwark against republicanism and socialism in France. Lyons pointed out that 'selfishly, we ought to remember that his influence in the gov't is the principle security we can have for free trade'.[3] The British ambassador never tired of reporting that only the emperor stood between France and the republicans.[4]

Bismarck was thoroughly detested by the same British statesmen who feared his removal from office. Like Napoleon, Bismarck was a buffer against the democratic spirit. 'Lord Clarendon is inclined to share H.M.'s [the Queen of Prussia's] apprehensions, as democracy in Germany means Socialism, i.e. the subversion of all those laws by which Society is held together.'[5] In 1866 the foreign secretary would have seen with pleasure the dismissal of Bismarck, not so in 1870. Stanley valued Bismarck because he would successfully unify Germany; Clarendon was hoping for time to avoid the war which it would provoke. As Loftus commented, the latter hope was vain:

As the war of 1866 decided the question of supremacy in Germany —the question now at issue is as to the supremacy in Europe between France and Germany. France feels that she has hitherto enjoyed a certain ascendancy in Europe, and that since 1866 she no longer enjoys the same position. A powerful military neighbour has risen up to contest this supremacy with her—and the feeling that she has been displaced makes every French man boil with jealousy

---

[1] Clarendon to Loftus, private, 8 June 1870, Clar. Pap. C 474.

[2] Lyons to Clarendon, private, Paris, 24 May 1870, PRO FO 361/1; Newton, ibid., pp. 290–1.

[3] Ibid.

[4] Clarendon was only too aware of this. 'A revolution in France [he wrote] might condense the floating disaffection that is on the increase in England. It is therefore important for us on every account to help the Empr. out of his scrapes, as far as possible' (Clarendon to Stanley, private, Florence, 21 Dec. 1867, RA J 39/131).

[5] Clarendon to Victoria, Wiesbaden, 21 Aug. 1869, QVL, 2nd ser., i. 623–4.

and hatred against Prussia. This can only be eradicated by time. But time cannot be purchased.[1]

On the eve of war Parliament and most British statesmen recognized with no little pleasure the great alteration in the balance of power. There was but slight sympathy for the position of France. Even the shock of the Hohenzollern acceptance of the Spanish throne did not change the direction of English sentiment, though it was obvious that it would further modify the balance of power. There was still indelibly stamped on the British imagination the imprint of an aggressive and dangerous France. The first years of the Second Empire only confirmed this picture, and Napoleon in large measure was forced to reap what his uncle sixty years before had sown. The seeming insensitivity of successive English governments to Prussian ambition in the 1860's reflected the aftertaste left by the Napoleonic wars and the recurrent fears of invasion by France. This had become an almost racial prejudice. In Dilke's words: 'Our true alliance . . . is not with the Latin peoples, but with men who speak our tongue, with our brothers in America, and our kinsmen in Germany and Scandinavia.'[2]

The queen and especially her secretary Grey, who reinforced her prejudice, wished naturally enough to act according to their German feelings. Grey preached alliance with Prussia and the queen checked any desire for such a step only because 'times have much changed; great foreign alliances are looked on as causes of trouble and anxiety, and are of no good'.[3] No one represented this attitude more than Stanley, whose popularity in England stemmed from the fact that he was a symbol of it. He made little attempt to hide his satisfaction at the prospect of German unification and rationalized his inaction on the basis of interest. Clarendon, who hated and mistrusted Bismarck, was pro-French and justified it by the necessity for French co-operation in the East and her value as a possible ally against the United States. Granville's feelings were smothered by correctness and emasculated by tact. His initiative in the July crisis was blunted by propriety. Gladstone, however,

---

[1] Loftus to Clarendon, private, Berlin, 3 Apr. 1869, Clar. Pap. C 478.

[2] Speech at the beginning of July 1870 by Dilke to the electors of Chelsea (S. Gwynn and G. M. Tuckwell, *The Life of Sir Charles W. Dilke* [New York, 1917], i. 104).

[3] Victoria to Prince of Wales, 29 Nov. 1869, *QVL*, 2nd ser., i. 632.

N

seemed satisfied with his qualifications for office: 'We are happy in being able to fill the office with a man who has the deep calm of Ld. Aberdeen, a strong sense of justice, much foreign knowledge, and singular tact.'[1]

When London learned of the Hohenzollern acceptance there was surprise and disappointment with Prussia's action, not because France had been injured but because war might result. It was not reasonable to expect England to sympathize with France on the basis of continental changes which she desired almost as much as Berlin. Clarendon himself had seemed more preoccupied with indications that Spain was interested in Portugal rather than with the prospect of a Hohenzollern in Madrid.

I think it necessary [he wrote to Layard] to draw your special attention again to this matter, and to instruct you to watch carefully any indication of a disposition to interfere with Portugal, wh., in case of need, you will clearly intimate wd. be viewed with much dissatisfaction by H.M's govt.[2]

Any connexion in Clarendon's mind between this concern and Hohenzollern plans in Spain must remain a moot question. Direct British interest in the Iberian peninsula was confined to Gibraltar, the advancement of free trade, and the preservation of an independent Portugal. The foreign secretary instructed Layard:

While abstaining from anything like an endeavour to influence the course which the Spanish nation may adopt for the reorganization of its government, you will not disguise the satisfaction which has of late . . . been shown [in England to the disposition] in Spain to act on the principle of toleration in matters of religion and of progress in matters of commerce.[3]

On Prim's desire for Gibraltar Clarendon was unequivocal:

Prim, cannot be aware of the obstacles we should have to contend against in any attempt to comply with his request, or how sensitive

---

[1] Gladstone to General Church, 3 July 1870, Glad. Pap. ccccliii, letter-book 1869–70.

[2] Clarendon to Layard, 17 May 1870, PRO FO 72/1231, no. 104.

[3] Clarendon to Layard, 8 Nov. 1869, PRO FO 72/1206, no. 2. The British Cabinet had seen with satisfaction the fall of Isabella. They had also favoured the provisional government because of its free trade policy (Kalnoky to Beust, London, 7 Oct. 1868, England, HHSA, no. 58 c; same to same, London, 20 Oct. 1869, ibid., no. 59 A–D).

and vigilant the British public are on the question of Gibraltar, esp. at this moment when opening of the Suez Canal makes it of utmost importance to us, with reference to free commun. with India, not in any way to weaken ourselves in the Mediterranean. . . . Parliament would not permit the cession of Gibraltar.[1]

The election of Leopold would not endanger these interests and would end the possibility of a republic,[2] which was an unpleasant alternative to most of the leaders of the British Government. Only the possibility of French objections prejudiced the candidacy in English eyes, and then only in the eyes of a few like Clarendon.

[1] Clarendon to Layard, private and confidential, 15 Mar. 1870, PRO FO 361/1.
[2] Ffrench to Clarendon, Madrid, 29 Oct. 1869, PRO FO 146/1317, no. 176.

X

WAR

The Candidacy becomes Public

IN Madrid many knew of Leopold's acceptance on 1 July, and the next day Paris had also heard the news.[1] On 3 July Napoleon and Gramont began to take steps to frustrate the candidacy through Mercier in Madrid and, Benedetti being away, Le Sourd in Berlin. Thile told the latter that the Prussian Government was ignorant of the whole affair,[2] but on the same day Gramont and Ollivier talked with Werther, the Prussian ambassador, and told him France could not permit the candidacy. As Werther was on his way to see the King of Prussia at Ems, the two French leaders instructed him to ask William to forbid the candidacy.[3] It was at this point in the affair, at 6 p.m. of the fourth, that Hammond sent the following telegram to Lyons:

Negotiations are being carried on between Prim & Saldanha. The latter will endeavour to persuade K. of Portugal to abdicate in favour of his son who is to be proclaimed K. of Sp. & Portugal, Saldanha to be regent in Portugal & Prim regent in Spain.[4]

Events had taken the lead of the British Government and would move so quickly that the efforts of Granville to arrest them were both too late and too little.

It was not until late afternoon of 5 July that London received any information. The first news came probably from Layard in a telegram which arrived at the foreign office at 5.50 p.m.[5] Lyons sent official and private reports of his conversation with Gramont:

The Duc de Gramont undoubtedly wished me to be convinced that France would go to war with Spain and Prussia rather than

[1] Steefel, pp. 101–3. [2] Ibid., p. 107; Lord, pp. 30–31.
[3] Ibid., pp. 31–34.
[4] Hammond to Lyons, telegram, 4 July 1870, PRO FO 146/1448, no. 575.
[5] Anderson, p. 84, footnote.

allow a Hohenzollern to reign at Madrid. . . . He would however be
very grateful for any exertion we might make to induce the King of
Prussia . . . to put an end to it. He said . . . a Prussian was an insult
and an injury to all France.[1]

On the same day Napoleon asked Gladstone through the
Rothschilds to aid in the withdrawal of the candidature. The
prime minister disapproved of it but was not inclined to interfere with Spain's freedom to choose her own sovereign.[2]

On 6 July Gramont, after conferring with Napoleon,
Ollivier, and the council, read the Government's statement
to the chamber. France would not 'permit a foreign prince on
the throne of Charles V and would 'know how to discharge . . .
[its] duty without faltering or weakness'.[3]

A big step towards war had been taken, and the British
Government was proceeding at a leisurely pace some distance
behind. There was some hesitation particularly among British
newspapers to take the quarrel seriously. The *Daily News*,
The Times, *Manchester Guardian,* and *London Graphic* either
thought that no French interests were threatened or that the
peace of Europe was not in danger.[4]

La Valette repeated to Granville the request for support that
Gramont had made the day before to Lyons. England was
asked to use its influence at Berlin and Madrid to prevent the
candidature. Granville's reply was so correct it was almost
impertinent. The foreign secretary expressed his surprise at
news of the project, his regret at the strong language used to
Werther, and his assent to the request to 'use what influence'
England 'had with Prussia and Spain'.[5] Consequently, on the
evening of 6 July, Granville wrote a draft telegram to be sent
to Madrid:

It is not for England to recommend any particular sovereign for

---

[1] Lyons to Hammond, private, Paris, 5 July 1870, Lyons Pap. RC 2; Lyons to
Granville, 5 July 1870, PRO FO 27/1805, no. 685.

[2] Morley, ii. 235.

[3] Lyons was surprised and complained of Gramont's language. The latter
attempted to justify France's reaction and requested British advice at Berlin and
Madrid to put a stop to the candidature (Lyons to Granville, Paris, 7 July 1870,
PRO FO 27/1805, no. 698).

[4] D. N. Raymond, *British Policy and Opinion during the Franco-Prussian War* (New
York, 1921), pp. 27–29.

[5] Granville to Lyons, 6 July 1870, PRO FO 27/1791, no. 14; same to same,
private, 6 July 1870, PRO FO 362/4; Newton, pp. 294–5.

Spain, or in any way to interfere with the choice of the Spanish
people; but wishing as they do, well to Spain, H.M.'s Govt cannot
but feel anxious as to the consequences of the selection now made.[1]

The wire, which was actually sent on 7 July as Granville informed Lyons, was short and to the point.

Use every pressure which will not offend the Spanish govt: but
which in your judgment will promote the abandonment of the
Hohenzollern project.

You will say nothing that would provoke them to adhere to it.[2]

On the same day Granville told Rances, the Spanish minister,
that the project could result in war and 'such a choice secretly
made' should have been avoided.[3]

On the evening of the sixth Granville also wrote a dispatch
to Loftus, which was probably not sent until 9 July.

I venture to hope that the K. [of Prussia] & his advisers will find
it consistent with their own views of what is best for Spain effectually to discourage a project fraught with risks to the best interest
of that country.

I cannot but add the reflection that the strict secrecy with which
these proceedings have been conducted as between the Spanish
ministry & the Prince who has been the object of their choice . . . has
given, what Her Majesty's Government cannot but admit to be so
far as it goes just cause of offence.[4]

The foreign secretary sent his draft to Gladstone who returned
advice both public and private:

I have put in pencil such shadings as I had to suggest in the text
of your proposed dispatch to Loftus.

I send herewith a proposed addition, for your judgment. The last
part is cribbed fr. an able article in the Times of today. The earlier
parts fr. Lyons.

I am doubtful whether this dispatch should go till it has been seen
by the cabinet, indeed I think it should not.

---

[1] Granville to Layard, telegram, 6 July 1870, PRO FO 72/1231.
[2] Granville to Lyons, telegram, 2.45 p.m., 7 July 1870, PRO FO 27/1791, no.
75; Granville to Layard, telegram, 2.25 p.m., 7 July 1870, PRO FO 72/1231.
'Both Lowe & Cardwell having seen y[our] telegram to Layard thought it went
rather far. I argued the case a little' (Gladstone to Granville, 8 July 1870, Glad.
Pap. ccccliii, letter-book 1869–70).
[3] Granville to Layard, 7 July 1870, PRO FO 146/1449, no. 5.
[4] Granville to Loftus, 6 July 1870, British State Papers, lxx (1870), 25. Morley
points this out in his biography of Gladstone (Morley, ii. 325–6). Gladstone to
Victoria, 9 July 1870, RA A 40/30.

The Queen recollects being told something about this affair by Clarendon—without result—last year.[1]
I think Gramont exacts too much. It would never do for us to get up a combination of powers in this difficult & slippery matter? I may add that we have not in any measure admitted that the assumption of the Spanish throne by Prince Leopold would justify the immediate resort to arms threatened by France. On this topic however you are not to enter at present in communicating with the Prussian Govt.
I cannot but add the reflection that the strict secrecy with which these proceedings have been conducted . . . seems inconsistent with the spirit of friendship or the rules of comity between nations, & has given what H.M.'s govt cannot but admit to be so far as it goes just cause of offence . . . [which the] withdrawal of the Prince . . . can alone effectively repair.[2]

The crisis was therefore a week old before Prussia was officially informed of the opinion of the British Government. On the seventh of July, Bismarck wrote a draft telegram to Bernstorff which anticipated England's belated reaction to the crisis:

We have in fact no interest in interfering in Spanish affairs, and there is no question of our support when Prussia has no concern in the matter. If France wants to interfere that is her business, if she wants to make war on us because the Spaniards elect a German as King, it would be quite unjustifiably quarrelsome. We shall never wage a war of the Spanish succession.[3]

On the following day Bernstorff called upon Granville and repeated Bismarck's instructions.[4]

The ambivalent attitude of England in the first week of the Hohenzollern crisis has been accurately described by Sorel: 'In England, public opinion declared itself against the candidature of prince Leopold. The Times formally condemned it. But in recognizing the legitimacy of French grievances, the English

[1] Victoria had either a bad memory or more probably was embarrassed at telling Gladstone of the communication concerning the candidature made in March 1870, as the prime minister had not been informed of it at the time it was made.
[2] Gladstone to Granville, 8 July 1870, Glad. Pap. cccliii, letter-book 1869-70. The article in *The Times* referred to by the prime minister stressed the 'great discourtesy' and secrecy of the negotiation which provoked France. In 1866 when Leopold's brother became the ruler of Roumania, Clarendon felt that Austria could not permit a Prussian lieutenant on her frontier.
[3] Bonnin, p. 227.
[4] Granville to Lyons, 8 July 1870, *British State Papers*, lxx (1870), 31.

wished above all to maintain peace.'[1] Both Granville and Gladstone exhibited this ambivalence. The former wrote:

It is difficult to believe that the Prussian Govt. have not had a hand in the business, & the secrecy with which the matter has been conducted was certainly offensive to Fr, & not courteous to other powers. On the other hand it seems unpardonable on the part of Fr to have made such a menace & a public one at the very outset. I have no doubt of their present intention to go to war, rather than allow the Prince to be seated on the throne. But if Pr. pretends to know nothing about it . . . their way of going to war is not very clear.[2]

Lyons privately expressed his complete lack of sympathy with the French Government's reaction to the candidacy.

The explosion of chauvinism in France is very unfortunate and very alarming. The govt. undoubtedly desire and hope at the present moment to carry their point without actual war; but they have burnt their ships and left themselves no possible means of escape. . . . They enormously exaggerate the injury to their interests . . . but they have taken up the question as a point of honour.[3]

Nor was the French Government any more pleased with Britain's lack of understanding. La Valette complained to Granville about his 'coldness'.[4] The foreign secretary then asked Cowley to intercede for him. 'Cowley is gone to La Valette as if out of curiosity & will let me know what his tone is & he probably would be able to reassure La Valette about me better than a colleague or my chief could do.'[5] Yet Paris continued to ask for English support in arranging an end to the affair. On 8 July Gramont spoke of 'a voluntary renunciation, on the part of the Prince . . . [as] a most fortunate solution'.[6]

The King of Prussia at Ems, upon receiving news of the

---

[1] Albert Sorel, *Histoire diplomatique de la guerre Franco-Allemande* (Paris, 1875), i. 70. There was little doubt in England that the candidacy had been long prepared by Bismarck. Bray, Hohenlohe's successor in Bavaria, told Howard this (Howard to Granville, most confidential, Munich, 8 July 1870, PRO FO 9/202, no. 141). Gramont told Lyons the same thing (Lyons to Granville, private, Paris, 8 July 1870, Lyons Pap. RC 2).

[2] Granville to Russell, 7 July 1870, Gooch, ii. 370. For Granville's justification of his actions prior to the outbreak of war see Fitzmaurice, ii. 33.

[3] Lyons to Granville, private, Paris, 7 July 1870, Lyons Pap. RC 2.

[4] Granville to Gladstone, 7 July 1870, Glad. Pap. lxxxii. 68–70.

[5] Same to same, ibid., pp. 71–72.

[6] Lyons to Granville, Paris, 8 July 1870, *British State Papers*, lxx (1870), 32–33.

French reaction to the candidature, inclined towards a renunciation by Leopold.[1] Bismarck, at Varzin, started a press campaign,[2] the purpose of which was to embitter what his king
wished to allay. Napoleon was conducting his own newspaper
campaign, and was more active in seeking Russian, English,
Austrian, Italian, and Belgian[3] assistance in ending the candidature. Pressure was also brought to bear in Madrid and
Benedetti, who was away at Wilbad, was ordered to go to
William at Ems. The king granted Benedetti an interview on
9 July and told the French ambassador that he could not
exercise his authority to induce Leopold to withdraw, but that
he was awaiting word from Leopold and Karl Anton concerning France's objections.[4]

On 10 July William and Benedetti met again. The French
ambassador urged upon the king the gravity of the situation
and another meeting was arranged for the following day. The
king meanwhile sent Colonel von Strantz to Sigmaringen to see
Karl Anton and explain that a renunciation by Leopold would
be quite acceptable. At the same time Strat, the Roumanian
minister in Paris, at the behest of Napoleon and Olozaga, the
Spanish ambassador, went to Sigmaringen to persuade Leopold
to withdraw.[5] The threat of war and the mounting pressure on
Karl Anton was too much. On 12 July he wired Olozaga at
Paris that he was withdrawing acceptance in the name of his
son.[6]

The British Government had belatedly held a Cabinet on
the ninth when Granville informed his colleagues of the situation. As Morley has pointed out, the only other Cabinet was
held on the fourteenth.[7] Granville wrote uncertainly to Lyons
that 'The Cabinet entirely approved all that we have done'.
He asked Lyons to 'remember what a novice' he was and to
give him 'any advice' that occurred to him.[8] Granville did not
want for either advice or opinion. Layard commented that it

---

[1] Steefel, pp. 120–1.

[2] M. Busch, *Bismarck: Some Secret Pages of His History* (London, 1898), i. 35–45.

[3] Lumley wired on 9 July that 'Napoleon has requested King of the Belgians to
induce Prince of Hohenzollern to renounce the throne of Spain. The King has
written today to the Prince' (Lumley to Granville, telegram, most secret, 9 July
1870, PRO FO 10/306).

[4] Lord, pp. 48–51.   [5] Steefel, pp. 130–1, 138–9.

[6] Ibid., pp. 142–3.   [7] Morley, i. 326.

[8] Granville to Lyons, 9 July 1870, PRO FO 362/4.

was 'somewhat remarkable . . . that the French government
should not have taken an early opportunity of signifying . . .
their views' concerning the candidature.[1]

Loftus thought 'the French menace . . . unwise and dangerous'
and hoped for a Hohenzollern withdrawal, but he felt that
'the essential thing will be to calm French govt & to stop
irritating language of French press'.[2]

With the concurrence of Gladstone and the Cabinet,
Granville sent instructions to Lyons which, though lacking
in sympathy, were calculated to prevent war:

> Her Majesty's government are not able to perceive how the
> nomination of Prince Leopold of Hohenzollern to the throne of
> Spain is a matter of such importance to a great and powerful nation
> like France as to warrant carrying to extremes a national feeling of
> resentment.
>
> Her Majesty's government feel confident that the Imperial
> government will act with moderation and forebearance in the
> further conduct of this affair.[3]

Lyons spoke to Gramont as instructed. The foreign minister
pointed to inflamed opinion in France as justification for his
Government's conduct. If, he said, Leopold would withdraw
all would be over; if not, France would declare war on Prussia.[4]
Privately Lyons reiterated the seriousness of the crisis to
both Granville and Layard.

> If the Hohenzollern's renunciation is announced in 24 or 48 hours,
> there will be peace for the moment—if not there will be an imme-
> diate declaration of war against Prussia. . . . The French are getting
> more and more excited. They think they have got the start of
> Prussia this time in forwardship of preparation. . . . If the excitement
> goes on, the French may choose to pick a quarrel on the form of the
> renunciation or some other pretext, even if the Prince retires.[5]

Lyons was as explicit to Layard.

> Notwithstanding the assurance of Gramont's . . . I am not quite
> sure that even Hohenzollern's renunciation wd. stop them.

---

[1] Layard to Granville, Madrid, confidential, 9 July 1870. PRO FO 72/1234,
no. 7.

[2] Granville to Lyons, 9 July 1870, PRO FO 27/1791, no. 18.

[3] Granville to Lyons, ibid., no. 19.

[4] Lyons to Granville, Paris, 10 July 1870, PRO FO 27/1805, no. 726; same to
same, telegram, ibid.

[5] Lyons to Granville, private, Paris, 10 July 1870, Lyons Pap. RC 2.

How Prim could suppose they wd endure a secret plot between him and Prussia coming upon them as a surprise it is difficult to conceive.[1]

On the same day, the tenth, Granville asked Gladstone about the possibility of the queen making an attempt to arrange a Hohenzollern withdrawal.[2] The prime minister thought it a good idea and made a further suggestion to the foreign secretary: 'If in the meantime you have authentic accounts of military movements in Fr., would it not be right formally to ask their suspension.'[3] It is curious that at this moment Gladstone planned to go to a funeral in Scotland. Granville begged him to remain: 'In so strained a state as Europe is now in, the slightest thing may lead to great consequences and it is possible that it may be a . . . disadvantage to me & to the *chose publique* if anything occurs during the 36 hours you are absent.'[4] Meanwhile anticipating Gladstone's favourable reply on the matter of using the queen's influence, Granville wrote to Victoria asking her to appeal to Leopold to withdraw.[5]

Victoria's feelings in the crisis were the feelings of most people in England who were aware of events during these first two weeks of July. France was reverting to the irresponsible and unjustifiable conduct of old. But as Granville's request was seconded by one from her cousin, the King of the Belgians,[6] the queen, in view of the probability of war unless the candidature were refused, wrote to the count of Flanders, whose wife was Leopold's sister.

On 11 July Malmesbury, a personal friend of Napoleon, expressed a minority opinion in the House of Lords.

This negotiation, it appears has been going on totally unknown to France . . . and the consequence is, that not only the manner in which the negotiation has been carried on, but also its substance, has been most offensive to France. . . . Negotiations should have been carried on above board and in a fair manner. . . . I would also ask

---

[1] Lyons to Layard, Paris, 10 July 1870, ibid.

[2] Granville to Gladstone, 10 July 1870, Glad. Pap. lxxxii. 74.

[3] Gladstone to Granville, 10 July 1870, A. Ramm, *The Political Correspondence of Mr. Gladstone and Lord Granville 1868–76* (London, 1952), i. 108; ibid., Morley, ii. 327.

[4] Granville to Gladstone, 10 July 1870, Glad. Pap. lxxxii. 75–78.

[5] Granville to Victoria, 10 July 1870, *QVL*, 2nd ser., ii. 24–25.

[6] King of the Belgians to Victoria, Brussels, 10 July 1870, ibid., pp. 25–27.

where and when Her Majesty's Government were first informed of these negotiations?

Granville replied that he wished to reserve his 'opinion as to the general question', that he first learned of the affair on the evening of the fifth, and that in order to preserve peace he had endeavoured 'without dictation & without any undue interference with the position of other countries, to impress upon them to the utmost the necessity of examining this important subject under all its serious phases'.[1] In answer to a question put in the Commons, Gladstone said that the British 'Government are not aware that the Government of the King of Prussia has committed itself or bound itself to any approval of such a candidature'.[2] It would seem that Gladstone was making the same distinction as Bismarck in separating William I into two parts, as King of Prussia and as head of the Hohenzollern family. On 9 July William admitted to Benedetti that he had 'authorized the prince to receive the Spanish offer'.[3] This was guessed or known in London before 11 July, when both Granville and Gladstone were questioned in parliament.[4]

Also on the eleventh Hammond wrote a private letter to Cowley:

The frank avowal of the King of Prussia, that he had been consulted by Prince Leopold and had assented, dispels any doubt which might have been entertained after Prussian denials, of the King's complicity. . . . I should think Howard's report is right that Bismarck is at the bottom of it.[5]

Granville wrote to the queen: 'It would have been better if the King had been able to say that he was out of the matter, that he had not given his consent, or taken any part in the matter'.[6]

[1] Hansard, *Parliamentary Debates* (3rd series), cciii. 2–4. Sir Thomas Biddulph was one who shared Malmesbury's opinion.

[2] Ibid., p. 33.

[3] Steefel, p. 127.

[4] Granville received a letter from Lumley on 10 July in which this extreme franco-phobe wrote that 'it would appear . . . that the king of Prussia has to a certain extent consented to the arrangement' (Lumley to Granville, most secret, Brussels, 9 July 1870, PRO FO 10/306, no. 126).

[5] Hammond to Lyons, private, 11 July 1870, PRO FO 391/13.

[6] Granville to Victoria, 12 July 1870, RA I 63/36.

Before Karl Anton's renunciation of 12 July the official attitude of the British Government was the same as Bismarck's, that Prussia was not involved and that it was a question between the Spanish Government and the Hohenzollern family. The maintenance of this idiotic fiction by London, though motivated by the desire to avoid a Franco-Prussian war, must have only further irritated the French. All that the British Government managed to do during the crisis before the renunciation was to increase French anger against Prussia and confirm Bismarck in his official ignorance of the affair. French exasperation with this last in part accounted for the demand for future guarantees after 12 July. In view of the already great French indignation, however, the British Government must have realized that to have wholeheartedly admitted the justice of France's case[1] might have led more quickly to war. Granville's sympathy for France was smothered by advice to her not to be precipitate, and the pressure which might have been applied in Berlin was used at Madrid and Paris.

Karl Anton's Renunciation and War

On the afternoon of the eleventh war seemed imminent to Lyons. 'Your Lordship is aware that it is a question of hours, because the French think they have got the start of the Prussians in preparations.'[2] The news of the Hohenzollern renunciation next day did little to improve the situation, for France was still not satisfied:

The French Government [Lyons wired] hold that it put an end to all dispute with Spain but they do not at present admit that in the form in which it has been given, it removes their complaint against Prussia. . . . They will determine at a Council to-morrow what course to take and announce it to the Chamber immediately afterwards. I have urged in the strongest possible manner that

---

[1] Granville, of course, refused to do this and wrote to Lyons that England had never officially admitted the legitimacy of French grievances (Granville to Lyons, 13 July 1870, PRO FO 27/1791, no. 46). On Granville's general attitude see S. William Halperin, *Diplomat under stress: Visconti Venosta and the crisis of July, 1870* (Chicago, 1963), pp. 42–43, 81–85.

[2] Lyons to Granville, Paris, telegram, 11 July 1870, PRO FO 27/1805, no. 733. Granville wrote to Lyons that 'the feeling against the precipitation of the French is getting strong. I do not know how you and I can make *effectual* remonstrances against the French . . . but the more we fire at them . . . the better' (Granville to Lyons, private, 12 July 1870, PRO FO 362/4).

they are bound to accept the renunciation as completely putting an end to the dispute with Prussia as well as with Spain.[1]

Lyons reminded Gramont of the latter's assurance that 'if the Prince withdrew his candidature, the affair would be at an end'. He further pointed out that if war occurred 'public opinion throughout the world [would be] against' France.[2]

Lyons's telegram, sent at 7.55 p.m. must have reached Granville about 10 or 10.30, for he passed it on to the queen at 10.50. Gladstone after reading the telegram wrote to Granville at 11.30 p. m.

It seems to me that Lyons should be supplied with an urgent instruction by telegram before the Council of ministers tomorrow.

France appealed to our support at the outset. She received it so far as the immediate object was concerned. . . . Under these circumstances it is our duty to represent . . . the immense responsibility which will rest upon France if she does not at once accept, as satisfactory & conclusive, the withdrawal of the candidature of Prince Leopold.

It is not I suppose needful or desirable to tell her that by her rash & violent conduct she has already created a strong revulsion of opinion against her.[3]

However, on 12 July, the day before the council of ministers met, Gramont and Ollivier suggested to Werther that William should write a letter of explanation to Napoleon,[4] and Napoleon and Gramont instructed Benedetti to secure a future guarantee from the King of Prussia. The council was informed of this last step when it met on the following day.

Following Gladstone's advice, Granville wasted little time in

---

[1] Lyons to Granville, telegram, 12 July 1870, Mosse, pp. 384-5.

[2] Lyons to Granville, Paris, 12 July 1870, PRO FO 27/1806, no. 738. Gramont wired to La Valette of the insufficiency of the renunciation for France (Gramont to La Valette, Paris, telegram, 13 July 1870, *Orig.* xxviii. 295; ibid., pp. 311-13). In the Windsor papers Gramont attached a condition to the withdrawal of Leopold. 'The Duc de G[ramont] said in conclusion that if the P[rince] of Hohenzollern should, on the advice of the K. of Prussia withdraw his acceptance of the Crown, the whole affair would be at an end' (Lyons to Granville, Paris, 10 July 1870, RA I 63/26).

[3] Gladstone to Granville, 12 July 1870, Glad. Pap. lxxxii. 80-81; same to same, 12 July 1870, Morley, ii. 328.

[4] After the French demand for future guarantees, Bismarck was impatient for news from Werther in Paris. He feared that the French were obstructing telegraphic communication, and asked Granville to telegraph in cypher to Werther to ask the Prussian ambassador what information he had last sent to Berlin (Bismarck to Bernstorff, Berlin, telegram, 13 July 1870, *GW* vi B, no. 1609).

wiring instructions that Lyons was to deliver before the council met on the morning of 13 July. The telegram was sent off about 2.00 a.m.

France asked us to exert our influence at the outset. We did so to the utmost as far as the immediate object was concerned. It could not have been more immediately and energetically given.

It is therefore our duty to represent the immense responsibility which will rest upon France, if she enlarges the ground of quarrel and does not at once accept as satisfactory the renunciation of Prince Leopold.[1]

Lyons received it at 9.30 a.m. and as the council at St. Cloud began at 9.00 a.m. he embodied the communication in a letter delivered to Gramont while the council was in session.[2] Since the decision to ask for future guarantees had been taken before the council convened, British pressure to accept the renunciation as satisfactory was too late. However, the advice might have had some effect, for the council at St. Cloud decided to declare itself satisfied even if it turned out that the King of Prussia refused any guarantee.[3] Sorel has indicated that Granville's words strengthened the position of the French ministers at the council who were for peace.[4] Gramont, however, was not happy with the interference of England and told Lyons so. The latter wrote hastily:

I have not time to think whether what France now demands of Prussia can be given and ought to be given.

Gramont said that your telegram wh. I communicated to him by letter during the council was 'peu bienveillant'.[5]

On the afternoon of the thirteenth Gramont read a statement to an already excited chamber. He announced that the Spanish ambassador had officially informed him of Leopold's withdrawal but that nothing more could be said as negotiations

---

[1] Granville to Lyons, telegram, 13 July 1870, PRO FO 27/1791; same to same, 13 July 1870, PRO FO 27/1791, no. 45. Granville repeated these words to La Valette on the morning of 13 July and begged him to ask his Government not to quarrel about 'forms' (Granville to Lyons, ibid., no. 50; La Valette to Gramont, London, telegram, 13 July 1870, *Orig.* xxxviii. 302–4). During the day Brunnow suggested the renunciation as a satisfactory settlement (Hansard, *Parliamentary Debates* [3rd series], cciii. 1409–10).

[2] Lyons to Granville, telegram, 13 July 1870, PRO FO 27/1806.

[3] Steefel, p. 162.   [4] Sorel, pp. 141–2.

[5] Lyons to Granville, private, Paris, 13 July 1870, Lyons Pap. RC 2.

with Prussia were still taking place.[1] Both Granville and Lyons
expressed their disappointment with the statement.[2]

Gramont justified the position of the French Government to
Lyons and asked the British ambassador for the support of the
English Government in persuading the King of Prussia to
associate himself with and to guarantee Leopold's renunciation.[3]

Opinion in England was mounting against France and
Granville was conscious of it.

My colleagues & the House of Commons are getting very angry
and G[ladstone] wishes me to use stronger language to the French
Govt than would in my opinion be useful.

I do not, like everybody else suspect the French of having had
a project of going to war. But having got into the wrangle, having
found their warlike preparations so popular, & having roused
effectually the feeling of France & Prussia, they do [not] like to
abstain from a fight, which they think will come & in which during
the next six weeks their enemies would be unprepared.[4]

On the same day, the thirteenth, Bismarck told Loftus that
if French military preparations continued Prussia would be
forced to ask for explanations and some guarantee against
attack.[5] The Crown Prince of Prussia wrote of German feeling
to Victoria:

By Leopold of Hohenzollern's renunciation . . . all pretext for war
on the part of France is removed. . . . Should fresh demands be made
upon us, however, he [Napoleon] will meet with a unanimous
expression of German feeling & anger that will cost him dear.
Already German feeling is wounded, as I have seldom seen it
amongst peaceful people.[6]

On the morning of 13 July, William and Benedetti had their
famous meeting at Ems. By the same evening Bismarck had
sent the Ems telegram to the newspapers, which published it

---

[1] Lyons to Granville, Paris, 13 July 1870, PRO FO 27/1806, no. 753; Steefel,
p. 162.

[2] Same to same, ibid., no. 754; Granville to Lyons, 13 July 1870, PRO FO 27/
1791, no. 51; Granville to Bloomfield, private, 13 July 1870, PRO FO 356/33.

[3] Lyons to Granville, Paris, 13 July 1870, PRO FO 27/1806, no. 754.

[4] Granville to Lyons, private, 13 July 1870, PRO FO 362/4.

[5] Loftus to Granville, confidential, Berlin, 13 July 1870, PRO FO 146/1450,
no. 27. Loftus thought it 'evident' that Bismarck 'regretted the too pliable disposition' of his king (ibid.).

[6] Crown Prince to Victoria, 13 July 1870, QVL, 2nd ser., ii. 29–30.

the following morning. When Lyons wired Gramont's request that England should support French efforts with the King of Prussia a Cabinet was held. But though it met after the Ems telegram had already been published the existence of that document was not yet known to the queen's ministers.[1]

The Cabinet which met at 12.30 p.m. on the fourteenth decided to suggest mutual concessions to France and Prussia.[2] Granville refused Gramont's request to support 'an engagement covering the future', but recommended to the King of Prussia and to Paris that if this demand were dropped by France, he, the king, might inform the French of his consent to Leopold's renunciation.[3] Both the queen and Gladstone, instead of favouring a compromise, wished to place more pressure on France: 'What if you [Granville] were to telegraph to Lyons . . . that . . . it will be impossible for us to conceal the opinion that the cause of the quarrel having been removed France ought to be satisfied.'[4] The queen telegraphed to the foreign secretary: 'Do not relax your efforts to induce the French to accept the Prussian answer as satisfactory.'[5]

At noon on the fourteenth the French council had met to consider the Ems telegram. Lyons consequently had been unable to see Gramont to give him Granville's compromise suggestion:

I have been oscillating between the Affaires Étrangères and the Corps Legislatif all day, but Gramont has not been at either since he went early to a council wh. the Emperor came to Paris to hold at the Tuileries.

After the article in the North German Gazette war seems absolutely inevitable. The Prussians seem to be bent upon it as well as the French.[6]

[1] The first news of the Ems telegram came probably in a telegram received from Lyons at 6.30 p.m. on the fourteenth (Lyons to Granville, Paris, telegram, 14 July 1870, PRO FO 27/1806).

[2] Gladstone to Victoria, 14 July 1870, QVL, 2nd ser., ii. 32.

[3] Granville to Lyons, telegram, 2.30 p.m., 14 July 1870, PRO FO 27/1791; same to same, telegram, 2.45 p.m., ibid.; same to same, ibid., 362/4. A telegram from Howard is interesting. 'The Bavarian foreign minister wishes that England should offer her mediation in order to obtain from Prussia . . . the assurance that the King approves the renunciation' (Howard to Granville, Munich, telegram, 14 July 1870, PRO FO 9/202; no. 7).

[4] Gladstone to Granville, 14 July 1870, Glad. Pap. ccccliii, letter-book 1869–70; same to same, 14 July 1870, Morley, ii. 329.

[5] Victoria to Granville, Osborne, telegram, 14 July 1870, QVL, 2nd ser., ii. 32–33.

[6] Lyons to Granville, private, Paris, 14 July 1870, Lyons Pap. RC 2.

Later, on the evening of the same day, the council met again at Saint-Cloud where it was decided to call out the reserves.¹ Still, though the peace party was no longer in the ascendant, war had not been irrevocably decided upon.

Early on the morning of the fifteenth, the French council voted unanimously for war, and Lyons had no opportunity to see Gramont before he made this declaration before the chamber. As the ambassador reported, it would have made little difference even if he had been able to intercept him.

If however I had been able to speak to him I could have found nothing to add to the arguments I had already so pertinaciously urged in favour of peace nor could I have hoped to shake a resolution already deliberately adopted by the Emperor and his Ministers.²

On the same morning Bernstorff communicated to Granville a telegram from Bismarck:

Bismarck regretted that H.M. Govt. should have made yesterday's proposal to the King [of Prussia] and that he [Bismarck] could not recommend it to the King for His acceptance. I [Granville] immediately concerted with Gladstone the mediation telegram. I do not anticipate any success from it—but we shall be able to shew that we have left no stone unturned.³

At the very moment Gramont was reading to the senate the council's decision for war,⁴ Granville telegraphed to Lyons what he knew was of no use.

War seems imminent. We deplore this great calamity. . . . We therefore appeal to the 23rd protocol of Paris in 1856, the more so as the question is brought within narrow limits.

Her Majesty's Government suggest to France and to Prussia in identic terms that before proceeding to extremities they should have recourse to the good offices of some friendly power or powers acceptable to both.

We are ready to take any part which may be desired.⁵

¹ Steefel, pp. 199–203, 206–7.
² Lyons to Granville, 15 July 1870, PRO FO 27/1806, no. 767, Mosse, p. 387.
³ Granville to Lyons, private, 15 July 1870, PRO FO 362/4; Granville to Victoria, telegram, 15 July 1870, *QVL*, 2nd ser., ii. 33.
⁴ Lyons to Granville, telegram, 2 p.m., 15 July 1870, PRO FO 27/1806.
⁵ Granville to Lyons, telegram, 1.25 p.m., 15 July 1870, PRO FO 27/1791. A few hours before Lyons wired to Granville suggesting the use of the 23rd protocol of the peace of Paris of 1856 (Lyons to Granville, Paris, telegram, 1 a.m. 15 July 1870, PRO FO 27/1806). Granville to Lyons, telegram, 15 July 1870, *Orig.* xxviii. 397–9. On 17 July, Gramont thanked London for its efforts for peace, but declined

The proverbial barn door had been locked. Lyons personally did not even bother to communicate the mediation proposal.[1] The queen seemed much less inclined to accept the inevitable than her foreign secretary. On 15 July she asked Granville whether she together with the sovereigns of the other European powers might collectively appeal to the King of Prussia and the Emperor of France.[2] When the foreign secretary replied that he wished 'to await the effect of the appeal' to the Paris protocol,[3] the queen suggested she personally intercede with Napoleon. Granville merely informed La Valette of the queen's general desire for peace.[4]

With hostilities certain British opinion in Parliament and the Press almost unanimously condemned France for provoking war.[5] Victoria's anger with France was matched by Disraeli's. In the Commons he branded France as 'the aggressor', a sentiment shared by 'the House on both sides'.[6] On 16 July *The Times* expressed the dominant British feelings of anger and indignation.

The greatest national crime that we have had the pain of recording in these columns since the days of the First French Empire has been consummated. War is declared—an unjust but premeditated war. This dire calamity, which overwhelms Europe with dismay, is, it is now too clear, the act of one man in France. It is the ultimate result of personal rule.[7]

The proclamation of British neutrality was an official formality which hardly masked English exasperation with France.[8] Granville, who was more alive to France's case than Gladstone, wrote to Lyons:

I am annoyed at the language of Disraeli, of the Times and of the Press in general.

The feeling was certainly French a week ago, but as soon as it was

the use of the protocol because of the Ems telegram (Gramont to La Valette, Paris, telegram, 17 July 1870, *Orig.* xxix. 41–42).
  [1] Lyons to Granville, Paris, 16 July 1870, PRO FO 27/1806, no. 782; Lyons to Gramont, Paris, urgent, 15 July 1870, *Orig.* xxvii. 399–400.
  [2] Victoria to Granville, telegram, 15 July 1870, *QVL*, 2nd ser., ii. 33.
  [3] Granville to Victoria, telegram, ibid., pp. 33–34.
  [4] La Valette to Gramont, London, telegram, 15 July 1870, *Orig.* xxviii. 397.
  [5] Raymond, pp. 71–86.
  [6] Gladstone to Victoria, 15 July 1870, *QVL*, 2nd ser., ii. 34; same to same, 15 July 1870, Morley, ii. 335; Hansard, *Parliamentary Debates* (3rd series), cciii. 343–5. [7] Raymond, pp. 73–74.
  [8] Victoria to Crown Princess of Prussia, 20 July 1870, *QVL*, 2nd ser., ii. 44.

thought they were the most determined of the two to go to war, there has been a great reaction—Public opinion, however varies rapidly, & I should not be surprised if in another week or two we shall be ardent gallicans.

The last week seems like a feverish dream—The end is sad.[1]

After reading *The Times* on 16 July, Lyons communicated his annoyance to Granville. 'The article in the Times is written in total ignorance of the facts, or is a wilful perversion of them. It will produce a most unpleasant effect here. The "Times" is read by the Emperor.'[2]

Britain's Responsibility

Morier, the British diplomat, thought at the time that England might have averted hostilities. 'The war could have been prevented if for twenty-four hours the British people could have been furnished with a backbone.'[3] In a more dispassionate and recent analysis Mosse has concluded 'that no action psychologically or constitutionally open to British Ministers could have prevented the outbreak of the Franco-Prussian war'.[4] The question is largely unanswerable since what could have been done can never be certainly known. We can only fruitfully consider what was done. Britain did not prevent the Franco-Prussian war. What did she do?

Though belatedly and without appreciating the seriousness of the quarrel, Granville on 7 July advised Madrid to find another king, admitted to Berlin on 9 July that the secrecy of the candidature was a 'just cause of offence', and on the same day told Paris that the British Government could not see how a Hohenzollern king of Spain could be 'a matter of such importance to . . . France'. British influence in removing the candidature was slight, and Gladstone's support for the fiction of the

---

[1] Granville to Lyons, private, 16 July 1870, PRO FO 362/4. Granville had written to the queen of Bismarck's complicity in the Hohenzollern conspiracy and of France's 'violent language' and hasty conduct (Granville to Victoria, 15 July 1870, *QVL*, 2nd ser., ii. 34–35).

[2] Lyons to Granville, private, Paris, 17 July 1870, Lyons Pap. RC 2. Granville sent the following to Lyons: 'I did all I could with Delane, but you may judge from the article of today with how little effect. They are not to be influenced when they think the public cat is jumping in any particular way' (Granville to Lyons, private, 18 July 1870, PRO FO 362/4).

[3] Morier, ii. 153–4.   [4] Mosse, pp. 387–8.

innocence of the Prussian Government in the affair irritated France.

When London learned late on the evening of the twelfth that France would not be satisfied with the renunciation as given, though Lyons had alluded to this possibility two days before, Granville instructed the British ambassador, early on the morning of the thirteenth, to tell Gramont before the French council met on that day of the 'immense responsibility' France was undertaking. As the decision to ask for guarantees had been made before the council assembled, Granville's advice merely buoyed up for the moment the French peace party but could do nothing to affect the intentions of Napoleon and Gramont. Granville's compromise suggestion of 14 July—that France should drop her demand for future guarantees and that the King of Prussia should assent to the renunciation—was negated by the publication of the Ems telegram which preceded it. The suggestion to appeal to the protocol of the Treaty of Paris on 15 July was a useless formality which Granville recognized when he made it.

After 12 July British efforts to preserve the peace were exercised too late to affect the decisions leading to war. This was not due to apathy. Events had moved so quickly that by the time London learned of one set of circumstances the situation had changed. Yet what action Granville and the Cabinet did take was calculated to solve a dispute over fishing rights, not a controversy between two European powers of which war was a distinctly possible if not a probable outcome. Granville nevertheless justified his action in the House of Lords: 'Although during the last 10 days we have used the strongest language compatible with their [Spain, France, and Prussia] dignity and our self-respect, I am happy to state I believe that language has not affected . . . friendly relations up to this time.'[1]

Malmesbury later expressed his views on the inevitability of the war: 'Where was the specific cause of war to be found? . . . What they are fighting for it is difficult for either of them to say, except that two nations were determined to make war upon each other. . . . Europe, in fact, was too small for these great potentates to live quietly side by side.'[2]

---

[1] Hansard, *Parliamentary Debates* (3rd series), cciii. 382.
[2] Ibid., p. 1058.

There was never a thought on England's part of siding with France, and consequently little pressure was put on Prussia. Neither Granville nor Lyons, however was willing to antagonize France beyond preaching moderation to her. If a Franco-Prussian war had to occur, then to most British statesmen it was preferable and necessary to keep England out of it. Beyond this it was wise not to provoke France for the sake of Belgium. A French defeat of Prussia would endanger that small country sufficiently without the addition of friction with England, whose goodwill would then have been the last thread by which Belgian independence hung. According to one of England's German experts a French victory was not unlikely. 'There is little doubt that the Prussians are not yet ready & that a great portion of Ger. will be occupied'.[1] Unprepared for war herself, strict neutrality was the only course for Britain to follow.

With the war officially begun on 19 July, the British Government and Parliament showed their concern for Belgium. Most people, and Gladstone most prominently, were certain that France was responsible for the war and this only increased British uneasiness about her small channel neighbour. Yet Granville, and even more Lyons, recognized Prussia's responsibility. At the end of July the British ambassador justly reviewed the evidence:

Prussia threw the first stone, by bringing on the Hohenzollern question. France made a peaceful settlement difficult by Gramont's irritating declaration on the 6th. The cause of the change from a mild to an irritating declaration was the arrival of the report from the chargé d'affaires at Berlin, that Thile pooh poohed the French remonstrance and said that the question n'existait pas pour le gouvernement Prussien? Then came the great fault of France in not accepting the renunciation . . . as a final settlement—but even at the last moment the declaration of the 16th wd have concluded with a phrase leaving the door open to the mediation of a congress, if the article in the North German Gazette had not arrived.[2]

During the crisis itself, however, fear of involvement and anxiety for Belgium checked British exertion and pressure on both Prussia and France. Bismarck would now use British sentiment for Belgium as a final lever to extirpate any sympathy for France.

[1] Morier to his father, 20 July 1870, Morier, ii. 154.
[2] Lyons to Granville, private, Paris, 31 July 1870, Lyons Pap. RC 2.

XI

AFTERMATH

Belgium

ON 13 July the King of Belgium wrote to his cousin, Queen Victoria, that England might propose to Prussia and France, as the price of British neutrality, a public declaration on their parts to respect Belgian neutrality.[1] Granville also had Belgium on his mind:

> I have [he wrote Lyons] some thoughts of asking the Cabinet if war is declared, whether it would be wise to ask Both Govts. whether they are prepared to respect the neutrality of Belgium. It is always safer, or at least generally so, to do nothing, but both, in doubt, would be more likely to give a favourable answer than either flushed with victory. Let me know what you think.[2]

On the fifteenth Lyons talked with Gramont after his declaration to the chamber on that day. The foreign minister assured the ambassador that France would respect Belgian neutrality no matter what occurred.[3] Granville greatly appreciated this 'spontaneous declaration'.[4] The British Government, however, were still anxious. Gladstone wanted to have the means to send 20,000 men to Antwerp in case of need.[5] Lyons too expressed the continuing uneasiness:

> Belgium [he wrote] is what I am most anxious. I don't think her zealous friends take the right way to help her. By constantly crying out that France is going to occupy her they accustom mens minds to the notion, and in fact discount the indignation wh. ought to be

---

[1] King of Belgium to Victoria, 13 July 1870, *QVL*, 2nd ser., ii. 30–32.

[2] Granville to Lyons, private, 13 July 1870, PRO FO 362/4.

[3] Lyons to Granville, Paris, 15 July 1870, PRO FO 27/1806, no. 779. Gramont also said France would adhere to the neutrality of Luxemburg and Holland (Granville to Lyons, 20 July 1870, PRO FO 27/1792, no. 98).

[4] Granville to Lyons, 16 July 1870, PRO FO 27/1729, no. 72. Granville must have also spoken to Bernstorff, since Bismarck expressed his annoyance that he did not think it should have been necessary for Prussia to confirm her respect for Belgian neutrality (Bismarck to Bernstorff, Berlin, telegram, 17 July 1870, *GW* vi B, no. 1657).

[5] Gladstone to Cardwell, 16 July 1870, Morley, ii. 339; same to same, private, 24 July 1870, PRO FO 30/48, 2/7.

reserved for some real attack. . . . I would rather too that the Belgians themselves did not come to us upon every trifling matter wh alarms or annoys them. If we interfere, we fritter away our influence [which] . . . should be kept in reserve for great occasions. . . . We can effect more by leaving our intentions a little vague, than by making distinct declarations to wh. everyone feels we must, when the time comes, act up to or not according to circumstances and especially according to public opinion in England.[1]

When Gramont offered Beyens, the Belgian envoy, a written promise to respect Belgium, Lyons advised Beyens to accept it.[2] The Belgian Government, however, decided not to press for it as Napoleon had already written in the same sense to the King of the Belgians.[3]

There was growing feeling in London that the best way to safeguard Belgium was by announcing that the violation of her territory would bring England into the war. Bismarck chose this moment to unleash the Benedetti draft treaty. On 20 July the Prussian minister privately informed Loftus of a French proposition to trade south Germany for Belgium.[4] On the day before, Bernstorff, as instructed by Bismarck, told Gladstone and Granville that he wished to read without authority from his Government a secret communication. Bernstorff said that the treaty had been proposed by Benedetti in 1867 and again in 1869, that Bismarck had not sent it to him, and that the original in Benedetti's writing was in the possession of the Prussian Government. Gladstone replied that such a communication was 'an insult to the govt. to which it was made'.[5]

The following day, 20 July, Granville asked Bernstorff why an 'experienced diplomat' like Benedetti would have left 'such an extraordinary document' in the hands of the Prussian Government unless there had been 'some preliminary discussion'. If, as Bernstorff said, the proposal was 'indignantly refused' by Prussia, why, the foreign secretary asked, was it

[1] Lyons to Granville, private, Paris, 17 July 1870, Lyons Pap. RC 2.
[2] Lyons to Granville, very confidential, Paris, 18 July 1870, PRO FO 27/1806, no. 811.
[3] Lyons to Granville, very confidential, Paris, 22 July 1870, PRO FO 27/1807, no. 868.
[4] Loftus to Granville, telegram, most confidential, 20 July 1870, Mosse, p. 312. Reports of this kind had been circulating since 1865 but not from so high or important an authority.
[5] Granville to Lyons, confidential, 25 July 1870, PRO FO 27/1792, no. 130.

made again. Bernstorff said that he knew nothing more about it.[1]

Bismarck was now spreading the news. One person to be let into the secret was Nothomb, the Belgian minister to Berlin. The result of this was a letter from Leopold to Victoria referring to the French wish 'to dominate the world'.[2] Another and more useful contact was made with Mr. Delane, the editor of *The Times*. On Bismarck's orders the treaty was given to him by Baron Krause of the Prussian Embassy.[3] The British editor had 'no doubt as to the authenticity of the draft',[4] and consequently the draft treaty was published in *The Times* on 25 July. It burst like an exploding bomb upon London, albeit a bomb the existence of which had been often suspected.

Gladstone wrote to Victoria:

Your Majesty will, in common with the world, have been shocked & startled at the publication in today's 'Times' of a proposed project of treaty between France and Prussia.

A large portion of the public put down this document as a forgery, & indeed a hoax; Mr. Gladstone fears it is neither. . . . Probably the object of the Prussian Govt. was to prompt them [Gladstone and Granville] to become the agents for making it known to the world.[5]

Granville recorded at the time that 'from its nature it might be deemed incredible that such a proposal should have been made by one party, & in any way considered by the other'.[6] It must be said for both Gladstone and Granville that they suspected Bismarck almost as much as Napoleon III. They were concerned but not fooled. In a short note the prime minister explained his suspicions: 'The draft treaty gives the precedence to the King of Prussia . . . . This is the form in which a Prussian

---

[1] Ibid. Bernstorff was ordered to tell Granville that the Benedetti treaty was only one of various offers made by France to Prussia. Rouher, according to Bismarck, continually tried to draw Berlin into a treaty, which efforts Bismarck kept secret for the sake of peace (Bismarck to Bernstorff, Berlin, telegram, 28 July 1870, *GW* vi B, no. 1713).

[2] King of Belgium to Victoria, 24 July 1870, *QVL*, 2nd ser., ii. 45.

[3] A. I. Dasent, *John Thadeus Delane, Editor of The Times* (New York, 1908), ii. 266–7; Bismarck to Bernstorff, Berlin, telegram, 23 July 1870, *GW* vi B, no. 1703. Bernstorff was instructed not to let the date of the treaty become public (ibid., no. 1704).

[4] Delane to Disraeli, 25 July 1870, Disraeli Pap., box 124.

[5] Gladstone to Victoria, 25 July 1870, *QVL*, 2nd ser., ii. 46.

[6] Granville note, 25 July 1870, Ramm, i. 116.

draft treaty would be drawn. The Emperor would have precedence in a French draft.'[1]

In the House of Commons Disraeli said he would 'look upon the extinction of Belgium as a calamity to Europe and an injury to this country'.[2] On 26 July Granville reported to the House of Lords that La Valette told him an hour ago that the treaty 'had been originated by M. de Bismarck . . . but it never had any serious basis, and was rejected by both parties'.[3] Gramont told Lyons that Bismarck had offered to occupy Belgium and 'so give Fr. a pretext for entering'.[4] Gladstone, following his earlier suspicions, was quite sure of himself in writing to Cardwell.

> I believe firmly that the original comm[unication] to G[ranville] & me was a trap laid for us by Bismarck, who probably thought he would so stir our fears & Indignation as to make us become the instrument of publication. This we had sense enough to avoid.[5]

Granville's feelings for Bismarck and Napoleon were of a kind which 'it is better not to put on paper'.[6] Victoria was more indignant with France than her two ministers and wanted to ask for explanations.

Bismarck's success with the queen was not duplicated with the queen's ministers. The plea of the King of Prussia for English support instead of neutrality was a futile one.[7] In the House of Lords on 28 July Granville without asserting Prussian responsibility implied that but for the Ems telegram war might have been prevented.[8] Both Gramont and La Valette attempted to convince Granville and Lyons that any iniquity intended towards Belgium came from Prussia.[9]

---

[1] Gladstone memorandum, ? July 1870, Glad. Pap. lxxxii. 206; Granville to Ponsonby, 26 July 1870, *QVL*, 2nd ser., ii. 52–53. Bulwer Lytton felt that the responsibility for the draft treaty was Benedetti's (Hansard, *Parliamentary Debates* [3rd series], cciii. 1356). Gathorne-Hardy felt that Bismarck had outwitted Benedetti: 'I doubt if the Emperor has really lent himself to the schemes of robbery proposed' (*Gathorne-Hardy: A Memoir*, ed. by A. E. Gathorne-Hardy [London, 1910], i. 297. [2] Ibid., pp. 882–3.
[3] Ibid., p. 225; Granville to Lyons, 26 July 1870, PRO FO 27/1792, no. 135.
[4] Lyons to Granville, Paris, 26 July 1870, Newton, i. 303–4.
[5] Gladstone to Cardwell, 26 July 1870, Glad. Pap. ccccliii, letter-book 1869–70.
[6] Granville to Ponsonby, 26 July 1870, *QVL*, 2nd ser., ii. 52–53.
[7] King of Prussia to Victoria, Berlin, 26 July 1870, *QVL*, 2nd ser., ii. 50–52.
[8] Hansard, *Parliamentary Debates* (3rd ser.), cciii. 1054.
[9] Granville to Lyons, 29 July 1870, PRO FO 27/1792, no. 147; Lyons to Granville, confidential, Paris, 29 July 1870, PRO FO 27/1807, no. 950.

If the British Government were not willing to attribute the intended rape of Belgium entirely to France, it was felt necessary nevertheless to speak out. On 29 July Gladstone expressed to Granville his feeling 'that if we are to form Engagements about Belgium it should be done before any great battle takes place to alter the relative position of the 2 parties'.[1] The Cabinet met on 30 July to decide upon a course of action and the decision reached was Gladstone's, apparently supported by the rest of the Cabinet:

But it seems to them [the Cabinet] that a great public & European advantage might be gained if at this time both France & Prussia could be brought to enter into engagements respecting Belgium which would fill up what is wanting or uncertain in their declarations of neutrality.

The Cabinet have therefore agreed that Lord Granville should ask each of these Powers separately whether it is willing not only to respect the neutrality of Belgium, but to join in upholding it if it should be invaded by another Power.[2]

Consequently Granville wrote to Lyons and Loftus to suggest either a 'treaty or protocol' to respect Belgian neutrality.[3]

Gramont expressed his immediate readiness to sign such a treaty with England, but Lyons was himself against such 'an absolute engagement' because it 'would have less weight' than the uncertainty of what Britain would do if Belgian territory were violated.[4] At this moment, however, Granville and Gladstone were as much concerned with the effect such a treaty would have on London as on Paris and Berlin. 'It is only in connection with Belgian neutrality that evidence exists that the Government was aware of the necessity of responding to Parliamentary and public pressure'.[5] The publication of the

---

[1] Gladstone to Granville, 29 July 1870, Ramm, i. 117–18. Hammond was strongly opposed to making any such engagements (Hammond to Granville, 29 July 1870, PRO FO 30/29, no. 104, Anderson, pp. 277–8). In April 1867 during the Luxemburg crisis Cowley offered as a suggestion an Anglo-Saxon guarantee of Holland and Belgium (Cowley to Stanley, private, Paris, 23 April 1867, RA I 71/125). Victoria agreed with Cowley. 'If France would join in case of war, in such a guarantee as Lord Cowley suggests, England should not hesitate to enter into it' (Grey to Stanley, private, 26 April 1867, ibid. 155).

[2] Gladstone to Victoria, 30 July 1870, QVL, 2nd ser., ii. 53–55.

[3] Granville to Lyons and Loftus, 30 July 1870, PRO FO 27/1792, no. 153, 55.

[4] Lyons to Granville, confidential, Paris, 1 Aug. 1870, PRO FO 27/1808, no. 981.

[5] S. Lambert, 'The Influence of Parliament upon the Foreign Policy of the

Benedetti treaty, Gladstone wrote, 'has wholly altered the feeling of the House of Commons'.[1] Granville justified the Government's decision to Lyons:

> There is much to be said against what we are doing as to Belgium, but how can we do nothing in the face of this draft treaty—when the English public think there was six to the one, and half a dozen to the other.
> It appears to be the most likely way of preventing what we dread.[2]

There was some feeling in the House of Commons, as exhibited by Mr. Fawcett and Mr. Gilpin, against 'threatening' France and Prussia as both countries had declared their intention to observe Belgian neutrality.[3] However, there was greater and more distinguished feeling for some action to defend this neutrality. Disraeli, who advocated armed neutrality, was no less vocal for Belgium:

> It had always been held by the Government of this country that it was for the interest of England that the countries on the European coast extending from Dunkirk and Ostend to the islands of the North Sea should be possessed by free and flourishing communities ... and should not be in the possession of a great military Power.[4]

On 2 August Gladstone anxiously wrote to Granville:

> I hope you will be able now to prosecute the treaty with France full gallop. There is an intense desire in the Ho[use] that we shd say or they shd know something about Belgium. We are sure to be pressed again unless we speak, & every time we are pressed, the demand for confidence will seem more exacting & supercilious. Is it impossible that a draft shd go to Lyons today for him to execute? As to the particular points—1. I think you cannot in the treaty limit yourself to sea defence. . . . 2. [There should] be a clause providing for the occasion of other powers. . . . 3. As to the termination of the treaty . . . what if it be made to last until a treaty of peace is ratified, & 12 months after to allow for settling down & disarming?[5]

Gladstone Government 1868–74' (University of London thesis, 1949), pp. 111–12. Lambert feels that Parliament and opinion had little effect on foreign policy from 1868 to 1874 except on the question of Belgium (ibid., p. 132).
[1] Gladstone to Bright, 1 Aug. 1870, Morley, ii. 341.
[2] Granville to Lyons, private, 1 Aug. 1870, PRO FO 362/4.
[3] Hansard, *Parliamentary Debates* (3rd series), cciii. 1362–4.
[4] Ibid. 1289–93.
[5] Gladstone to Granville, 2 Aug. 1870, Glad. Pap ccccliv, letter-book 1869–70.

The following day Granville sent a draft convention for the consideration of the French Government.[1] On the fourth, the foreign secretary again justified to Lyons the attempt to create a new treaty for Belgium. The argument he used was Gladstone's and is contained in the prime minister's letter to Bright of 1 August:

> There is no time today to argue with you. . . . There are objections to what we are doing. But I believe there are more such to any other course. We cannot declare that we are not bound to stir for Belgium— We cannot even say nothing in the present frame of mind of the British public. If we merely say we will defend Belgium, we incur the same risk as by our proposal, but in a greater degree—For we bind ourselves, to do that singlehanded, which on our plan we shall only do in conjunction with a powerful nation. I cannot doubt that this alliance will act as a powerful check on either party doing that which we wish to avoid—and makes junction on their part more difficult.
>
> If both parties agree, the thing will be much criticized, but I suspect will be approved by Public opinion, which is exasperated and alarmed by these revelations and recriminations as to the Draft project.
>
> Please hasten the convention as much as you can.[2]

Gladstone spoke of the disappearance of Belgium as 'an extinction of public right in Europe'.[3]

On 6 August Granville was informed by Bernstorff that the King of Prussia accepted the English draft treaty on Belgium.[4] France was proving more recalcitrant, Gramont objecting to the proposed duration of the treaty of twelve months after the ratification of peace.[5] Granville, however, refused to give way.[6] Defeat in the field at Weissenburg and Worth modified French reluctance.

> The news stuns me. It is not merely a great action lost & won—It is the greatest apparently which France has received as a military

---

[1] Granville to Lyons, 3 Aug. 1870, PRO FO 27/1792, no. 182.

[2] Granville to Lyons, private, 4 Aug. 1870, PRO FO 362/4.

[3] Gladstone to Bright, 4 Aug. 1870, Morley, ii. 342; same to same, 8 Aug. 1870, Glad. Pap. ccccliv, letter-book 1870–1.

[4] Granville to Lyons, 6 Aug. 1870, PRO FO 27/1792, no. 204; Bismarck to Bernstorff, Mainz, telegram, 4 Aug. 1870, *GW* vi B, no. 1724.

[5] Lyons to Granville, confidential, Paris, 5 Aug. 1870, PRO FO 27/1809, no. 1010; same to same, telegram, 6 Aug. 1870, ibid., no. 1024.

[6] Granville to Lyons, 6 Aug. 1870, PRO FO 27/1792, no. 203; same to same, ibid., no. 205.

power for more than 100 years, in the vital point of credit & reputation. . . . But further it raises the question whether it will be followed by a revolution—If ever there was a govt made war, it is this: & France may call the author to account. . . . If the Napoleonic Govt is alive I suppose they will make no more difficulty about signing with us.[1]

French hesitation to sign the Belgian draft treaty was complemented by criticism in Parliament for offering it.[2] It was not merely the harping of a few isolationists against foreign entanglements but the questioning of men like Lyons and Disraeli. The latter argued that 'where there is a treaty guarantee so explicit as that expressed in the treaty of 1839, I think the wisdom of founding on that another treaty . . . may be open to doubt'.[3] Gladstone's reply in the House of Commons indicated that what the prime minister wished to avoid was a situation where England faced the prospect of defending Belgian neutrality alone:[4]

In accordance with our obligations, we should have had to act under the Treaty of 1839 without any stipulated assurance of being supported from any quarter . . . whereas by the Treaty now formally before Parliament . . . we secure powerful support in the event of our having to act—a support with respect to which we may well say that it brings the object in view within the sphere of the practicable and attainable, instead of leaving it within the sphere of what might have been desirable, but which might have been most difficult . . . to have realized.[5]

The treaty with Prussia was signed on 9 July and that with France two days later. From the peace and quiet of Knowsley Stanley wrote of it to Disraeli:

The Belgian treaty is on the face of it a compromise between those who wanted to do nothing and those who wished to threaten war if Belgium were touched. Lowe and Gladstone must both have been overruled, or rather yielded to the pressure of opinion. Local feeling here is strongly Prussian.[6]

[1] Gladstone to Granville, 7 Aug. 1870, Glad. Pap. ccccliv, letter-book 1870–1.
[2] Hansard, *Parliamentary Debates* (3rd series), cciii. 1739–43, 1752, 1779.
[3] Ibid., p. 1703.   [4] Ibid., p. 1705.
[5] Ibid., pp. 1787–9.
[6] Stanley to Disraeli, Knowsley, 14 Aug. 1870, Disraeli Pap., box 112. The treaties signed with France and Prussia had three identical articles. First, England would go against whichever power (France or Prussia) violated Belgium's neutrality with the stipulation that England's intervention would be restricted to

Britain had committed herself to a definite course of action to meet a future contingency, and in so doing departed from one of the fundamental precepts of British foreign policy in the nineteenth century. 'Canning deprecated the laying down of "fixed resolutions for eventual probabilities", and declared that "cases must arise upon facts which it is utterly beyond the powers of human foresight to combine and calculate beforehand." '[1] Palmerston had written that 'it is not usual for England to enter into engagements with reference to cases which have not wholly arisen'.[2] In January 1872 Granville wrote that 'the policy of successive Governments in this country has been to avoid prospective understandings to meet contingencies which seldom occur in the way which has been anticipated'.[3] To have made treaties, as England did in August 1870, to meet a future possibility was unusual. That the treaties were made in a period when sentiment was so vocally opposed to involvement would have been extraordinary had anything but Belgium been at stake.

Neutrality and Mediation

With Belgium secured, British concern in the Franco-Prussian war was limited to restricting its scope and preserving a strict neutrality. The first was endangered by the possibility of Denmark and Italy joining France. This and the rumours of an Austrian alliance with Napoleon subsided after the Prussian military successes. English neutrality so punctiliously pursued by Granville was impugned by Bismarck and the King of Prussia,[4] who constantly complained of the foreign secretary's

Belgium. Secondly, France and Prussia agreed to co-operate with England in the event of a violation of Belgium's neutrality by one or the other. The third article made the treaties binding on all three powers for a period of twelve months after the ratification of peace between France and Prussia (Hertslet, iii. 1886–9).

[1] Temperley and Penson, p. 88.
[2] Ibid., p. 137.　　　　　　　　　　　　　　　　[3] Ibid., p. 344.
[4] 'The interest of England with Germany stands in such intimate relation that public opinion ought to be informed as to the true state of the case. . . . I trust that the press which carries so much weight may be influenced to arouse national sympathy for Germany and that through your wise advice assistance may be afforded to us whilst it can still be useful.
'P.S. We have today received intelligence that notwithstanding England's declaration of neutrality horses, coals and even ammunition in the shape of millions of cartridges are being shipped to France from England, whilst we expected a decree

preference for France. Granville protested and proclaimed his innocence. Prussian irritation was not assuaged, for it was a result of the very neutrality Granville so carefully pursued. Berlin wanted assistance or at least sympathy, and officially Britain could not give it.[1]

With the defeat at Sedan and the formation of a government of national defence, sympathy for France grew in England,[2] though it did not affect the official neutrality of the Government. On 6 September Favre, the French foreign minister, told Lyons that France would agree to an armistice if one were proposed by a neutral power.[3] Gladstone, conscious of his blunder about southern independence during the American Civil War, saw 'but two really safe grounds for mediation, a drawn battle; the request of both parties'.[4] Granville agreed, especially as 'any suggestion would probably be considered a menace by Prussia'.[5] Nevertheless the foreign secretary instructed Lyons to encourage the French 'to send proposals through us, with a certain elasticity in them'.[6] Britain would transmit; she would not mediate.

forbidding the exportation of all war material' (King of Prussia to Victoria, Berlin, 26 July 1870, RA I 63/176).

[1] Whatever the foreign secretary's personal feelings were towards Prussia or Germany, he did not like Bismarck. This can be seen from an undated memorandum of 1870. 'I am inclined to believe 1st that Bismarck hates England. . . . 2nd that there is an engagement with Russia to let her act in the East. . . . 4 that Bismarck has long wished for friendly relations with the United States to neutralize our influence in Europe' (Granville memorandum, 1870, PRO FO 30/48, 5/29). Irritated because he could not obtain active British support, Bismarck complained of Birmingham arms going to France and implied that England should influence Denmark, Austria, and Italy to remain neutral (Bismarck to Bernstorff, Berlin, telegram, 18 July 1870, GW vi B, no. 1669; same to same, 22 July 1870, ibid., no. 1699; same to same, 29 July 1870, ibid., no. 1715; same to same, Mainz, 4 Aug. 1870, ibid., no. 1728; same to same, Bar-le-Duc, 26 Aug. 1870, ibid., no. 1767).

[2] The sympathy was hardly complete. The Times on 8 Sept. thought that the cession of Alsace and Lorraine and the payment of a million francs would be a moderate settlement (Sorel, p. 314).

[3] Lyons to Granville, very confidential, telegram, Paris, 6 Sept. 1870, PRO FO 27/1814.

[4] Gladstone to Duke of Argyll, 6 Sept. 1870, Morley, ii. 344. Gladstone felt the uselessness of mediation until France and Prussia approached 'a fundamental approximation of views'. Until then the prime minister felt that any mediation might result in 'mischief' (Gladstone to Chevalier, private, 6 Sept. 1870, RA I 65/61).

[5] Granville to Lyons, private and confidential, 6 Sept. 1870, PRO FO 362/4.

[6] Granville to Lyons, private, 7 Sept. 1870, ibid.; same to same, confidential, 7 Sept. 1870, PRO FO 27/1793, no. 368A.

Favre grasped at the crumb and begged London to ask
Bismarck if he would agree to talks to arrange an armistice.[1]
Granville immediately requested Bernstorff to forward the
information.[2] On the thirteenth Granville received Bismarck's
reply. The Prussian minister wanted a 'guarantee' that the
French armies would recognize treaties signed by the provisional
government at Paris.[3] Granville thought that Bismarck's
disinclination to negotiate was due to Favre's circular of 6
September, which disavowed the cession of any French territory.[4]

On 13 September Thiers arrived in London to appeal to the
British Government for support in securing peace. His plea
to Granville was a compound of interest and sentiment. The
foreign secretary replied that mediation was inappropriate
until both parties wished it.[5] A second interview on the following day failed to move Granville from his rigid neutrality but
did result in the foreign secretary's efforts to procure an interview for Favre with Bismarck.[6] On 18 September, without
having received a definite reply from Bismarck, Favre set out
for Prussian headquarters. He spoke with the Prussian minister
on the nineteenth and twentieth but could not accept the
terms offered for an armistice, which were the cession of
Strasbourg, Toul, and Verdun.[7]

Granville's lack of initiative and his cautiousness were
manifestations of his own personality, as well as being a reflection of his concern for Belgium and the Black Sea. Gladstone's
influence upon and contact with his foreign secretary was close
and constant.[8] Wishing to substitute abstractions like European

---

[1] Lyons to Granville, Paris, telegram, 9 Sept. 1870, PRO FO 27/1815.
[2] Granville to Lyons, 10 Sept. 1870, PRO FO 27/1793, no. 408. Lyons sent a
copy of Granville's note to Prussian headquarters in the field (Lyons to Granville,
Paris, telegram, 13 Sept. 1870, PRO FO 27/1815). He was authorized to do so by
Granville because of uncertain telegraphic communications with Prussian headquarters.
[3] Granville to Lyons, telegram, 13 Sept. 1870, PRO FO 27/1793; Bismarck to
Bernstorff, Rheims, telegram, 12 Sept. 1870, *GW* vi B, no. 1792.
[4] Ibid.   [5] Granville to Lyons, 13 Sept. 1870, ibid., no. 433.
[6] Lyons to Granville, Paris, telegram, 14 Sept. 1870, PRO FO 27/1815; same to
same, ibid., 27/1816; Granville to Lyons, telegram, 15 Sept. 1870, PRO FO 27/
1793.
[7] Wodehouse to Granville, Paris, telegram, 21 Sept. 1870, PRO FO 27/1817;
Bismarck to Bernstorff, Ferrières, telegram, 23 Sept. 1870, *GW* vi B, no. 1826.
[8] Morley, i. 388. In the period prior to 1871, Gladstone and Granville, whose

law and public right for the more mundane but realistic workings of power politics, Gladstone only confirmed Granville in the policy of strict neutrality. Buchanan's warnings of possible Russian plans to abrogate the Black Sea clauses of the Treaty of Paris[1] and uncertainty about Belgium[2] made any antagonism towards Prussia an expensive luxury. Such antagonism would have resulted had England interposed her mediation with any force. Consequently, on 15 September, when Victoria wrote a draft letter to be sent to the King of Prussia asking him to end the war by the offer of lenient terms to France, Granville blunted the point of the message and delayed sending it even when pressed.[3] He still smarted from the previous Prussian complaints about his French preference.[4]

On 22 September Bernstorff informed Granville that Bismarck would insist upon the annexation of Alsace and Lorraine.[5]

personalities were so different, worked well together on foreign policy. In fact they almost cancelled each other out. Gladstone's enthusiasm was emasculated by Granville's propriety, and the latter's diplomacy was supported by the prime minister, depending on the circumstance, with either righteous indignation or moral affirmation. For a very clever and provoking analysis of Gladstone and foreign policy see A. J. P. Taylor, *The Trouble Makers* (London, 1957), pp. 67 ff.

[1] Buchanan to Granville, confidential, 21 Sept. 1870, J. H. Rose, 'The mission of M. Thiers to the neutral powers in 1870', *Transactions of the Royal Historical Society*, xi (1917), 49–50; Buchanan to Granville, most confidential, 4 Oct. 1870, PRO FO 146/1459, no. 386.   [2] Morier, ii. 179–80.

[3] Victoria to King of Prussia, 15 Sept. 1870, RA I 65/116; Victoria to Granville, ibid., no. 117; Granville to Goschen, 17 Sept. 1870, ibid., nos. 132, 133; Ponsonby to Victoria, 18 Sept. 1870, ibid., no. 148; Granville to Victoria, 21 Sept. 1870, ibid., no. 157. Ironically Victoria was willing to do unofficially, by means of a personal letter from herself, what she was opposed to having done officially by her Government. A few days before she wrote the draft letter asking the King of Prussia for leniency for France, she wrote a more revealing memorandum, 'the great danger for us [she wrote] in interfering is to have the appearance of wishing to prevent Germany from making a lasting peace. . . . If we appear to try and protect France . . . it would not be listened to . . . and would only confirm the bad feeling in Germany which is barely subsiding towards us. . . . The great danger [is] of [a] victorious & powerful Germany, becoming altogether estranged toward us. . . . [The] Queen . . . must . . . warn most solemnly and positively against the danger of alienating Germany from us' (Victoria memorandum, 9 Sept. 1870, RA I 65/68; ibid., *QVL*, 2nd ser., ii. 623). The memorandum was sent to Granville (Ponsonby to Victoria, 9 Sept. 1870, ibid., no. 68; Granville to Victoria, 12 Sept. 1870, ibid., no. 94).

[4] Granville was probably aware that Bismarck resented his efforts in forwarding French requests and that he also considered such work as a contribution to the prolongation of the war (Bismarck to Bernstorff, Meaux, telegram, 16 Sept. 1870, *GW* vi B, no. 1812).

[5] Mosse, p. 338; Lyons to Granville, Tours, telegram, 24 Sept. 1870, PRO FO 27/1817; Granville to Victoria, telegram, 22 Sept. 1870, RA I 65/170.

Gladstone had thought that the Prussian terms for an armistice, the possession of Strasbourg, Toul, and Verdun, were 'most moderate',[1] and his first reaction to Bismarck's circular demanding Alsace and Lorraine as the price of peace was a cool and unsympathetic one towards France:

> You know that if it [the war] had been successful France would have demanded territory, and got it. . . . She cannot plead the doctrine of inviolability.
> Were I in your place [the bishop of Winchester] I would suggest to him [Guizot] that the best chance . . . of keeping Alsace & Lorraine would be to plead the sentiments of the people of those provinces & to work the question on that basis rather than on the principle of inviolability.[2]

The prime minister advised Granville to make no reply to Bismarck's circular because 'there are not now any actual negotiations for peace or armistice . . . [and] I do not think that in any case we can dispose of the question of the circular without the cabinet'.[3]

On 27 September Favre asked for the 'active' intervention of the European powers. This request and the Prussian demand for Alsace and Lorraine were discussed at a Cabinet meeting held on 30 September. The British ministers declined to accept the appeal of Favre. A long and strenuous discussion then ensued upon a memorandum drawn up by Gladstone. 'My opinion certainly is that the transfer of territory & inhabitants by mere force calls for the reprobat[ion] of Europe, & that Europe is entitled to utter it, & can utter it with good effect.'[4] The prime minister's wish to join the other neutral powers in a protest against the contemplated annexation, without reference to the

---

[1] Gladstone to Granville, 26 Sept. 1870, Glad. Pap. ccccliv, letter-book 1870–1; Lyons to Granville, Tours, 27 Sept. 1870, PRO FO 27/1817, no. 1606.

[2] Gladstone to Bishop of Winchester, 26 Sept. 1870, Glad. Pap. ccccliv, letter-book 1870–1. For Gladstone's views on the cession of Alsace and Lorraine see Paul Knaplund, *Gladstone's Foreign Policy* (New York, 1935), pp. 54–65, 270–9.

[3] Gladstone to Granville, ibid. According to Granville, Gladstone, Cardwell, Lowe, Forster, Hartington were all opposed, with himself, to any official British mediation. Only Chichester Fortescue disagreed (Granville to Victoria, 12 Sept. 1870, RA I 65/94).

[4] Gladstone to Bright, 1 Oct. 1870, Glad. Pap. ccccliv, letter-book 1870–1; same to same, 1 Oct. 1870, Morley, ii. 346. Gladstone's objections to the annexation were not entirely moral ones. 'This violent laceration & transfer is to lead us from bad to worse, & to be the beginning of a new series of European complications' (Gladstone to Bright, 10 Oct. 1870, ibid., lxxxi i. 253).

inhabitants involved, was opposed by Granville and most of the Cabinet. Goschen supported the prime minister in a letter to Granville: 'A despatch in the sense suggested by Mr. G[ladstone] was desirable. . . . I see great danger ahead in the unbounded success not only of the German arms, but of Bismarck's unscrupulous, cynical, and cruel policy.'¹ Granville and the majority of the Cabinet remained firm, and Gladstone's attempt to protest was defeated.²

In October, Salisbury spoke out in an article in the *Quarterly Review*. His reasoning was far different from Gladstone's, but like the prime minister he wished to prevent the annexation of Alsace and Lorraine:

The first object of a treaty of peace should be to make future war improbable. . . . On the other hand, a ceded territory would be a constant memorial of humiliation.

Is there no neutral that will make one effort to rescue Europe from such a future of chronic war? Will England make no sign? Has it really come to this, that the disposal of the frontiers of France and Germany is a matter to us of purest unconcern? Is not the crisis worth some little risk? . . . They [the government] are yielding a mistaken obedience to the doctrines of a commercial school whose foreign policy has always been detested by the nation.³

Granville justified his reticence to Goshen. To 'lay down a general principle at an inopportune moment . . . could have only one practical meaning, viz. that, although we cannot prevent it, the Prussians are not to take any territory away from the French'.⁴ The foreign secretary was more explicit in a detailed letter to Gladstone:

I am personally better inclined to the French than you are. My objection to doing at present what you propose is that it is impossible . . . to do so, without being considered to throw our weight into the

---

¹ Goschen to Granville, 3 Oct. 1870, A. D. E. Elliot, *Life of G. J. Goschen* (London, 1911), i. 130–2.

² Fitzmaurice, ii. 62; Morley, i. 346; Granville to Lyons, private, 5 Oct. 1870, PRO FO 362/4. Gladstone also opposed the not a 'stone or fortress' declaration of France (Gladstone to Granville, 7 Oct. 1870, Glad. Pap. ccccliv, letter-book 1870–1). 'The general feeling throughout England seems to be in favour of non-intervention and the decision of the cabinet is approved by The Times and Daily News and Morning Post, but opposed by the Standard which does not point out in what way any such interference at present could be of the slightest use' (Ponsonby to Victoria, 2 Oct. 1870, RA I 66/40). ³ Cecil, ii. 34–36.

⁴ Granville to Goshen, 5 Oct. 1870, Elliot, i. 132–3.

French scale against Germany. Palmerston wasted the strength derived by England from the great war by his brag. I am afraid of our wasting [it] . . . by laying down general principles when nobody will attend to them, and when in all probability they will be disregarded. We have reserved our full liberty of action, and can protest whenever we like. But there are symptoms of both sides wearying of the war; they may come to us at last.[1]

The prime minister's irritation with Granville was a product of frustration, a frustration born of inactivity and a feeling of uselessness.

Y[ou]r reply convinced me . . . we shd do better not to give utterance to any sole opinion. What I afterwards proposed was an overture for a joint declar[atio]n but that proposal also is in abeyance. Yest[erday] I made another suggest[ion] to you, wh. rests upon another ground, namely the supposit[io]n that Ld. Lyons may be . . . able to draw them [the French government] back, without any formal recommend[ation], fr[om] their extreme claims. . . . In moral forces, & in their growing effect upon European politics, I have a great faith.[2]

For these 'moral forces', Gladstone was 'prepared to throw overboard the special British interests'.

I do not believe in them, I mean as connected with the affairs of the European continent. Take the one which comes nearest home, namely the hypothesis of a maritime aggrandisement of any of the great powers. That in my view cannot be formidable to us without being more formidable to others.[3]

The prime minister's internationalist proclivities were out of place in a world of nationalism. Curiously Gladstone wished to intervene in the main for moral considerations, and Granville wished to wait till the exhaustion of both sides resulted in a Franco-Prussian appeal for mediation.

[1] Granville to Gladstone, 7 Oct. 1870, Fitzmaurice, ii. 63. If Granville was more pro-French than Gladstone, the latter was not particularly a Germanophile (Gladstone to Granville, 12 Oct. 1870, Glad. Pap. ccccliv, letter-book 1870-1). In 1860 Gladstone wrote that 'alliance with France is the true basis of peace in Europe' (Morley, ii. 14-15).

[2] Gladstone to Granville, 8 Oct. 1870, Glad. Pap. ccccliv, letter-book 1870-1. On 11 Oct. 1870 Granville asked Lyons to point out to the French that a 'rigid adherence' to yield-no-territory-or-fortress was a 'great obstacle' to peace (Granville to Lyons, telegram, 11 Oct. 1870, PRO FO 27/1794).

[3] Gladstone to Granville, 11 Oct. 1870, Glad. Pap. ccccliv, letter-book 1870-1.

Gladstone continued to press Granville to induce 'the neutral powers or some combination of them' to propose mediation.[1] He reassured the foreign secretary about Prussia. 'I do not feel [as Granville did] a great apprehension of Bismarck's wishing to pick a quarrel with us and fight us with the aid of the United States'.[2] One reason for Granville's strict neutrality was the desire to avoid offending Prussia. Even Gladstone recognized the possible trouble that Bismarck could cause in connexion with Belgium and Holland.[3] Apparently the British Government was less concerned about French ill feeling.[4]

On 16 October Chaudordy, Favre's counterpart in Tours, told Lyons in strict confidence that 'he did not regard some cession of territory as altogether out of the question'.[5] On the same day Granville wired Buchanan to ask Gorchakov if England and Russia could devise peace terms and prevent the siege of Paris.[6] The Russian minister felt that the opinion of a neutral unsupported by military intentions would be disregarded, and that Alsace was the 'minimum concession' which Germany would accept. Russia refused to co-operate.[7]

On the nineteenth Granville instructed Lyons to ask whether France would authorize England to request Bismarck to state his terms for peace.[8] Chaudordy replied that England must act on her own initiative, France could not 'authorize' her to do so.[9] At a cabinet meeting on the following day it was decided to propose an armistice. To save Paris from the horrors of war Granville on grounds of humanity suggested an armistice to both sides, with a further hope that it might lead to the election of a constituent assembly.[10] French acquiescence was

---

[1] Same to same, 15 Oct. 1870, ibid. lxxxii. 153–4.

[2] Same to same, 16 Oct. 1870, ibid., pp. 155–6. Bismarck was angry with British mediation, however unobtrusively it was offered. He told Bernstorff that the making of peace was a matter for France and Germany and not any other powers (Bismarck to Bernstorff, Versailles, 15 Oct. 1870, *GW* vi B, no. 1868).

[3] Ibid.

[4] Lyons to Granville, Tours, 16 Oct. 1870, PRO FO 27/1818, no. 1677.

[5] Same to same, private and secret, Tours, 16 Oct. 1870, Lyons Pap. RC 2.

[6] Granville to Buchanan, telegram, 16 Oct. 1870, PRO FO 30/48, 5/22; same to same, 16 Oct. 1870, PRO FO 146/1461, no. 262.

[7] Buchanan to Granville, confidential, 17 Oct. 1870, PRO FO 146/1461, no. 401.

[8] Granville to Lyons, telegram, 19 Oct. 1870, PRO FO 27/1794, no. 549.

[9] Lyons to Granville, telegram, Tours, 20 Oct. 1870, ibid., 27/1818, no. 1695.

[10] Granville to Lyons, 20 Oct. 1870, PRO FO 27/1794, no. 555; Granville to

hampered by the difficulty of communication between Tours and Paris and the failure of Thiers to keep in touch;[1] France also continued to resist any territorial cessions,[2] upon which Prussia was adamant. At the beginning of November the Cabinet agreed it could do little more to obtain either peace or an armistice.[3] This decision was reached immediately before Russia announced the repudiation of that part of the Treaty of Paris neutralizing the Black Sea.

The Russian complication had little effect upon England's policy with respect to the Franco-Prussian War. If anything it confirmed Granville's position of strict neutrality. On 29 October he criticized Gladstone for the latter's 'occasionally compromising conversations with foreign ambassadors'.[4] The prime minister, however, was more active in conversation than in policy. At the beginning of December he wrote Granville that 'I do not see what you can do at present about an armistice, nor do I think the Defence Govt. is united in desiring one'.[5] On 3 January the prime minister in another connexion thought that 'a protest fr. this country agst a ... measure of the Germans, in the present state of p[ublic] feeling, wd place [us]within one step of war'.[6]

With the new year the mountain came to Mohammed. It became apparent to many Englishmen that there were corollaries of German unification that were of questionable value. Stanley was one who was unmoved:

I cannot understand the feeling which leads some of our friends

Loftus, 20 Oct. 1870, PRO FO 64/682, no. 226. The British were genuinely concerned about Paris (Gladstone to Bright, 18 Nov. 1870, Glad. Pap. ccccliv, letter-book 1870-1).
    [1] Granville to Lyons, telegram, 23 Oct. 1870, PRO FO 27/1794, no. 564; same to same, 25 Oct. 1870, ibid., no. 578; same to same, 26 Oct. 1870, ibid., no. 579.
    [2] Same to same, 4 Nov. 1870, PRO FO 27/1795, no. 635.
    [3] On 8 November Wodehouse left Paris, and with his departure Britain had no official representative in that city. At approximately the same time Thiers and Bismarck could reach no agreement at Versailles (Lyons to Granville, very confidential, Tours, 10 Nov. 1870, PRO FO 27/1820, no. 1785; Bismarck to Bernstorff, Versailles, 6 Nov. 1870, GW vi b, no. 1908). Bernstorff was told to inform Granville that English mediation only encouraged France to resist. This probably affected the Cabinet's decision (Bismarck to Bernstorff, Versailles, 11 Nov. 1870, GW vi B, no. 1911; same to same, Versailles, telegram, 16 Nov. 1870, ibid., no. 1918).   [4] Granville to Gladstone, 29 Oct. 1870, Fitzmaurice, ii. 64-65.
    [5] Gladstone to Granville, 6 Dec. 1870, Glad. Pap., ccccliv, letter book 1870-1.
    [6] Same to same, 3 Jan. 1870, ibid.

to wish that England should take part in the war. . . . There is no
pretext for saying that France is asked to make greater concessions
than naturally follow at the end of an unsuccessful war—A war,
moreover, in which she was the aggressor. And as a matter of policy,
the German alliance will be safer and more solid than that with the
French Empire.[1]

Granville on the other hand wrote to Lyons: 'I see no chance
of peace—I cannot say how my heart bleeds for the misery of
France—I lie in bed thinking whether there is nothing to be
done'.[2]

The foreign secretary undoubtedly recognized the change
in the public mood, for a month later he decided to question
Bismarck. 'I have written to Loftus a disp[atch] to ask
Bismarck for his terms of peace, and a declaration of his readiness to negotiate. But I do not wish the French to know it at
present.'[3] There was probably little connexion between Granville's letter and the armistice arranged a week later.

On 17 February a long debate in the House of Commons
expressed sympathy for France and considerable disenchantment
with the policy of abstention that England had been pursuing
during the war. Herbert criticized the Government's 'attitude
of indifference'. Instead of waiting for a basis of negotiation,
it should have found one. He felt that England ought to speak
out against 'violent annexation' as 'extravagant and impolitic',
and proposed that the Government should act with the other
neutral powers to obtain moderate terms of peace.[4] Peel agreed
generally with Herbert in a speech marked by pity for France,
criticism of the Government, and distrust of Germany.

I should much like to know if . . . our policy of isolation—of selfish
isolation—has been productive to us of any advantage.

I believe that this country . . . in the last two years in the councils
of Europe, has achieved more unpopularity than was accomplished
by the policy of any statesman within the last 30 or 40 years.

I look on the unification of Germany as a great peril to Europe.

---

[1] Stanley to Disraeli, Knowsley, 22 Jan. 1871, Disraeli Pap., Box 112. Morier
was another who felt British interests had been served by the German victory
(Mosse, pp. 357–8).

[2] Granville to Lyons, private, 20 Dec. 1870, PRO FO 362/4.

[3] Same to same, private, 21 Jan. 1871, ibid.

[4] Hansard, *Parliamentary Debates* (3rd series), cciv. 387–96. British opinion and
attitudes towards Germany are excellently delineated in R. J. Sontag, *Germany
and England* (New York, 1938).

. . . We have at this moment the unification of Germany under a
military despotism.[1]

There were others, like Cartwright, Goldsmid, Royston,
Horsman, and Muntz, who opposed any interference by
England. Sir Henry Hoare felt that Germany now threatened
Belgium and Holland, and that England should obtain 'just
terms' for France.[2] Cochrane, Corrance, Torrens, and Bass
agreed that the annexation of Alsace and Lorraine would be
immoderate.[3]
   The change in British feeling towards France and Prussia at
the beginning of 1871 was marked.[4] The queen noted it with
dismay and sadness, whilst Granville himself reflected it. 'How
hard the conquerors have been, and what a mistake in a great
nation like Germany to give up all direction of its affairs to
one bold unscrupulous man.'[5] British disillusionment with
Germany was not yet complete however. It had only begun
and did not match the all-pervading dislike and mistrust of
France before 1870. As with France, so with Germany, British
policy did not always reflect sentiment. Clarendon, Stanley,
and Granville recognized the necessity of co-operation with
France in the East, as Salisbury did with Germany after the
Franco-Prussian War. 1871 was a turning point, not merely
because the terms of peace were hard[6] but because it was felt
that Germany was intent upon crushing France.[7] The change
would come full circle in the twentieth century, when the
German unification Britain had desired in order to preserve

----

[1] Ibid., pp. 396–408.
[2] Ibid., pp. 429–31.
[3] Ibid., pp. 431–46.
[4] Mr. Martin to Victoria, 29 Oct. 1870, RA I 66/126.
[5] Granville to Lyons, 1 Mar. 1871, PRO FO 362/4. 'He [Mr. Forster] is
evidently anxious about the movement for sympathy with France, and for declaring war with Germany' (Ponsonby to Victoria, 12 Jan. 1871, RA I 68/29). 'The
feeling here—towards Prussia is as bitter as it can be. It is a gt. grief to me—& I
can do nothing! . . . For it is alas! the people—who from being vy. German up to
3 months ago—are now vy. French!' (Victoria to Crown Princess of Prussia,
1 Mar. 1871, RA U/32).
[6] Bismarck attempted to combat this feeling in England (Bismarck to Bernstorff,
Ferrières, telegram, 30 Sept. 1870, *GW* vi b, no. 1838).
[7] Bismarck admitted this to Odo Russell. He told the English minister that 'the
more completely France was vanquished the better in the end for Germany and the
more lasting the peace' (Russell to Granville, private, Versailles, 18 Dec. 1870,
RA I 67/104).

the balance of power became German hegemony, which proved even more dangerous than that exercised in the past by France.

Gladstone and Granville, whatever their feelings about the humbling of France, did not wish to see her crushed. But even if Britain had had the military capacity to intervene to prevent it she might have still lacked the will to do so. Granville was not the man to lead the Cabinet or the country where it would not go. He was better at preventing what he thought would be foolish or rash. Gladstone's vision of foreign policy was just that, a vision. It was too broad, except where Belgium was concerned, to implement. The Government had successfully defended Britain's interests on the Continent by restricting their scope. The embarrassment brought on by the bravado of Palmerston and Russell had been replaced by an ignominy born of self-effacement. Britain's influence in Europe would only revive with the return of Disraeli to power in 1874.

XII

CONCLUSION

ISOLATION or non-intervention are terms too imprecise to have real meaning.[1] The 'splendid isolation' of Rosebery and Salisbury tells us as little as does the use of the term non-intervention to describe the policy of Castlereagh, Canning, and Palmerston. Castlereagh and Canning were generally opposed to forcible intervention in the internal affairs of independent states and with Palmerston devised non-intervention as a formula to combat the continental predominance of the three conservative powers. Clarendon, Stanley, and Granville rejected the intrusiveness and the hectoring of Palmerston and Russell. Their version of non-intervention, the avoidance of verbal meddling, was calculated to accord with the public mood[2] and make allowance for the military inadequacy of Britain. Only the Cobdenites and the Manchester School, a vocal but distinct minority, interpreted non-intervention as almost complete withdrawal. In 1864 Disraeli referred to the Government's view of the balance of power as 'founded on the obsolete tradition of an antiquated system'.[3] But in 1867 he was willing to 'destroy and shatter to pieces the decaying theory of noninterference'.[4]

In the first half of the nineteenth century there were two general attitudes expressed by British foreign secretaries concerning Prussia. Castlereagh and Canning enunciated one when they opposed a Germany dominated by Prussia because that power was so 'peculiarly [a] military' one.[5] Palmerston

---

[1] See Strang, pp. 167 ff.

[2] Apart from the Court and Parliament, the politically conscious in England, those who formed 'public opinion', were not very numerous. 'In the fifties its [*The Times*] circulation of 50,000 to 70,000 was three times as large as that of its five chief competitors put together. Not one of these could boast a circulation exceeding 7,000. The paucity of these figures gives one a tangible idea of the very small number of persons who were able to take any serious interest in political events' (Erich Eyck, *Gladstone* [London, 1938], p. 124).

[3] Hansard, *Parliamentary Debates* (3rd series), clxxvi. 371.

[4] Disraeli to Victoria, 16 Aug. 1867, Buckle, iv. 473–4.

[5] Temperley and Penson, pp. 25–27.

presented the other view. Just before he died, he was willing to interpret a more powerful Prussia as an offset and buffer between France and Russia. Stanley acted upon the same premise. It was not merely an acquiescence in what could not be prevented; it was an acceptance of that which was not undesirable, although with Clarendon after 1867 it was also a recognition of the futility of resisting the inevitable.

Clarendon followed the view of Castlereagh and Canning. He would not admit any desire on his part for the enlargement of Prussia. His pro-Austrian feelings before to the war of 1866 were a reflection of his contempt for Bismarck and Bismarck's iniquitous conduct. The possibility both of Bismarck's dismissal before he could arrange his war and an Austrian victory if he did, restrained the foreign secretary's mediatorial ardour. The unreliability of France as an ally for peace and the apparent willingness of Napoleon to allow the conflict to occur were Clarendon's justification for his failure to prevent hostilities. His personal aversion to Prussian aggrandizement was easily counterbalanced by the lack of will to prevent it. By 1869 he conceded the inevitability of the Prussian unification of Germany and only hoped that it would be gradual, so as not to provoke France to war.

Stanley felt that a unified Germany was in Britain's interest because it would offset the power of France and Russia. Though he was very much predisposed towards both Prussia and Bismarck, he would not join the latter against France, and even admitted the reasonableness of Luxemburg as compensation for Napoleon.

Granville, like Clarendon, disliked and distrusted Bismarck but was no more willing than his predecessor to prevent Bismarck from unifying Germany. His lack of sympathy for France in July 1870 was due to the general feeling which he shared, that however wounded by the Hohenzollern conspiracy France was using it to make war.

After 1866 war between France and Prussia was expected annually. In this situation Clarendon and Stanley justified their inaction to Victoria by explaining that their purpose was to maintain unfettered the freedom of action for Her Majesty's Government. This is exactly what they did not do, as time and again they both indicated that England would be neutral, first in an Austro-Prussian conflict then later in a Franco-Prussian war. At a much later date Salisbury would write:

> Several times during the last sixteen years Count Hatzfeldt has tried to elicit from me, in conversation, some opinion as to the probable conduct of England, if Germany or Italy were involved in war with France. I have always replied that no English Minister could venture on such a forecast. The course of the English Government in such a crisis must depend on the view taken by public opinion in this country, and public opinion would be largely, if not exclusively, governed by the nature of the *casus belli*.[1]

Apparently there was no doubt in the minds of Clarendon, Stanley, and Granville that British opinion, regardless of the 'nature of the *casus belli*', would be opposed to taking sides. We must now consider the reasons why this was so, or why they acted as if it were.

Foreign Policy and Mid-Victorian England

Upon the death of Palmerston in 1865 the following appeared in *The Times*: 'The name of Lord Palmerston, once the terror of the Continent, will long be connected in the minds of Englishmen with an epoch of unbroken peace and unparalleled prosperity.'[2]

During the foreign secretaryships of Clarendon, Stanley, and Granville, England remained, on the whole, at peace and her prosperity continued unabated, with a minor reversal in 1866. Any difference between the policy of Canning and Palmerston and that pursued after 1865 lay in the social or ideological content of its formulation. Canning, at least metaphorically, balanced the conservative old world with the new, and Palmerston was famous for defending the cause of liberalism on the Continent. The Cabinets between 1866 and 1870, on the other hand, wished Bismarck and Napoleon III in power because it was felt that both were bulwarks against 'a Red and anarchical government'. In 1866 Loftus wrote that 'Goltz [the Prussian ambassador at Paris] wd. be a more dangerous man than B[ismarck], for he is a more liberal one'.[3] In Castlereagh's and

---

[1] Temperley & Penson, pp. 519–20.
[2] G. M. Young, *Victorian England. Portrait of an Age* (London, 1936), p. 108.
[3] Loftus to Clarendon, Berlin, 21 Apr. 1866, RA I 44/55.

Canning's day liberalism on the Continent was the liberalism of 1689 and 1832, giving property the vote and constitutions. By the end of Palmerston's life, with the emergence of socialism, democracy had acquired social and economic implications which were not congenial to property, whether represented by Conservative lords like Stanley or Whig aristocrats such as Clarendon. A liberalism perverted by nationalism seemed more satisfactory than a democracy which questioned the sanctity of private property. An unprincipled Bismarck was better than a democratic Lassalle. It was difficult to take sides when it was felt necessary to support both Bismarck and the Second Empire.[1]

Denuded of its moral vestments British policy became more difficult to justify to British opinion when active interference on the Continent had to be explained. Disillusionment with war after the Crimean conflict of 1854 was due only in part to 'bad medical services at Scutari'. Perhaps more important was the feeling that the Crimean War had been fought for nothing. That Russia had been kept out of the Principalities seemed less important once the war was over than the fact that the Turk had made no reforms and still oppressed his Christian subjects.

In 1864 Russell and Palmerston could not carry a pacific Cabinet to war. Consequently when Palmerston bluffed and his bluff was called, England was embarrassed and her prestige received a rude jolt. The loss of Brtish prestige as a result of the débâcle of 1864 induced both political parties to pursue a policy of caution in order to avoid further rebuffs and a consequent decline in reputation. Conscious of this, Clarendon, Stanley, and Granville devoted themselves not to raising Britain's credit but to an attempt to prevent any further diminution of it. In this they failed because their self-effacement was an acknowledgement of England's diminished influence and this only magnified the problem. Clarendon, at least, realized this but saw no way to counteract it.

In 1864 the unsuccessful interference of Palmerston and Russell discredited intervention and British opinion subsequently opposed it because intervention had become a

---

[1] It has been argued that the fall of the Bonapartes at Sedan removed the chief British objection to the French regime. See W. L. Langer, *European Alliances and Alignments* (New York, 1956), p. 13. Actually the British Cabinet wanted Napoleon III in power.

temporary synonym for meddlesome and potentially dangerous behaviour. After 1864 caution in diplomacy was imposed on the Government by Parliament, and the Government responded readily enough. After 1866 the pattern hardened and this free choice ceased to exist. What had begun as a national reaction ended by becoming a fixed domestic necessity.[1]

In 1866 the advent of important reform measures was complicated by the already existing party instability. The latter only made parliamentary majorities more precarious. Gladstone's difficulty in reconciling the Whigs to a liberal course at home was matched by Disraeli's frustrations in remaking a party destroyed by the split with the Peelites. Gladstone was much put out because a debate on foreign policy required 'five hours of time which ought to have been given to the Reform Bill'.[2] The Austro-Prussian dispute in 1866 coincided with the introduction of Gladstone's Reform Bill, whilst the Luxemburg crisis was concurrent with Disraeli's manoeuvring to pass the Reform Bill of 1867. The Belgian railroads affair of 1869 and the Hohenzollern candidacy of 1870 occurred when Parliament was taken up with the Irish Church Bill and Land Act.

It is sometimes argued that foreign affairs were ignored by most Englishmen, whose concern had been captured by domestic issues.[3] Actually it was because foreign policy had become an important issue domestically that British ministries in this period were obliged to make it compatible with parliamentary opinion. Ironically what made it so important was the re-emergence of reform as an active political issue. Votes needed to pass a reform bill might be squandered or alienated by the intrusion of foreign issues. Therefore it was important to avoid the discussion of such questions, and the way to do this, a discovery made by both parties, was by insisting that British interest and honour were not involved in continental imbroglios, so that no action need be taken to meet them. Both parties could better preserve precarious parliamentary support by restricting or eliminating the possibility of criticism.

---

[1] This was Kalnoky's view (Kalnoky to Beust, London, 21 Jan. 1868, England, *HHSA*, no. 6 B).

[2] Gladstone to Victoria, 11 June 1866, RA B 22/71.

[3] Professor Langer, though he only mentions it in passing, alludes to the English as 'far too much wrapped up in domestic problems to have much interest in foreign affairs' (Langer, p. 8).

It was essential to show the House of Commons that there was no foreign policy to criticize, and what better way to do so than by asserting that England was not involved—even though sometimes she was. A Cabinet that intervened could be censored; one that advertised its abstention and lack of commitment was safe so long as it proclaimed at the same time that no British interests were adversely affected by continental changes, even when they were.

Concern for parliamentary reform diminished the pertinence of continental questions. For the time being Englishmen saw foreign affairs as 'a branch of Liberal and Conservative politics tinged with emotion, a matter of taste, not a question of existence'.[1]

The apparent transformation of British policy in the five years before the war of 1870 was not only a manifestation of withdrawal but an estimate of means, an estimate seen as clearly by Disraeli as by Gladstone. The military change was European, not English, with the mass armies of Prussia and France. Without a close ally, and there is real doubt that Britain wanted one, she could not compete, and if the European powers at times ignored her it was due to the fact that the nature and degree of English interference were limited by the size of her army. Until the Franco-Prussian war the military force of England was reduced in the interests of economy. In the words of Trevelyan, England was 'concerned not to gain security by improving . . . [the army], but to save money by cutting it down'.[2] Court has demonstrated the strictly economic ends of Victorian finance.

Victorian public finance . . . was the finance of landowners and of wealthy professional and business people, anxious to limit their liabilities and confident they could invest to good effect every penny of their income that the State did not take. Under their leadership, the State became a careful spender and even a considerable saver. . . . The National Debt fell almost without a break from the years following the Crimean War until the end of the century.[3]

The possibility of British interference was further reduced by the relative inapplicability of naval pressure in this period

[1] G. M. Trevelyan, *English Social History* (London, 1942), iv. 24.
[2] Trevelyan, iv. 80.
[3] W. H. B. Court, A *Concise Economic History of Britain* (Cambridge, 1954), pp. 268–9. For the military expenditure of Gladstone and Disraeli see Morley, ii. 374.

and the desire not to offend the European powers whose forces were not on a peace footing. England's wealth and industry were dedicated to peace and further profits. There was neither the will nor the desire to translate this potential strength into military power, nor the appreciation of the importance of such a transformation.[1] In 1864 Cobden argued in Parliament that 'we have not the material strength to protect the weak against the strong'.[2]

Seen in this light, Clarendon's attempt to bring about Franco-Prussian disarmament was not without a certain amount of self-interest. The reduction of the military forces of Prussia and France would make the job of opposing an enemy or of controlling an ally a more realistic one. Clarendon had not forgotten 'drifting' into the Crimean War. In 1866 Russell's energy, which often counteracted his wisdom, was neutralized by Clarendon's tact, propriety, and diplomatic experience, which usually imparted grace to his cautiousness. As the Austro-Prussian crisis coincided with the attempted passage of the Reform Bill, an unpopular, that is an active policy, was a luxury incompatible with keeping office. Russell's vanity as premier and Clarendon's party feelings, particularly his dislike of Derby to say nothing of Disraeli, confirmed them in the pursuit of an easily justified foreign policy.

The Conservatives were no less hamstrung. Disraeli, who was almost as vocal on government economy as Gladstone, was strengthening a party led by a convinced isolationist. Lacking a majority in the House of Commons, any policy, however unobtrusive, was a precarious one. Stanley, to a certain extent under Clarendon's tutelage, was by nature careful and cautious. This made the foreign programme of the Conservatives, which was at best circumspect, amount to the almost total effacement of England in the eyes of Europe. If Stanley was vocal about Britain's abstention, it was because in his hands it resulted as much from personal conviction as from political expediency[3]—

---

[1] The exception that the Radicals and Gladstone made was one for self-defence. 'What Cobden urged was that existing naval armaments were enough to ward off any sudden attack and that, if danger threatened, our superior industrial resources would enable us to arm faster and more effectively than any potential aggressor' (Taylor, *The Trouble Makers*, pp. 51–52). [2] Ibid., p. 66.

[3] Disraeli's attempts to stir Stanley to action were in part motivated by party considerations (Monypenny and Buckle, iv. 468).

although he probably realized that his public popularity derived from his image as a man of peace.

Gladstone's view of policy was either swamped by rhetoric or drained almost dry by abstraction, but for the most part it was dictated by the budget.[1] Ironically Gladstone, almost alone, was willing to continue the meddling and interference of Palmerston, though he himself would not have so characterized it. In 1866 he wished to censure Bismarck's conduct in the crisis leading to war. He scolded Clarendon when the latter seemed indisposed to stand up for Belgium in 1869. In July 1870 he wanted to place more pressure on France than Granville thought expedient and he also differed from the foreign secretary in his vocal opposition to the Prussian annexation of Alsace and Lorraine. The prime minister's 'zest for financial economy inclined him towards Cobden; his moral fervour tempted him to universal interference'.[2]

Where Palmerston wished to intervene for British interests, Gladstone would do so for moral or emotional reasons, and neither wished to go to war. If Gladstone had been a check on the impetuousness of Palmerston, Granville neutralized Gladstone's moral fervour. Granville, who appreciated more keenly the implications of power politics, was the epitome of tact. In his hands policy was executed by a diplomacy which was calculated to offend no one.[3] British insignificance in Europe in this period was partially due to the personality and character of her foreign secretaries. Clarendon, Stanley, and Granville might obstruct with caution; they could not lead with confi-

---

[1] For a sympathetic appreciation of Gladstone's later views on foreign policy one should consult W. N. Medlicott, *Bismarck, Gladstone, and the Concert of Europe* (London, 1956).

[2] Taylor, *The Trouble Makers*, p. 57. Taylor's estimate of the foreign policy of Gladstone is as brilliant as it is correct. 'But whereas they [the Cobdenites] were rational and modestly reluctant to interfere with others, he [Gladstone] was emotional and convinced of his own peculiar inspiration. He was by nature an interferer, by training a man of Power' (pp. 69–71). In Magnus's opinion 'Gladstone never understood that high moral principles, in their application to foreign policy, are often more destructive of political stability than motives of national self-interest' (Philip Magnus, *Gladstone* [London, 1954], p. 287).

[3] There is some evidence, though hardly conclusive in nature, that Granville's inaction during the Franco-Prussian War was influenced by the hope that continued French resistance would limit the scope of the Prussian victory. On Granville's attitude during July 1870, see S. William Halperin, *Visconti-Venosta and the Crisis of July, 1870* (Chicago, 1963).

dence. Stanley's popularity derived from his embodiment of the public mood. Abstention had become temporarily popular, and neither he nor any minister dared oppose it by exercising any initiative.[1]

The changed and changing political structure of Britain affected policy. A decline in the normal aristocratic interest in Europe was a manifestation of the concern for a greater danger at home—the threat of democracy. A middle-class England was more willing to subordinate any policy to the demands of the budget. Stanley told Apponyi that 'finances govern the world'.[2] This was not merely the expression of a desire for peace in order to enjoy the fruits of trade and commerce. The political balance of power within England and interests outside Europe seemed more relevant than most changes on the Continent. British trade was king because it was also world-wide.[3]

British foreign policy was dedicated to peace. Whether this dedication, as some have argued, was due to a purely selfish desire to maintain trade and industry,[4] or whether commerce was seen as a causative factor in the Victorian idea of progress and improvement to which the avoidance of war was a basic assumption, is a moot question.[5] The desire for peace, in any case, was a worthy desire. The will to preserve it was lacking. Prosperity in Britain had bred complacency, a state of mind

---

[1] In 1868 Disraeli wrote the following to Gathorne-Hardy: 'The commercial Liberals . . . look with the greatest alarm to Lord Russell's return to the F.O., or even that of Ld. Clarendon. They think the peace of Europe depends upon Stanley's remaining' (Monypenny and Buckle, v. 29). 'Throughout the middle classes and in the eyes of the plain man Derby [Stanley, the fifteenth earl] stood for prudence and common sense in politics' (ibid. vi. 232).

[2] Apponyi to Beust, London, 25 Sept. 1867, England, HHSA, no. 69.

[3] For the tremendous expansion of English trade and the nature of that trade with France and Germany see B. R. Mitchell and P. Deane, *Abstract of British Historical Statistics* (Cambridge, 1962), pp. 279–335; Crowe to Granville, Düsseldorf, 22 Oct. 1872, PRO FO 83/394; Mansfield to Granville, Warsaw, 15 Nov. 1872, same to same, PRO FO 83/394 and 395, October to December 1872; Strang, p. 133.

[4] Victoria and Stanley were foremost among those who connected commerce with peace, particularly after the effects on Lancashire of the American Civil War. Stanley expressed annoyance that the possibility of a war between France and Prussia disturbed 'trade and so forth' (Stanley to Grey, private, 9 Aug. 1867, Stan. Pap., Queen).

[5] On the tendency toward humanitarianism in nineteenth-century England see A. Briggs, *The Age of Improvement 1783–1867* (New York, 1962), p. 2; G. Kitson Clark, *The Making of Victorian England* (Cambridge, 1962), p. 282.

which, though difficult to document, was nevertheless real. Young's impression of England at this period seems a little too strong but it is still revealing—'an ignorant pride which forgot that Prussia had an army, a thoughtless prosperity which did not reckon with American wheat'.[1]

[1] Young, pp. 82–83. Britain did react though perhaps not consciously. 'Imperialism was a middle-class reaction to the steady increase in the wealth and armaments of the Continental Powers which threatened Great Britain's prestige; and it constantly gained support as the century drew to a close' (Magnus, p. 218).

BIBLIOGRAPHY

MANUSCRIPT MATERIALS

Arundel, England, Lyons Papers.
Bodleian Library, Oxford, Clarendon Papers.
British Museum, London, Gladstone Papers.
Haus-, Hof-, und Staatsarchiv, Vienna, political and diplomatic letters, England 1866–1870.
Hughenden Manor, High Wycombe, England, Disraeli Papers.
Knowsley, Prescot, England, Derby Papers.
Knowsley, Prescot, England, Stanley Papers.
Public Record Office, London, Bloomfield Papers. (Cited as PRO FO 356.)
Public Record Office, London, Cardwell Papers. (Cited as PRO 30.)
Public Record Office, London, Clarendon Papers. (Cited as PRO FO 361.)
Public Record Office, London, Cowley Papers. (Cited as PRO FO 519.)
Public Record Office, London, Granville Papers. (Cited as PRO FO 362.)
Public Record Office, London, Hammond Papers. (Cited as PRO FO 391.)
Public Record Office, London, Russell Papers. (Cited as PRO 30.)
Public Record Office, London, Foreign Office, diplomatic correspondence.
Material consulted by countries: *Bavaria*: FO 9 (1866–70); *Belgium*: FO 10 (1866–70); *France*: FO 27 (1866–71), FO 146 (1866–71); *Germany*: FO 30 (1866–70); *Prussia*: FO 64 (1866–71), FO 244 (1866–71); *Saxony*: FO 68 (1866–70); *Spain*: FO 72 (1866–71); *Turkey*: FO 78 (1866–70); *Württemberg and Baden*: FO 82 (1866–70); domestic, consular, and commercial for above countries; general: FO 83 (1869–72).
Royal Archives, Windsor Castle.
A 22, Biddulph Papers, 1850–72.
A 34, Russell, 1865–6.
A 35–36. Derby, 1866–8.
A 37, Disraeli, 1868.
A 38–46, Gladstone, 1868–74.
A 77, Prime Minister's letters, addenda, 1866–84.
B 11, 21–26, minister's letters, 1865–74.
C 15, Victoria to Russell, 1865–6.
C 32, change of government, 1866–8.
D 24–26, Ireland, 1868–70.
E 15–18, Army, 1866–71.
E 52, Navy, 1865–76.
F 9–15, parliamentary reform, 1851–68.
G 56–57, Eastern question, 1866–7.
H 1–5, Eastern question, 1867–74.
H 41, Russia, 1864–74.
I 43–48, 71, family and political letters to and from Victoria, 1866–70.
I 63–68, Franco-Prussian War, 1870–1.

I 87, Austria, 1865–71.
J 51–52, Spain, 1857–73.
J 81–83, Napoleon III.
J 85, France, 1870–3.
J 92, French royal family, 1869–1901.
L 1–4, Royal Family, 1841–98.
L 13, political letters, 1855–75.
O 11–12, Egypt, 1860–81.
Q 11, United States, 1866–7.
Q 21, foreign affairs, 1866–1900.
S 31, letters to Disraeli, 1860–81.

PUBLISHED SOURCES

Die Auswärtige Politik Preussens, 1858–1871. Edited by the Historischen Reichskommission under the direction of Erich Brandenburg, Otto Hoetzsch, and Hermann Oncken: 10 vols. Oldenburg, 1933–9.

BENEDETTI, LE COMTE: *Ma Mission en Prusse.* Paris: Plon, 1871.

BLOOMFIELD, GEORGIANA, BARONESS: *Reminiscences of Court and Diplomatic Life.* 2 vols. 2nd ed. London: Chapman & Hall, 1884.

BOLITHO, HECTOR, ed.: *Letters of Queen Victoria from the Archives of Brandenburg —Prussia.* New Haven: Yale University Press, 1938.

BONNIN, GEORGES, ed.: *Bismarck and the Hohenzollern Candidature for the Spanish Throne.* London: Chatto & Windus, 1957.

BUCKLE, GEORGE EARLE, ed.: *The Letters of Queen Victoria: A Selection from Her Majesty's Correspondence and Journal between the years 1862 and 1878.* 2nd ser. 2 vols. New York: Longmans, Green, 1928.

BUSCH, MORITZ: *Bismarck: Some Secret Pages of His History.* 3 vols. London: Macmillan, 1898.

GATHORNE-HARDY, A. E., ed.: *Gathorne-Hardy: First Earl of Cranbrook; A Memoir.* 2 vols. London: Longmans, Green, 1910.

GOOCH, G. P., ed.: *The Later Correspondence of Lord John Russell, 1840–1878.* 2 vols. London: Longmans, Green, 1925.

HANSARD: *Parliamentary Debates.* 3rd ser. London, 1864–71.

HERTSLET, EDWARD: *The Map of Europe by Treaty.* Printed for Her Majesty's Stationery Office. 4 vols. London, 1875–91.

LOFTUS, LORD AUGUSTUS: *Diplomatic Reminiscences, 1862–1879.* 4 vols. London: Cassell, 1892–4.

LORD, R. H.: *The Origins of the War of 1870.* Cambridge: Harvard University Press, 1924.

MALMESBURY, 3RD EARL OF: *Memoirs of an Ex-minister: An Autobiography.* 2 vols. London: Longmans, Green, 1884.

ONCKEN, HERMANN: *Die Rheinpolitik des Kaisers Napoleon III von 1863 bis 1870 und der Ursprung des Krieges von 1870–1871.* 3 vols. Berlin: Deutsche Verlagsanstalt, 1926.

Les Origines diplomatiques de la Guerre de 1870–1871: published by the French Foreign Office. 29 vols. Paris, 1910–30.

RAMM, AGATHA, ed.: *The Political Correspondence of Mr. Gladstone and Lord Granville, 1868–1876*. 2 vols. London: Royal Historical Society, 1952.
RICH, N. and FISHER, M. H., eds.: *Holstein Papers: memoirs, diaries and correspondence of Friedrich von Holstein 1837–1909*. Cambridge: Cambridge University Press, 1955.
RINGHOFFER, KARL, ed.: *Bernstorff Papers: the life of Count Albrecht von Bernstorff*. 2 vols. New York: Longmans, Green, 1908.
TEMPERLEY, H. and PENSON, L. M.: *Foundations of British Foreign Policy, from Pitt to Salisbury*. Cambridge: Cambridge University Press, 1938.
THIMME, F., ed.: *Bismarck: Die gesammelten Werke*. 15 vols. Berlin: Stollberg, 1924–35.
WELLESLEY, F. A., ed.: *Secrets of the Second Empire, private letters from the Paris Embassy: selections from the papers of H. R. C. W. Cowley*. New York: Harper, 1929.

HISTORICAL STUDIES

ANDERSON, MARY: 'Edmund Hammond, Permanent Under-Secretary of State for Foreign Affairs 1854–1873.' University of London dissertation, 1956.
BANNING, E.: *Les Origines et les phases de la neutralité belge*. Brussels: Alfred de Ridder, 1927.
BARTLETT, C. J.: 'Clarendon, the Foreign Office and the Hohenzollern Candidature, 1868–1870', *English Historical Review*, lxxv. 276, 1960.
—— *Great Britain and Sea Power 1815–1853*. Oxford: Clarendon Press, 1963.
BAXTER, J. P.: *The Introduction of the Ironclad Warship*. Cambridge: Harvard University Press, 1933.
BERNSTEIN, P.: 'The Rhine Problem during the Second Republic and Second Empire.' University of Pennsylvania dissertation, 1955.
BEYENS, BARON NAPOLEON: *Histoire du Second Empire vu par un Diplomate Belge*. 2 vols. Paris, 1924–6.
Bismarck's Pen: The Life of Heinrich Abeken. Edited by his wife. London: G. Allen, 1911.
BOURNE, K.: 'The Foreign Secretaryship of Lord Stanley, July 1866–December 1868.' University of London dissertation, 1955.
BRIGGS, A.: *The Age of Improvement 1783–1867*. New York: David Mckay, 1962.
BUSCH, M.: *Our Chancellor*. 2 vols. London: Macmillan, 1884.
CASE, L. M.: *French Opinion on War and Diplomacy during the Second Empire*. Philadelphia: University of Pennsylania Press, 1954.
CECIL, ALGERNON: *British Foreign Secretaries 1807–1916*. London: G. Bell, 1927.
CECIL, LADY G.: *Life of Robert, Marquis of Salisbury*. 4 vols. London: Hodder & Stoughton, 1921.
CLARK, C. W.: *Franz Joseph and Bismarck: The Diplomacy of Austria before the War of 1866*. Cambridge, 1934.
CLARK, G. KITSON: *The Making of Victorian England*. Cambridge: Harvard University Press, 1962.

COURT, W. H. B.: *A Concise Economic History of Britain*. Cambridge: Cambridge University Press, 1954.

CRAIG, G. A.: 'Britain and Europe 1866–1869: A study in the application of non-intervention.' Princeton University dissertation, 1941.

—— 'Great Britain and the Belgium Railways Dispute of 1869', *American Historical Review*, l. 738, 1945.

DASENT, A. I.: *John Thadeus Delane, Editor of the Times: his Life and Correspondence*. New York: Scribners, 1908.

DAWSON, W. H.: *Richard Cobden and Foreign Policy*. London: G. Allen, 1926.

ELLIOT, A. D.: *Life of G. J. Goschen 1831–1907*. 2 vols. London: Longmans, 1911.

EYCK, E.: *Bismarck and the German Empire*. London, 1950.

FITZMAURICE, E. G. P.: *Life of the Second Earl of Granville*. London: Longmans, 1905.

FOOT, M. R. D.: Great Britain and Luxemburg 1867', *English Historical Review*, lxvii. 352, 1952.

GRENU, R.: *La question belge dans la politique européenne de 1866 à 1870*. Published by the Comité des travaux historiques et scientifiques. Paris, 1931.

GWYNN, S. and TUCKWELL, G. M.: *Life of Sir Charles W. Dilke*. 2 vols. New York: Macmillan, 1917.

HALPERIN, S. WILLIAM: *Visconti-Venosta and the Crisis of July, 1870*. Chicago: University of Chicago Press, 1963.

HEADLAM-MORLEY, J. W.: *Studies in Diplomatic History*. London: Methuen, 1930.

—— 'Treaties of Guarantee', *Cambridge Historical Journal*, ii. 151, 1926.

HIGGINSON, T. W.: *English Statesmen*. New York: Putnam, 1876.

HINSLEY, F. H.: *Power and the Pursuit of Peace*. Cambridge, 1963.

HOUSTON, D. W.: 'The Negotiations for a Triple Alliance between France, Austria and Italy 1869–1870': University of Pennsylvania dissertation, 1959.

HOWARD, M.: *The Franco-Prussian War*. London: Rupert Hart-Davis, 1962.

HYMANS, P.: *Frère-Orban*. Brussels: J. Lebèque, 1905.

JOLL, J.: *Britain and Europe 1793–1940*. London: N. Kaye, 1950.

KNAPLUND, P.: *Gladstone's Foreign Policy*. New York, 1935.

LAMBERT, S.: 'The Influence of Parliament upon the Foreign Policy of the Gladstone Government 1868–1874.' University of London dissertation, 1949.

LEE, SIR S.: *King Edward VII: A biography*. 2 vols. New York: Macmillan, 1935.

LEWIS, M.: 'Armed Forces and the Art of War: Navies', *The New Cambridge Modern History*, vol. x. Cambridge, 1960.

LINGLEBACH, W. E.: 'Belgian Neutrality: its origin and interpretation', *American Historical Review*, xxxix. 48, 1933.

MAGNUS, P.: *Gladstone: A Biography*. New York: J. Murray, 1954.

MARDER, A. J.: *Anatomy of British Sea Power*. New York, 1940.

MARTIN, B. KINGSLEY: *The Triumph of Lord Palmerston: A Study of Public Opinion in England before the Crimean War*. London: G. Allen, 1924.

MAXWELL, SIR H.: *The Life and Letters of Lord Clarendon*. 2 vols. London: E. Arnold, 1913.

MEDLICOTT, W. N.: *Bismarck, Gladstone and the Concert of Europe*. London, 1956.

MONYPENNY, W. F. and BUCKLE, G. E.: *Life of Disraeli*. 6 vols. London: Macmillan, 1916–20.

MORLEY, J.: *Life of William Ewart Gladstone*. 3 vols. New York: Macmillan, 1903.

MOSSE, W. E.: 'The Crown and Foreign Policy', *Cambridge Historical Journal*, x. 205, 1951.

—— *The European Powers and the German Question 1848–71*. Cambridge: Cambridge University Press, 1958.

—— *The Rise and Fall of the Crimean War System 1855–71*. London, 1963.

—— 'Public Opinion and Foreign Policy, 1870', *The Historical Journal*, vi. 38, 1963.

—— 'Queen Victoria and her Ministers in the Schleswig-Holstein Question' 1863–4, *English Historical Review*, lxxviii. 263, 1963.

NEWTON, LORD: *Lord Lyons, A Record of British Diplomacy*. 2 vols. London: E. Arnold, 1913.

PENSON, L. M .: 'Obligations by treaty: their place in British foreign policy 1898–1914', *Studies in Diplomatic History and Historiography in Honour of G. P. Gooch*. London, 1961.

PFLANZE, OTTO: *Bismarck and the Development of German Unity*. Princeton: Princeton University Press, 1963.

PRIBRAM, A. F.: *England and the International Policy of the European Great Powers 1871–1914*. Oxford: Clarendon Press, 1931.

RAYMOND, D. N.: *British Policy and Opinion during the Franco-Prussian War*. New York: Columbia University Press, 1921.

RENOUVIN, P.: *Histoire des relations internationales: Le XIXe siècle de 1815 à 1871*. Paris: Hachette, 1954.

ROSE, J. H.: 'The mission of M. Thiers to the neutral powers in 1870', *Transactions of the Royal Historical Society*, vol. xi. London, 1917.

SONTAG, R. J.: *Germany and England*. New York: D. Appleton Century Co., 1938.

SOREL, A.: *Histoire diplomatique de la guerre franco-allemande*. 2 vols. Paris: Plon, 1875.

STEEFEL, L. D.: *Bismarck, the Hohenzollern Candidacy, and the Origins of the Franco-German War of 1870*. Cambridge: Harvard University Press, 1962.

STRANG, LORD WILLIAM: *Britain in World Affairs*. New York: Praeger, 1961.

TAYLOR, A. J. P.: *The Trouble Makers. Dissent over Foreign Policy 1792–1939*. London: H. Hamilton, 1957.

—— *Struggle for the Mastery of Europe 1848–1918*. Oxford: Clarendon Press, 1954.

TEMPERLEY, H.: *The Foreign Policy of Canning 1822–7*. London, 1927.

—— 'The Treaty of Paris of 1856 and its Execution', *Journal of Modern History*, iv. 397, 1932.

THOMAS D. H.: 'English Investors and the Franco-Belgium Railway Crisis of 1869', *The Historian*, xxvi. 228, 1964.

THOMPSON, D.: 'The United Kingdom and its World-wide interests', *Cambridge Modern History*, vol. x. Cambridge, 1960.

TREVELYAN, G. M.: *Life of John Bright*. New York: Houghton Mifflin, 1924.

—— *English Social History*. London, 1924.

VERNER, W. W.: *Military Life of George, Duke of Cambridge*. 2 vols. London: J. Murray, 1905.

WALPOLE, S.: *The History of Twenty-five Years 1856–1880*. 4 vols. London: Longmans, 1904.

WARD, A. W. and GOOCH, G. P.: *Cambridge History of British Foreign Policy 1783–1919*. 3 vols. Cambridge: Cambridge University Press, 1923.

WEBSTER, C. K.: *The Foreign Policy of Castlereagh 1815–22*. London, 1925.

—— *The Foreign Policy of Palmerston 1830–41*. London, 1951.

WEMYSS, R.: *Memoirs and Letters of Sir Robert Morier, 1826 to 1876*. 2 vols. London: E. Arnold, 1911.

YOUNG, G. M.: *Victorian England: Portrait of an Age*. London: Oxford University Press, 1936.

INDEX